T0193409

I'VE NEVER BEEN TO HEAVEN

BEEN TO HEAVEN

(BUT I'VE BEEN TO OKLAHOMA)

Kurt Turner

authorHOUSE®

AuthorHouse™
1663 Liberty Drive
Bloomington, IN 47403
www.authorhouse.com
Phone: 833-262-8899

Published by AuthorHouse 10/05/2023

ISBN: 979-8-8230-1416-8 (sc)
ISBN: 979-8-8230-1417-5 (hc)
ISBN: 979-8-8230-1415-1 (e)

Library of Congress Control Number: 2023917054

Print information available on the last page.

To Linda L. Turner (1952–2021), my wife of twenty-one wonderful years, without whose help this book would never have been accomplished;

To James E. Williams, Jr., United States Marine Corp, wounded in Vietnam on December 27, 1967 died aboard US Navy hospital ship USS Repose, *December 27, 1967;*

To Shep Chase (1947–1999), one of the best friends I could ever ask for, Vietnam veteran;

And to Chris, Ryan, and Carrie, for the rough times I put you through by not handling my PTSD as I should have.

PREFACE

The USS *Repose* and Vietnam are now fifty-five years in the rearview mirror, but it seems to be a previous lifetime. Before reading this book, I invite the reader to, just for the time being, displace the movies you have seen related to the war. No movie can display the true emotions of the experience and lifetime of reliving any war. Only those who have experienced it can tell the real experiences they endured. Movies are stories of individual battles and experiences that may be "based on a real story." You may have emotional experiences as you watch those movies. However, other than a scene or two, those scenes quickly and quietly fade into the past.

For those who experienced the events firsthand, the intrusive thoughts and even nightmares persist forever—until the lid is closed on our casket or our bodies are returned to ashes. When the bagpipes play out their sorrowful tune and the bugler's playing of "Taps" fades into the far distance following the twenty-one-gun salute, our souls are finally at rest.

Some who have served in time of war will have their family and friends believe that they left the scars of battle in some distant foreign land. They have the right to say that. They have the right to suppress or willingly repress the scars born of battle.

There are a few things I want you, the reader, to consider. One is the fact that each war is totally different than the ones fought previously. Therefore, I do not speak, at least not generally, for those who endured war before or after my own experiences. The weapons have changed as drastically as the reason the war was declared or fought without a declaration.

Most wars had the backing of the populous. One, in particular, did not. Therefore, its soldiers were unfairly scrutinized. Those who returned to their unforgiving nation were the scapegoats for government leaders who could not validate the reasons more than 58,400 soldiers returned to Dover Air Force Base in flag-draped caskets. While "shell shock" was prevalent long before this particular war, for those of who served in this particular war, the impact of war became not just that of the events of the war itself. We felt as if we were targets of demonstrators; of the press; and, most unfortunately, of the people for whom we fought.

I have never tried to convince anyone that I was a grunt who lived and fought in the unforgiving jungles filled with spiders, snakes, Vietcong and NVA soldiers. Life on a hospital ship was a completely different assignment. We, the Navy corpsmen, were the ones who did not watch our buddies get riddled with a hail of bullets or ripped apart by a land mine. We were the ones who received the wounded and the deceased. We were the ones who fought our hardest to heal the wounded to a point where they could be flown by helicopter to Da Nang, and eventually, if necessary, back to "the world."

Finally, there's one more consideration for the reader. This is my story. It is not the same story that any other individual can tell, any more than I can tell anyone else's story. Every veteran came back with different memories—or, in some cases, almost no memories at all. Some of our brains repressed those events, not wanting to remember or relive the horrid details of certain experiences. You are about to delve into a story that cannot be told once I leave this world for a place where there will be no memories of Vietnam and no tears will be shed, ever again. And the Good Lord knows I still shed those tears, more than a half century after the events that rocked my world as a teenager occurred.

Mine is a story of my experiences and how those experiences—some good and some bad—eventually shaped my life. But in the end, God turned some bad events into life-altering changes, so that even the bad was turned to good.

I had accepted Jesus Christ as my Lord and Savior before my

teenage years. But no single event brought me to Him as did that night of December 27, 1967, aboard the USS *Repose*. Thirty-two years later, that same singular event led me into an even much greater purpose when, as I was returning from "the Wall," that "small, still voice" called me into the ministry after a life of turmoil. The PTSD from which I suffered all those years would be culminated into an understanding of what His purpose was for me. It would also explain why my life was spared from a live grenade placed in my hands and my actions were executed by the Holy Spirit.

"For everything there is a season ... a time for every matter under heaven." My seasons were spelled out after thirty years. Most of my life is a story of the deaths of our fallen heroes and the deaths of family and friends. It is also a story of love, which, at one point, I was incapable of accepting or giving.

Having finally completed this book—more than twenty years in the writing—I look back and see why I was held back all those years. More seasons have come and gone, and I understand those seasons much better than I did when I began writing.

"There are those who have worn the scars of battle whether in victory or defeat, but let us never forget that the true heroes are those who never returned to let us witness their scars and their stories."

—KURT TURNER

INTRODUCTION

James E. Williams, Jr., was a hero, no matter how one might define the word. His name can be found among the 58,318 (as of May 2017) etched into the black granite wall at the Vietnam Veterans Memorial in Washington, DC. Wounded in Quang Tri province on December 27, 1967, James clung to life as he was flown by helicopter to US Navy hospital ship USS *Repose*, which was anchored offshore from Vietnam. At the time, I was serving as a hospital corpsman aboard the USS *Repose*, and my brief encounter with James E. Williams, Jr., would forever change my life.

Shepherd Lee Chase and I served together during our first two years of service as US Navy hospital corpsmen. We became friends during hospital corps school at Great Lakes, Illinois, and our friendship continued as we served together at Bethesda Naval Hospital in Bethesda, Maryland.

As you may know, many veterans have claimed medals that they received as they claimed to have achieved heroic acts (which cost them serious embarrassment later in life). Everything in my story is true, and all military events included have been verified through psychiatric examinations and testing, not by an independent physician but, rather, by the Veterans Administration. Claiming post-traumatic stress disorder (PTSD) and verifying it through the VA are two completely different things. Of those hospital corpsmen who have applied for PTSD (in fact, most of those who have applied), relatively few are verified to be 100 percent disabled because of this condition alone. I am not certain how many hospital corpsmen stationed on hospital ships have received disability under PTSD; I am sure there are very few.

The same is true of Agent Orange. We treated those who were covered with the dreaded chemical. Most are not aware that prostate cancer and ischemic heart disease (both of which I suffer from), along with many other diseases, are directly related to Agent Orange. Those who came in contact with it and suffer from any of these diseases are eligible for treatment by the VA regardless of income or other factors. To all who came in contact with the chemical, especially those who didn't realize it, my heart goes out to you.

For those corpsmen who served with the marines, I salute you, for my story isn't about bravery, while yours is!

PART ONE

Chapter 1

"For everything there is a season, a time for every matter under Heaven."

—Ecclesiastes 3:1

I was a typical small-town Midwestern kid who didn't know what the world was all about in the 1960s. I was born in Bellaire, Ohio, which was then a booming little town along the banks of the Ohio River, nestled in the foothills of the Allegheny Mountains. Small towns in Ohio and West Virginia were flourishing with job opportunities, and anyone able to perform any type of labor, be it driving a truck or possessing clerical skills—let alone engineering and other high-paying professions—could find immediate employment.

"Help Wanted" posters were short-lived, as jobs abounded. With few among the wealthy, most of the population was blue-collar working class. The steel mills were still booming, as steel was then known as a true American-made product that faced no challenge from other countries. Bellaire was home to one small and two large glass factories, and there was another large plant on the West Virginia side of the river. The Imperial Glass Company in Bellaire was one of the largest glass-making plants in the United States.

The coal-mining industry was at its height and was by far the largest employer throughout the area, including mines on both sides of the river in Ohio, West Virginia, and eastern Pennsylvania. These areas produced a grade of high-sulfur coal that was a target for politicians concerned with air quality. Sulfur emissions were blamed for—and unfortunately proven to be—damaging the quality of the air inhaled by residents, causing lung damage known as black lung disease and other breathing problems, including cancer.

The glass industry was also a victim of research that concluded lung damage was caused by fiber found in the molten glass. High school graduates, as well as many nongraduates who'd left school prematurely, were employed by mines, steel mills, and glass plants once they reached seventeen years of age. Many had no aspirations of a college education and dreamed of the money and retirement benefits their fathers and grandfathers had received. Little did they know that, as scientific research evolved, it would prove that the carcinogens from these two prominent industries were responsible for diseases—predominately lung cancer—along with various other injuries.

The dagger was driven deep into the local economy when global warming became a popular and controversial issue. Studies showed that local citizens not employed by the coal or glass industries were suffering from health issues similar to the miners. Many of the local industries burned coal as a source of producing electrical power, melting iron ore to produce steel products and to power locomotives. Therefore, coal was used by just about every industry across the Ohio Valley and the entire country.

A lump of coal taken from deep beneath the surface of the Alleghenies could meet its demise in a furnace a thousand miles from where it had formed millions of years before. Therefore, many areas where local coal was transported would opt for lower-sulfur coal from western states at a higher cost. The lower-sulfur coal presented somewhat lower health risk factors.

Numerous abandoned mines remain the present danger, because long underground tunnels are subject to collapse. Many cliffs remain to this day from longwall mines, where coal was collected from near the surface by extremely large shovels. Two of these were the famous Gem of Egypt and Silver Spade, which supposedly ended up near

Chicago. Their giant buckets lifted tons of earth and coal with each scoop.

As time passed, the only positive remnants were the ponds at the bottom of many of these cliffs that provide good catfish and bass fishing. However, that fails to make up for incidents of cattle and other animals, occasionally people, falling over and cars being driven over the edge of the man-made cliffs. Stories exist of cars being intentionally sent over these cliffs and sunken in the ponds to hide evidence in robberies and even murders. Eventually, the industry was forced into land reclamation, and the terrain was returned to a resemblance of how it had originally appeared.

The booming economy of the Upper Ohio Valley was on a downward spiral that eventually left my hometown and most towns in the area more or less ghost towns. Unfortunately, as the Vietnam War came to an end, so did most of the industries of the Upper Ohio Valley, including the world-famous Pittsburgh steel-producing companies.

The sad part for me was that I soon missed the exit to the Fort Pitt Tunnel, from which the panoramic view of the largest city in the area opened up to a site that is forever embedded in my memory. Practically every Sunday evening from April 1966 to September 1967, I headed to Bethesda National Medical Center. The highlight of the trips was peering out the window of the Greyhound bus, taking in the deep red glow of the sulfur and other carcinogens arising from smokestacks we now realize shortened the lives of steel workers and, to an extent, residents of the area.

I had not yet read Dante's *Inferno* but would later surmise that this could well have been the tenth level of hell. Dante traveled through the nine levels of hell, beginning on Good Friday, to return to Earth on Easter morning. In my mind's eye, I integrated those sights with the drawings illustrated in the book. For those not familiar with the classic, the thick reddish smoke belching from the smokestacks is among those things that will never be extinguished from my mind's eye. I am not sure which of the nine levels of hell this reminded me of, but I'm sure Dante Alighieri envisioned something like the scene I experienced when exiting the eastbound lane of the Fort Pitt Tunnel. Dante didn't have this scenario in mind in the year 1300, but if I were to revamp his book, I would have to sneak the scene in somewhere.

Soon, the Upper Ohio Valley would dwindle into the area known as the Rust Belt. Most of the steel mills in eastern Ohio, western Pennsylvania, northern West Virginia, and on westward to Indiana turned from well-kept buildings into rusted-out skeletal shells. Almost every mill shut down, along with the glass industry and coal mines, all of which took major hits. Today, the mines are up and down, depending on politics. I won't go there other than to say that politics run the mines one way or the other. One party receives most of the blame, but how much is perception and how much is reality remains a looming question.

After my father's sudden death in September 1957, I stopped applying myself in school and was only promoted every year because I was smart enough to pass each class without studying. I always labeled myself the smartest student in Bellaire High School who never studied and performed only mandatory homework while still receiving passing grades. I would verify that later with a 3.6 GPA in college, followed by a 3.95 in graduate school. I reverted back to high school days in one class in graduate school, taking for granted my professor wouldn't give a legitimate final exam, which was his common practice. Well he did, and I got burned! Why he mercifully gave me a B on the final, I'll never know. But he taught me a lesson that came in handy, as I took my remaining classes very seriously. My carelessness surely cost me a perfect 4.0 postgraduate average.

Although I was a city boy, I spent a good bit of time on my grandparents' farm. I learned many valuable lessons that I'd missed out on in the city. Before spending some time on a farm, I never realized what early settlers and those who continued to work the land and raise cows and other animals experienced. It is a difficult life—up and out of bed by daybreak. A breakfast of ham and eggs was typical, especially since both were products of the farm. Feeding and milking cows came next, along with slopping the hogs, feeding the chickens, and gathering eggs. All of this had to be done before nine o'clock in the morning. Planting and harvesting were time-consuming on a small farm without much equipment, and the equipment they did have seemed to constantly break down, which created even more work. Small-scale farmers are often limited to one tractor that was probably bought from another farmer, already well-used and just waiting to break down. Then the farmer would still have to purchase further equipment to add to the tractor for plowing, planting, and gathering.

Sundays on the farm were days of rest, outside of milking and feeding the animals. On a typical Sunday from spring through fall, after attending church services, my aunts, uncles, and cousins usually gathered at the farm for a great meal. Then the adults sat around talking while we kids played. We couldn't wait for Grandma to ring the dinner bell that announced lunchtime. Then we went back to playing until the bell rang again, announcing another homemade farm meal had been prepared. Because most of the food and milk were products of the farm, it seemed like Thanksgiving every Sunday. My favorite food was wild game, which included rabbit, squirrel, grouse, and quail.

Mom provided for my sister and me by getting a job at Bellaire High School Library (now known as Bellaire City Library) after Dad's sudden death. Mom was only thirty-seven when Dad died. We didn't have the luxuries most families did, but we had everything we needed. Dad had been employed at JCPenney as a carpenter and worked in sales during busy seasons. Back then—unlike today—stores performed their own maintenance, remodeling, and so forth. Dad also worked at the neighborhood gas station for several hours a week and had previously worked at one of the local steel mills. When he was drafted into World War II, he failed his physical due to an old leg injury. He had a very slight limp at times, but I never asked how he was injured or whether it was from an innate condition.

Concerning Dad, there are two specific sad moments I remember well. When a very good friend of his crashed in a small single-engine plane, Dad rushed to the hospital to see Andy. When he came home, Dad sat down and cried. All he said was, "Andy isn't going to make it." Fortunately, Andy did survive, although he lost both legs. He continued to run his car dealership and was able to maintain the business despite his handicap.

The other episode came when I was about seven years old. The family was in the basement, and Dad was sorting through old newspaper articles and photographs. He ran across one particular picture that contained several of his friends who had been drafted, passed their physicals, and were about to board a train headed for army basic training. As Dad recalled each of the five or six men, he told a short story about what each soldier did after the war. When tears welled up in Dad's eyes, I knew why he saved two of the stories until last. All he was able to say was, "Neither of them came home." They were casualties of World War II.

The thing I remember most about Dad is that, whenever the phone rang, he would take off to help a neighbor who had a water leak, a broken-down car, or whatever the situation no matter what time of day or night. After he died of a sudden heart attack (he had never visited a doctor in his forty-five years), Mom blamed it on his helping a friend drag out the man's belongings during a fire at his home. She refused requests for an autopsy because she wasn't going to let them, in her words, "butcher" him then, after going all his life without seeing a doctor. Although she blamed the fire event, she refused to blame Dad's friend for his death.

Some who lost a father at a very young age remember little about the man. Dad was a very loving, caring family man. I was skinny and scrawny, and except for a short stint in little league, I was never on an organized sports team until I was in the navy. Little League baseball, at that time, consisted of one age group being ages eight years-old to 13 years-old. I could not compete with thirteen-year-olds when I was eight. But Dad would play ball with me in the evenings. It certainly wasn't his fault I wasn't an athlete. When he wasn't helping a neighbor, friend, or relative on Saturday evenings in the summer, he would take Mom; my sister, Edith Ann; and me to stock car races or to a drive-in movie.

Before my time, Mom and Dad went to the West Virginia State

Prison in Moundsville to watch boxing matches featuring inmates, and sometimes, local boxers were invited to participate. I have fond memories of cuddling on the couch with Dad and falling asleep watching boxing on TV. I had the feeling that was Dad's favorite sport.

I remember going to Cleveland for a weekend series between the Cleveland Indians and Detroit Tigers. It was 1954, the year the Indians ran away with the American League pennant. They were heavy favorites after a record 111 wins but were swept by the New York Giants in a series that was immortalized by Willie Mays's famous catch, forever remembered as "the catch."

Among my fondest memories of my father were the times he took me hunting. I had gone squirrel hunting with him several times before my eighth birthday. One day, a package arrived, and I happened to be home. I picked up the box, ran in the house, and told Mom my rifle was here. The box was marked "Remington." Mom did her best to keep me from believing my .22 bolt-action rifle had arrived. Dad had to be a little disappointed that he didn't get to surprise me, but as usual, he was calm and cool. He said, "Open it up. And after dinner, we're going to go out to the farm and learn the proper techniques of handling and shooting a firearm." Soon afterward, I was hunting with Dad with my own rifle at my side. I never did get a clear shot at a squirrel or rabbit that fall and winter. But as I look back, I realize it was one of the best times of my life. Dad wouldn't live to see the following hunting season.

When I was nine years old, Mom allowed me to hunt groundhogs to help a farmer clear his cow grazing fields of the critters. With my .22 Remington rifle and a .410 shotgun, I bagged thirteen groundhogs. I had to have a very close shot to kill a groundhog with a .410, but I learned Indian style how to sneak up on the groundhogs. My neighbor made me a deal that, if I shot and cleaned a young groundhog, she would cook it for me. I never would have thought it would be my favorite dish except for rabbit. Mom would cook any other wild game but wouldn't cook groundhogs. To this day, I prefer rabbit to any gourmet meal. I don't have anyone left who will cook up a groundhog, so that is a memory of the past.

Not having a father to teach me to fight and stand up for myself was often costly. I was always picked on around the neighborhood and at school. The jocks in high school didn't want to pick on the farm boys and mostly stayed away from them. Being one of the smallest boys in school meant often getting shoved around at lunch break and after school. Then one specific afternoon on the way home from school during my junior year, the neighborhood bully, although a next-door neighbor and friend, started picking on me. I'd finally had enough and threw my books down and challenged him. He went to his house and slammed the door shut behind him so his mother couldn't hear me yelling and telling him to come out and fight. That was the end of an era for me. I never lost another (fair) fight the rest of my life. I learned that, when you stand up to the bullies, they are afraid they just might get their asses kicked, and they tend to avoid possible embarrassment.

So it was that I grew up fatherless, with no particular goal in mind, and having no idea what my future held. I met a girl at a playground dance after my junior year of high school, and we dated steadily. I had signed my papers to join the navy and would leave for boot camp on August 16, 1965, almost four months short of my eighteenth birthday. Chris said she would wait for me to return from the service (and she did).

Off I went to boot camp. It was thirteen weeks of hell. But in a sense, as I look back, I see it wasn't all that bad. Those thirteen weeks changed me from a small-town city boy into a man.

The flight to Great Lakes Naval Training Center from Pittsburgh to Chicago wasn't as bad for me as it was for my family. Unbeknownst to those of us on the Boeing 707, another plane headed to Chicago had crashed into Lake Michigan, killing all on board. Of course, this being well ahead of the time of cell phones, the passengers aboard my flight had no idea what was going on. But the media had reported that a plane from an unknown point of origin headed west to Chicago had crashed, killing all aboard. I believe the flight may have originated from somewhere in New York. I later saw remnants of the plane that crashed on August 16. In winter 1965, when I made my second trip to Great Lakes, this time headed for hospital corps school, I saw sections and pieces of the plane, which had been placed in a hangar as experts attempted to nail down the cause of the crash. I never did find out if they were successful.

The Great Lakes region had one of the hottest summers on record that year. Sailors would pass out during drills. We just left them there lying on the drill field until they woke up. To help one who had passed out meant a strict punishment, a threat to go back to day one of boot camp. Fortunately, all of those casualties in my company survived. I couldn't even imagine things happening today that were dished out then. Lawsuits and discrimination procedures weren't in style yet, and the military knew it.

I witnessed one recruit being kicked in the head by his company commander because he couldn't provide him with some ridiculous number of push-ups. This was not my company commander. Boatswain's Mate First Class Christianson was a great guy. At first, we thought he was a real bastard. But we soon found he wasn't as tough on us as other company commanders were on their recruits. And we respected him as much as we feared him. Sure, Christianson was tough on us at times. After all, we were lowly recruits, and we had to learn the responsibility of becoming United States military men.

There was another instructor whose name I cannot recall. He was obviously a drunk who the navy chose to keep until he reached retirement age. Once in a while he would get wound up and give his favorite speech. "Remember why you are here, sailors. This is war ... and war is hell!"

As I look back, I realize I love the guy. It was easy to label him as a drunk. Later, I would discover his story. His wife and two children were on their way to pick him up after his shift (I do not know at which naval base). He stood watching their vehicle approach the intersection where they would pick him up daily. A vehicle ran a red light and T-boned their car, killing all three instantly in front of their husband/father. Ironic how one remembers things like this when you are receiving stressors from all angles, the likes of which you have never experienced before. This was one of the times that reminded me there is always someone suffering more than I am.

One hot day, another recruit and I earned the dubious task of burying the proverbial sand flea. After digging a large hole in the sand, Christianson asked us if we buried the sand flea face up. Everyone knows people are buried face up, so we answered in the affirmative. Of course, we were wrong and had to dig the imaginary flea up and bury him face down.

"Did you boys bury him facing east?"

"Of course, sir!" (We knew that humans are traditionally buried facing east). It was a battle we knew we couldn't win, so we took a chance that would either have us burying the damned flea all day or just do it right the next time.

"Sir?"

"Yes, Turner."

"Would you please tell us the proper method to bury a sand flea?"

"Why, certainly. I never thought you would have the balls to ask. Take the f—— thing over and throw it in the dumpster. Don't you dumbass recruits know better than to bury a sand flea? They ain't worth a shit to nobody, so what the hell did you listen to me for in the first place?"

I wanted so badly to say something like, "Well some thirty years from now, I'll tell the story about some lifer telling two of us recruits to do this. And we figured, after all those years in the navy, he was brain dead, so we just wanted to appease him." But we would have been there all night digging the grave over and over, so we just let him have his laugh. You soon learn that, in boot camp, the only wiseass is the company commander. You laugh at his corny jokes as if he was George Carlin. And you pretended you were in exercise-induced pain even if you could go on doing push-ups forever. You never lost sight of the fact that he was king, and you were the joker.

Even when we got on the train after graduation, a recruit who technically had earned a second stripe flipped his company commander off. Someone managed to have the train stopped and the company commander pulled him off it. I don't know his fate, but he may have become a recruit again and reentered boot camp for his stupidity. My guess is that he was restrained in front of all of us to teach us a lesson, and he boarded the next train without incident.

As the train eased away from the station, I lifted my white sailor hat and let Mr. Christianson see how long my hair had grown. At about an inch long, it was twice regulation boot camp length. Having been selected as a leader and serving what was called "permanent service week," instead of one week like everyone else, I wasn't with the company during the daytime and had pulled one over on him. I had spent almost the entire second month serving with the Catholic priest in a gravy job that should have lasted one week. I was inadvertently placed with the Catholic chaplain, although I had been selected as my company's Protestant religious petty officer (RPO). The chaplain was a good ol' guy and let me stay there in an air-conditioned office eight hours a day and listen to Chicago's famous WLS radio station. When he realized I couldn't set up for daily Mass, he told me to sit there and answer the phone.

For the first couple of weeks, I wondered who would call. One day, the phone rang, and on the other end was the priest. He told me, "Now, if anyone asks If you ever get calls, you can truthfully answer in the affirmative." No wonder I didn't consider boot camp to be all that bad. I recalled the words of my uncle Bill Farmer. "No matter how bad boot camp seems, you'll laugh about the whole thing once you're finished." My uncle Bill Turner advised me before I left for Great Lakes, "You can do anything you want in the service. Just don't get caught!"

Although I lucked out with the permanent service week job, I look back at the times we participated in marching, using army-style tactics such as crawling through tunnels while under fire (blanks of course). One thing we all earned was the sense of "team," as opposed to "self." This didn't really leave an impression until I was working on psychiatric wards and triage. There was no individual glory. Just like our brothers in combat, we failed as individuals and realized success when working as a team.

A young smart-ass from the state of Maine (I hadn't figured out exactly where that was at the time) and I became good friends. How the two of us hit it off at all is a mystery to me. We were exact opposites. Shep Chase was a drinker and hell-raiser. I wouldn't touch the stuff and was as quiet as the proverbial church mouse. But we formed a friendship that would last forever. Shep would come home with me on weekends while we were at Bethesda, and Chris would have a date lined up for him. Other weekends, he would go home with Alan Wallace, and he would have a girl lined up for him there.

Shep, Alan, and I were close friends and formed a relationship that would bond again later in life. One day while I was visiting Shep in Maine, we decided to attempt to track down Alan. After several phone calls to people named Wallace around the area where Alan lived in central Ohio, Shep struck gold. He had reached Alan's mother. She remembered Shep and that he was from Whitefield, Maine. She gave him Alan's phone number, and our relationship would rekindle. Shep and Alan would never physically meet again, but Alan and I see each other often, as he regularly travels from his home in central Ohio to the Virginia, Washington, DC area. His mother lived well into her nineties and died in 2021. I never got to meet her but often asked about her.

The three of us experienced so many great times that our impending orders to Vietnam seemed far off in the future. Thus, we lived the lives all young men in their late teens should live, without the fear of dying some thirteen thousand miles from home.

But that day was inevitable. Shep ran into some problems that were brought on by his drinking. He was not really guilty of doing anything wrong, except being in the wrong place at the wrong time. He ran into the middle of a military investigation he had no role in except for having contact with a suspect he didn't even know. Poor Shep got his orders for Fleet Marine Force, which meant jungle training in South America and a free ticket to a far-off land with a romantic-sounding name. A corpsman's life expectancy in Vietnam, when serving with a marine unit, was supposedly something like two hours. The corpsman was the favorite target of the VC (Vietcong) and NVA (North Vietnamese Army). This was understandable because he was the one who treated injuries and many times kept our soldiers on the battlefront.

Soon afterward, Alan got his orders to serve at the Naval Support Activity Hospital, Da Nang, South Vietnam.

Chapter 2

"Sunshine came softly through my a-window today."

—"Sunshine Superman," written and sung by Donovan in1966

"Sunshine Superman" was the first song I remember hearing after arriving at National Naval Medical Center (NNMC) in Bethesda, Maryland. Things went well for me at NNMC. I was only about six hours from home. I had virtually every weekend off and was home by Friday night, usually thumbing for rides. Then I left by Greyhound bus at 9:30 Sunday night, which got me back at about 6:00 a.m. Monday morning, in time for 7:30 muster. A friend who was also from Ohio (Youngstown) stayed on base almost every weekend and took my weekend duty (every other weekend) for five dollars, which, even at that time, was a super bargain.

While awaiting entrance to neuropsychiatric school, I spent my time working at the main information desk at nights. This was a cake job because things were usually quiet at night unless President Johnson was admitted for surgery or some other dignitary was aboard.

I thoroughly enjoyed most of the phone calls which usually went something like this:

> Q. What is the temperature of the water in the pool
> at the officer's club?

A. What could possibly make the difference at 2:00 a.m. when the pool is closed?

Q. I just discovered I'm out of birth control pills, and I need my prescription filled right now.

A: I don't think you understand how they work. I would suggest finding the proverbial aspirin instead and holding it between your knees until you get your prescription refilled later this morning.

One morning, I called a nurse following her request for a wake-up call. A man's groggy voice answered. Thinking I had the wrong number, I asked who it was. In his sleepiness, not thinking yet, he replied, "This is Dr. Smith."

To this (realizing he had also requested a wake-up call at this residence), I replied, "Good morning, Doctor. This is Hospitalman Turner at NNMC. It's time to get up. And while you're at it, how about getting Nurse Jones's ass out of bed too?"

It was great, because I knew he wouldn't dare say anything to me when he arrived for his shift. About two hours later, he walked past the desk and surprisingly said, "Good morning, *Hospitalman Turner.*" The emphasis was on "Hospitalman Turner," as in saying, "You got me, so let's leave it at that. I don't report you for disrespecting an officer, and you don't spread the story."

It was even more fun when Nurse Jones straggled in the door a few minutes later with her jacket collar pulled up over her face as far as she could get it. I felt like saying, "Well, honey, at least you aren't married like your doctor friend is." But, somehow, in the military, you learn to leave well enough alone while you're ahead. And at this point, I was securely ahead. This was the same doctor who I always addressed by intentionally mispronouncing his name. He took it as a joke until I did it when paging him over the public announcing system. The manner in which I handled the wake-up call probably saved my ass from losing a stripe. But I was prepared to claim a speech impediment, because his name was easy to pronounce (obviously, his real name wasn't Smith).

After spending my share of nightshifts at the main information desk, I was assigned to Barracks 12 as assistant master-at-arms, under BM-2 (Boatswain's Mate Second Class) Greene. He was one of the meanest-looking and gentlest men I ever met. "Greenie" was a career sailor just looking to bide his time and receive a pension. At least that was how I read him. He had a habit of calling for someone to report to the master-at-arms desk "on the double!" He always began with the words "this man." It would come out, "This man Turner, report to the barracks master-at-arms office, oooooooon the double!"

If you had never heard his voice before, you would just about shit your pants thinking, *Oh boy, am I in trouble!* Then when arriving at the desk, you would see this large black man staring down at you, apparently ready to bite your head off. Just as your bowels would prepare to erupt, he would smile and give you the message, which usually wasn't from him personally. And he always sent you off by having something pleasant to say.

Being the practical joker I was, I was dared one day by somebody to get on the squawk box and call out, "BM-2 Greene, get to the master-at-arms office—oooooooon the double!" Knowing I could sound just like him (I had his voice down pat) and knowing he had left the barracks, I got on the box, called for BM-2 Greene, and let out an exaggerated (even more so than his actual voice) "'oooooooon the double!"

Guess who showed up seconds later after flying down the passageway, just returning from wherever he had been? BM-2 Greene—in person!

I was speechless, and so was he. He stared at me for what I swear was an hour and then began laughing so hard he could hardly control himself. With his entire 250-pound frame, he pounded me on the back (I weighed about 145 pounds) and said, "Come here. If you're going to work with me and act like me, we're going to get this right!"

I thought he was going to take me outside and stuff my shirt with pillows and paint me black so nobody could tell us apart. Instead, I got on the squawk box and practiced announcing, "This man so-and-so, report to the barracks master-at-arms office ... oooooooon the double," until nobody could tell our voices apart. Soon, I had sailors flying to the office as fast as Greene did because they didn't know if it was Greene or me.

Although I never had a problem respecting rank and seniority, I learned from this gentle giant that people can earn respect from others, no matter what their rank, color of skin, or other attributes were. It wasn't Greene's size that earned his respect. It was his true demeanor and respect for others, regardless of rank, that got him the respect of every man in that building.

It was almost a sure bet that, if you did not specialize in a field after graduating from corps school, you would automatically become a field corpsman with the grunts. This is a position that, to me, holds the honor of all honors, maybe comparable to the Navy SEAL or Green Beret. But with it usually came your death certificate, signed by a Vietcong sniper. One of the first things we were told on arrival at Da Nang was that the life expectancy of a navy corpsman or army medic was seven seconds. While that was an obvious exaggeration, it served the intended purpose. Medical personnel were the lifeline of the troops. We not only kept troops alive but also, in many instances, got them back to the field to extend their tour of duty.

Fortunately, with my honors from boot camp as one of the four "most likely to succeed" in my company and my success in hospital corps school training, I was able to attend the class B training of my choice. This ended up being neuropsychiatric technician school. My first choice was actually X-ray technician school, but I was unwilling to extend for two years to enter that field.

The training was extensive and somewhat exhausting, as we learned to handle anything from character disorders to extreme and violent schizophrenia. My life was on the line more than once working with psychiatric patients, even before I finished school and left for Nam. We were taught man-to-man combat because we weren't likely to be in field combat situations but were often forced to defend ourselves when attacked one on one. I outscored the others in this class because I was the runt of the class, and I was damned if I was going to let the others pick on me.

One afternoon, I was locked in a "quiet room" with a very large young soldier who had just been shipped back to the States after killing all six of this tent mates point-blank with this M16 rifle. (Don't worry, Uncle Sam, I won't reveal names, as the families were likely notified that the six men had been killed in action.) "Lenny" was locked in a room by himself pending a hearing and transport to another (probably government but not military) hospital. When he ate meals, someone had to be present in the room with him, and someone else had to be watching from outside the small window. Well, as luck would have it, my backup disappeared at the time Lenny broke the handle off his plastic spoon, put it to my throat and said, "You know, Doc, I could kill you with this in a second."

My advanced training kicked in immediately (let alone my faith). In a situation where an NP (neuropsychiatric) technician would normally panic, I calmly and quietly said, "You don't need a weapon to kill me. You can do the job with your bare hands!"

It was the right thing to say. He grinned, and I'll never forget the look on this mass murderer's face as he looked at me and said, "I like you, Doc. You're cool. You don't know how close you came to dying, but I like you."

Normally, I wouldn't want to be liked by someone like Lenny. But God was with me, and I never forgot who got me through that incident and many more that followed at Bethesda and, eventually, in Vietnam.

One day, I walked onto the maximum-security ward (7D), where I spent most of my time while stationed at Bethesda. A Korean soldier, who was a new admit and who I hadn't seen before, met me inside the locked door as I reported to duty. His arm went up so fast I didn't even see it, and his hand came to rest at the tip of my nose. Fortunately, again, my training set in. Instead of the initial reaction of panic, which would be typical in this situation, I slowly reached out my hand and said, "Good morning. I'm Hospitalman Turner. Who are you?"

He was amazed at my coolness, and we became "friends," to the point that I was the only one who could talk to him when he was in a fighting mood—all because I'd shown him respect instead of panicking upon that initial meeting. Once again, God was there beside me.

The man was hospitalized after jumping from a government car on a crowded Washington, DC, throughway. When asked about his inappropriate behavior, he told the psychiatrists, "The goddess of beauty told me to do it." This was the only admission of a foreign soldier that I recall being admitted to section 7 (psych). He was only there a few days before he disappeared. Notices were sent to area media. That afternoon, a local barber called the police and said there was a foreign guy at his shop wanting a haircut. It wasn't his ethnicity that threw up a red flag to the barber. The man was wearing the "uniform of the day" for section 7 patients—dark blue pajamas and a robe that bore the words "Bethesda Naval Hospital." He was apprehended there. I have no idea what his disposition was, but we never saw him again.

Although it wasn't my forte, I also learned to fight violence with subdued violence. When a patient (Horace) attacked a nurse in the nursing station of good old "7D," I knew he had lost it. And I wasn't about to take him one-on-one, so I grabbed a fire extinguisher and turned his face into a frosty white. Only seconds before, he had been black. Now he was a black man with a snowman's face. When he thawed out, he shook my hand and thanked me for not letting him "kill the bitch!" Truth is, if I could have walked away, I might have momentarily considered doing so, because a few of the nurses were power hungry and flaunted their rank. This particular nurse belonged in that category.

By far, most of the nurses I worked with respected the corpsmen, whether NP techs other specialists or general corpsmen. But there were always those few who, just like in any job, considered themselves better than anybody ranked below them. Although they had some training working with psychiatric patients, very few could handle a patient who went ape shit.

Unfortunately, in that field of work, it happened often. In one incident, a five-foot seven, 150 pound patient sent several techs to the emergency room. The tech with the worst outcome received 101 stitches over various parts of his body. The weapon, a three-inch pocket knife. The wielder, a hospital corpsman who had trained with the Green Beret. It was a lesson that should have been learned but wasn't. In a facility such as this, the MP (military police) on duty should be stationed somewhere near the maximum security ward and should carry a weapon. This was a case of the infamous law that says there is a right way, a wrong way, and the navy way. I never did find out what set this man off, but nobody was able to talk him down. The event ended when two corpsmen who were off duty answered the alarm, rushed him with a mattress, and subdued him. He remained a patient there for a week or so before being returned to active duty.

A memorable time during my stint at Bethesda occurred after the death of my grandfather. I was home on a weekend pass when my grandfather died. I called the local chapter of the American Red Cross. I went through the steps they advised and was told I had been granted three extra days leave. After the funeral, I returned to my duty station, only to discover I was officially AWOL (absent without leave). Since I was well known at the front desk, I was permitted to go to my assigned barracks and stay until I was summoned in the morning.

Bright and early the next morning, an MP arrived at my dorm, and I was escorted to the captain's office. I was told the story was I'd flown home the prior Friday evening; fallen asleep on the plane, which was headed for Columbus; and ended up in Phoenix, Arizona. Usually, one does not laugh at a pre-court martial hearing, but the thought of being able to fly the friendly skies for three thousand miles while paying for a three hundred-mile flight was funny to me. Everyone there knew I thumbed home and never even considered flying. They knew there was something amiss. Fortunately, the captain's aide's chat with the American Red Cross representative cleared up the matter, and things were cool. Before I left, I discovered the captain not only had a sense of humor but was also thinking along my lines when he asked if I would secure one of those long-range flights for him at short-range price.

Another fiasco occurred on a night I returned to base; walked up to the main entrance of the hospital; and was grabbed by a marine military police and escorted, of all places, to the main information desk. People weren't allowed to enter the main entrance because President Johnson had been admitted there as a patient. Mr. Bad Ass Marine soon discovered, compliments of the "officer of the day," that he should have intercepted this sailor long before I reached the front door. The chief petty officer who was serving as OD (officer of the day) happened to be my boss at that time. By the time the MP had been reamed very well, I would not have wanted to meet him on the street the next day.

And so, the hours and days passed. Evenings consisted of anything from extra sleep to softball and basketball competition. The one thing that may surprise people is that I did not consume an alcoholic beverage during my military days. To this day, I have never been drunk a single time in my life. That's why I stuck around the barracks and read during the evenings when I wasn't playing sports.

The NP team had two entries in basketball, which gave me a chance to get in a good bit of playing time. Not having any varsity experience, I did quite well in playing point guard but didn't exactly have college or NBA scouts scurrying around the locker room seeking an interview.

Though I hadn't played a lot of organized baseball and had no experience whatsoever in softball, I managed to make the softball all-star team which consisted of players from neighboring bases in Maryland, Virginia, and Washington, DC. For an inexperienced little runt at five foot eight and 145 pounds (up from 117 when I entered boot camp), I was elated to receive the honors of being an all-star.

The first all-star game was held on a Saturday I was scheduled to work. The game was played on my home field at Bethesda. I had a friend who was willing to take my place at work for a few hours. This would have been approved with no questions asked 99 percent of the time. But the chief nurse of the psychiatric department (also known as the chief bitch)—one of those haggardly, overweight, sports-hating, men-hating "sweethearts"—nixed my request, and I wasn't to appear in my first all-star game after all.

Chapter 3

"The Times They Are a Changin'"

—Bob Dylan song, 1964

The times were quickly changing, and the clouds of war were thickening in Southeast Asia. The Vietnam War was escalating, and every member of the military, especially men (except for nurses) feared the worst when time for new assignments came. When time came for reassignment, we were given our "dream sheet" to fill out. Realistically, it was bullshit, spread thick and deep. I listed two naval hospitals, including Bethesda and Boston, plus Patuxent River Air Station in Maryland. The base sits on the Chesapeake Bay, which would not have been too much farther from home than Bethesda. We also had a "choice" of two duty stations overseas. I have no idea which ones I selected, other than one of the hospital ships. As I said, it would not have made a difference. Slots came open as those serving abroad finished their year, so I figured I would fit into the next available slot.

Once we hit the fourteen-month limit (the time that remained before our active duty time expired), we knew which direction we were headed—just not exactly where. We would be traversing westerly until west turned into the Far East. The good thing was, at that point, we did not have enough time left for jungle training. Therefore, we were headed to some sort of hospital setting in Vietnam. We would serve one more month at our current duty station before the mandatory thirty-day leave. It was mandatory on the military side to give us up to thirty days, assuming we had thirty days of accumulated leave. We could elect to take less time, but I have never met or been aware of anyone who did.

For too many of our heroes, this would be their final leave and final time with friends, family, and loved ones. Their last trip home would be to Dover Air Force Base in Delaware, with a ceremonial landing with full military honors.

One by one, we got our orders. Shep had left earlier. Some of my other friends, including lifelong "brother" Alan Wallace, left before that day in early September 1967 when I got my orders to serve on the USS *Repose* AH-16 (auxiliary hospital). This was one of two hospital ships where the dead and injured marines were sent from combat areas. I was familiar with the ships' names. And as I mentioned, on my dream sheet, I had requested one of these as my overseas "wish" slot. I do not remember which one. I figured I was a corpsman and an NP Tech. If I was going to leave the States, I might as well use my expertise. Hopefully, I'd be able to both help save lives and treat those who were mentally, emotionally, and physically scarred by combat.

The USS *Repose* and USS *Sanctuary* (AH-17) have, since, been scrapped. (You may be more familiar with the USNS *Comfort* and USNS *Mercy*, as both gained fame during the COVID-19 coronavirus pandemic of 2020.)

I had enjoyed my time at Bethesda. Well, that is considering the fact that I was a member of Uncle Sam's chosen few. I would have been happier if I was living at home, either working or going to college. But I had volunteered to put my time in and have never been sorry for eventually earning the title of "veteran'" I wish things had later taken a different course, but I will never have to hang my head because I refused to serve my country. I did what I felt compelled to do. My government, beginning with President Johnson, can kiss my patriotic red, white, and blue ass. But I love my country and the flag I served under and will be buried under.

At the end of October, 1968, I said so long to my remaining

buddies, figuring I would never see any of them again. Jack Sturiano was one of the three I'd see again later in life. As I mentioned, Shep and Alan had already departed for Vietnam.

Sturiano, a New Yorker, was a senior corpsman under whom I'd trained on ward 7C (neurology). He wasn't then a close enough friend to say an emotional goodbye to. We probably exchanged a quick handshake. However, through a twist of fate, after the death of Shep Chase, we met at my home. We kept in touch for a year or so. Then I got a letter from him stating he had joined the protest movement. He said goodbye without leaving a new address. He believed my opposition to this newfound movement would cost us our friendship. Well, Jack, we both fought for the right to believe in wherever life takes us. You have earned the right much more than others to know this! It is sad that we have corresponded for the last time.

One terrific result of being stationed at Bethesda was that my friendships from hospital corps school with Shep Chase and Alan Wallace would continue. These bonds would grow into a lifetime love as true "brothers."

The only good thing about getting orders to the Orient was the thirty days leave for which each soon-to-be-deployed soldier was automatically eligible. Unfortunately, as many believed, this was not "free" leave and was deducted from any accrued leave a serviceman had built up. There were a couple of reasons for this leave being automatically approved (as long as you had at least thirty days built up). One was that Uncle Sam knew that 58,220 weren't returning home alive. The other was that most of us who did return without our personal body bag, would be discharged upon arrival to the world. We might not be enclosed in that body bag, but we are still covered by it. Most of us continue to wear battle scars, whether physical or emotional. Being home for more than a week was something I had not experienced for some twenty-six months.

Chris and I were engaged that October. Looking back later in my life, I would come to a difficult realization. After all the death and devastation I had witnessed (and, adding insult to injury, the fact I was sent home without being debriefed), I believe Chris would have been fortunate if I'd returned in a body bag rather than being discharged. Even World War I and World War II soldiers and some from Korea had been debriefed on their way home while aboard ship. While the term "critical incident stress debriefing" hadn't been coined yet, I firmly believe the United States government was negligible in not debriefing those who served in combat or in a combat zone upon their return, whether they were being discharged or remaining on active duty.

Anyway, the thirty days flew by, and I'd received a change in orders. Instead of flying from Pittsburgh to Lackland Air Force Base in San Antonio, Texas, I was—per a new set of orders I received while at home—to fly to Los Angeles. From there, I was transported that Halloween evening to Norton Air Force Base near San Bernardino, California, where I would begin my flight to hell the following morning.

I remember very little about the transit base there at Norton Air Force Base. I arrived late at night; was up before daybreak; and boarded a plane without having to purchase a ticket, check in luggage, or go through any of the time-consuming pleasantries that normally preceded a flight. "Welcome to Flying Tiger Airlines!" the captain's voice boomed.

Somehow, Flying Tiger had quite a Southeast Asian connotation. The pilot wasted no time in lifting the big Boeing 707 into the air. And much too soon, the California shore was quickly approaching and then fading away, providing my first glimpse of the Pacific Ocean.

For the first time in my life (except for the short time over Lake Michigan on the way to basic training), I experienced seeing nothing but water below me for several hours. The truly magnificent sight soon grew old. But in about three hours, it was transformed into an even much more spectacular sight. As we approached Hawaii and the airport at Honolulu, the mountains were decorated in mist and rainbows that seemed to cascade from all directions. If one was on his way to war and did not believe in God, I don't know how the beauty that emanated from this scene could not touch his inner soul and proclaim that only God could create such a sight.

We had been allowed to disembark at Honolulu International Airport as the plane was refueled. Therefore, I can say I was in Hawaii long enough to get "leid." Of course, I'm referring to the leis the cute Hawaiian girls placed around our necks there on the tarmac. This was a terrific prepayment for the service I was about to give my country.

The flight from Honolulu to Okinawa was a horrendous ride. We ran into a terrific storm that shook the plane as if the Golden Dragon at the International Date Line had reached up and pulled us down hundreds of feet at a time, relinquishing and then regaining its grip to tease us into thinking we weren't going to survive its awesome power. But the pilot prevailed, and the dragon would have to reach out for the next plane, which surely wasn't far behind.

A few hours of nighttime on the island of Okinawa, and the flight was ready to resume. Where to? We weren't exactly sure until we reboarded the bird and noticed that the sweet, young, coffee-serving stewardesses had disappeared, only to be replaced by two male stewards who weren't the typical, polite coffee-serving hostesses we had come to enjoy on the previous legs of the flight. There would be no more stops before our final destination.

A few hours later, 150 or so sailors, marines, soldiers, and airmen went sailing into hell!

PART TWO

Chapter 4

"For each and every underdog, soldier in the night:
And we gazed upon the chimes of freedom flashing."

—*"Chimes of Freedom Flashing," Bob Dylan, 1965*

It was Halloween night again (because of the International Date Line), and the flare-lit skies above Da Nang Air Base lent credence to the occasion. It appeared as though we were heading into daylight already, although, this time, it was obvious it had nothing to do with time zone or the natural order of things in the universe. Just as in the song by Neil Diamond, "Night Becomes Day," the flares take on a whole different perspective.

Da Nang Airport at 2230 hours seemed as though it was basked in the tropical sun to which we would soon be introduced. The flares were spookily the first sign of war we experienced. Eerie shadows danced, and as each flare sunk in the night sky, another arose to replace it. It seemed as though every F-11 (Phantom jet), helicopter, vehicle, and building transformed into grotesque objects crawling slowly but purposefully along the ground at various speeds, according to the angle and height of the nearest flare. Eerie shadows distorted reality, morphing it into something from the underworld.

As our aircraft taxied to a stop on the godforsaken foreign tarmac after what seemed to be several hours, it was time to disembark. Here it was—the time every male teenager of the time envisioned and feared. Even for those who lived for this day—a chance to experience combat and legally kill another human being—the harsh reality set in that this might be the last minute of our life, or maybe the last day. We knew for certain that, for many on that plane, it would be the last year of their life. For us, 1968 was a goal, not a new year that was only two months away. Many of us and many of those in every group that landed here had kissed their families a final farewell and told them goodbye for the final time. Who would be the victims? Who would be the survivors? We each had an idea what our chances were according to statistics compiled by our MOs (modi operandi). But little did many of us realize that job descriptions would change upon arrival. Some would serve in a different role than expected. A division that had remained rather dormant for a while might be headed to the frontline as replacements arrived.

Many (marines) who expected to spend twelve or thirteen months in steady combat ended up spending their tour down south in a life of comparable "luxury" with a mama-san to clean their hooch, wash their clothes, and feed them. Then came those who expected to skate through a year of easy duty, only to end up in harm's way consistently. I don't know that anyone could have known with any certainty what life would dish out over the next year. All we could be certain of was that, a year from now, we wouldn't all be gathering for a reunion and boarding the same flight together again. Tiger Airlines did not provide us with a round-trip airline ticket. These flights came one at a time, as one-way reservations.

Then came the first step off the plane. And we were headed … where? Follow the leader. Where the hell was the leader going? Did he himself even know where he was headed? To a building? To a bunker? To another plane? To drop us off at a different air base?

Uncertainty abounded. Just follow the man in front of you. (Sorry, ladies. There's no sexism meant here. It's just that there were no females on this particular flight.) Do what you were told, just like in basic training. Trust your government and believe that each politician, each military officer, and all those entrusted with any power whatsoever knew exactly why in hell we were in this war and exactly what the hell we were doing here.

For many of us, basic training was two years passed. Many of us had been in class since then, learning and perfecting our advanced skills and becoming specialists in our field. Others had come here thirty days after basic training, having received their orders with their first stripe. "Congratulations, Marine. You have just earned the only stripe you will live to see. And here is a one-way ticket for a thirteen thousand-mile journey, compliments of Uncle Sam. And just think of it this way. If you survive, you will receive another ticket this time next year and maybe even another stripe. Of course, you might receive a free ticket for a medical flight before your time is up. But then you may only be half a person and live the rest of your life in one of our fantastic Veterans Administration hospitals. The good news is that your family won't receive a single medical bill for your treatment!"

We ended up in a building, a Quonset hut, used as a staging area. I couldn't believe the first thing I saw when I arrived there. It wasn't a stack of bodies or coffins lined up awaiting a flight home in the aircraft we had just abandoned. There, on a desk, sat a small television set on which *It's the Great Pumpkin, Charlie Brown* was playing.

Of course, I realize that movie wasn't comforting to a whole lot of those who had just arrived with me. But the last one I expected to see upon arrival at the asshole of the world was my idol, Snoopy, and the rest of the Peanuts gang. Snoopy remains one of my idols to this day. My office is full of *Peanuts* characters, pictures, and other memorabilia I've collected over the years. We even put up a Christmas tree every year and decorate it with nothing but *Peanuts* characters. Maybe Charlie, Lucy, Linus, Franklin, Pigpen, Woodstock, and the rest of the gang represent the friends I didn't have while growing up.

Charles Schulz was a genius. It's a shame so very few people understood the philosophy and religious context behind his cartoons and films. Mr. Schulz would have made a great president. He certainly wouldn't have seen things through the eyes of LBJ but, rather, through the eyes of his beloved characters. Yet, I don't believe he was a pacifist either. If you aren't familiar with Schulz's persona, try reading *The Parables of Peanuts* by Robert Short. I tried reading it once but laid it down. Then after college, I read it thoroughly. Parts of it were still over and beyond my pea brain!

While most guys had pinups and calendars with pictures of Marilyn and Raquel, mine was of good ol' Snoopy. When a study was done to find the number one pinup of those serving in Vietnam, the result surprised most people, but not me. It was Snoopy himself, the World War II flying ace, returned to be with his counterparts, in a different war, a different time, and seemingly even a different dimension. Imagine those poor broads, one who was long gone by the time of the study and the other, the sex goddess of her time, being beaten out by a dog! What a statement we were making without realizing it. I guess people still fail to realize it today.

Meanwhile, back to the "midnight sun" created by the flares over the Da Nang Air Base and being told where we would spend the night. I remember very little about that night. If I had to, I couldn't even tell you where I slept.

Again, I have no memory of that first night. I don't remember how far we walked to our temporary bunks. I don't remember hitting the sack my first night on foreign soil. I don't remember if they fed us first. I don't remember if I slept at all or if I prayed all night long (which is the most likely scenario). I don't remember getting up or eating breakfast the next morning. I don't remember shit!

I guess at some time in the morning hours, the sun rose to announce the dawn of another day. I don't remember seeing the sun that morning. Maybe things just continued to be a blur, and my mind couldn't process how quickly things were happening. It seemed like each moment was a first of something or other in my life. What I am sure of is that the blazing sun rose over the mountains east of Da Nang, giving a message—"enjoy the first day of the rest of your life. It may be one of the hottest days you'll experience, and it may be one of the few you have left!"

I was given the news that the *Repose* was anchored in the harbor, and those of us assigned to her figured we were an hour or so away from our intended duty station. Then we were told she was headed for Hong Kong and that we couldn't catch a ride in a chopper because the weather was too rough to allow a chopper to land. Later, we would discover that was the first lie we witnessed, as we experienced many choppers headed to and landing on the helipad of the ship, carrying enough supplies to cover the ensuing voyage. We stood there and watched in dismay as the diesel engines coughed up black smoke, preparing to get underway.

There was no free ticket to ride the "Great White Whore" for a voyage to another way-off country in the Orient. (I would discover the nickname for the large white floating bathtub with red crosses painted in several conspicuous areas identifying it as a floating hospital later on.) Maybe a return ticket on the next flight out of Da Nang would be a good idea, since we couldn't get a flight to our duty station about a half a mile away! No, how about an eight-day tour of duty in the rat-infested, hotter-than-hell food storage building where you can "work for food" until the ship comes back?

Many folks believe in destiny or karma. I believe in an omnipotent, all-knowing God who, despite my disappointment, knew something I didn't, which would be revealed to me in the future, or maybe not. Maybe God just let me experience one of the many disappointments that would lie ahead in the next year.

This is how the military makes a man/woman out of you. Sometimes a superior will do things just to prick you and see how angry they can make you. Sometimes, as in this instance, there is no personal involvement by another person. But I sucked it up and said, "That's OK." After today, I would only have 364 days left until I would leave the ship, which I was watching leave for Hong Kong. Who knew? Maybe I could do something for somebody in the next eight days that would leave a positive mark on myself or someone else. And in the end, I would be glad I was left behind. Always take a positive attitude and roll with the punches, especially in a situation in which you have no control.

Those of us who were placed in a holding group while we awaited assignment were mustered after breakfast, and we were sorted out like dirty linen. One was sent with this batch, and another went with the next batch. Once we were broken into groups, we went off with the particular group to which we had been assigned. I didn't get a chance to talk with many members of my company of twenty or so, but I figured this was the bunch that was assigned to ships. My main reason for figuring this out was because one of the corpsmen I'd met on the plane was in my group. Immediately, that group was broken down, and Mario and I were the only ones left in our new minigroup.

I remember throwing my seabag with all my earthly possessions onto a Jeep and being driven to a very large building with sheets of steel siding and a roof consisting of the same material. The driver stopped long enough to let me get out and grab my seabag, and I was headed down the road within seconds.

A grumpy sergeant, who appeared to be as happy to be here as I, greeted me by assigning me to a shit detail. The sweltering heat outside was bad enough, but the humidity was extremely oppressive inside the steel building, and the heat seemed to climb to yet another level. My detail was unloading and stacking boxes (of whatever happened to be in them) onto appropriate shelves. I knew what I had to say to him would end up with a snide remark, so I carried out my assignment until a whistle blew. I didn't know if the whistle meant incoming rounds were approaching or if it was for something that didn't involve me. So, I just played follow the leader and discovered we were all on a fifteen-minute break.

Speaking of "break," now was my chance. I slipped away into what seemed to be the main office of the warehouse and spotted a junior air force officer relaxing at his typical military green metal desk. He was sitting, feet up on the desk with a fan blowing air—hot but nonetheless air—into his face.

He looked up and made a derogatory remark about me being a sailor as opposed to all the soldiers in the area. I knew what I wanted to say, but I had to choose my approach and wording very carefully in order to let him know I respected his rank and, yes, even his branch of the military.

He seemed to know from experience what I had to say. But before I could say anything, he beat me to the punch. "What's the problem sailor? Is the work too hard for you? You think you're going to come in here for a week or so and get a pussy job like mine?"

"No thanks, I'm not better than anyone else here, but my MO" (in military terms, modus operandi referred to an individual's specialty) "is a corpsman and neuropsychiatric technician, and this isn't exactly what I went to two schools to prepare for. I didn't see any wounded boxes of cereal that looked like they needed first aid or any oranges that seemed to need crisis intervention." I wanted so badly to continue with, "So, the hell with this bullshit!"

I knew I had made my point. Saying anything else in addition to my statement would only piss him off. I stood my ground but wasn't going to let my announcement of being a corpsman make me look like an eccentric, so I let it go at that. If it came down to a pissing contest, I would be assigned to an even worse job. So I stopped there, stared him in the eyes, and waited … and waited. Finally, surprisingly enough, my point was accepted as legitimate. The assignment at Da Nang Hospital would serve as a temporary duty station until the ship returned from Hong Kong.

So, off I went, toting my seabag with all my worldly possessions flung over my shoulder. Looking just like the World War II flying ace, Snoopy, I headed for a building that was probably a mile or so away on an immense military base. The base was larger than most of the cities I had visited. There was a bus route, but I had no idea what bus would take me to the hospital, as I saw no such banner on any bus that passed by.

After the long walk, I reported to the duty officer. And to my amazement, I ended up, not on a psychiatric ward or medical ward, but at the VD clinic (yes, as in venereal disease). Fortunately, I wasn't involved in treating syphilis or gonorrhea. Instead, I was assigned to question soldiers who came to the clinic with complaints consistent with the various types of sexually transmitted diseases. What a skate job!

"Who did you have sex with?"

"Well, I figured you didn't remember her name."

"Of course, she was short, skinny, and had slanted eyes, and they all look alike!" (As if I was asking them to describe someone in the United States, where race, height, or color of hair might make a difference in describing a female suspect.)

"You say your friends did her too?"

"Of course, you don't remember which friends they were!"

"We need to know about your buddies so we can get them started on antibiotics."

"Look, man, I don't give a shit if your pecker rots and falls off. Tell me what I need to know or get the hell out of here! I'm a short-timer here and on my way to a real duty station. Cooperate or suffer the consequences. It's your choice."

"Next victim, front and center!"

Note to reader—I am sensitive now to racial and cultural issues. This account is written in past tense about a different era and a totally different situation.

The prostitutes were accounted for, rounded up, and given medication to clear up their VD as much as possible. They weren't harmed at all. It was better to work with them, by offering free medical attention, for the sake of our GIs, rather than to have them fear us and hide.

One fantastic event took place soon after I arrived at Da Nang Hospital. As I entered whatever building I was told to report to, I heard a voice call out, "Kurt Turner, you asshole!"

The coward was hiding behind a surgical mask, which I was about to remove so I could throw my first punch ever away from American soil. As I approached the faceless figure, he removed his mask and thus revealed the person who was about to become my worst enemy was, in fact, none other than Alan Wallace. We enjoyed a good laugh, and Alan became my guide for the first eight days of my Vietnam tour.

As of this writing, Alan and I still have a good time. We talk often and meet every couple of months when Alan travels to the

Arlington/DC area. He stops at McDonald's near my home for breakfast, and I meet him there at 7:00 a.m.

Soon, much too soon, war became a reality. Having spent more than a week in Da Nang helped me grow accustomed to some of the sounds of war. Air raid sirens wailed so often that, after a few days, I became somewhat immune to them. They served as such empty threats that only a few people scurried to bomb shelters when the sirens blared out a supposed danger from the Vietcong, who were always nearby.

My first and only experience with a bomb shelter came soon after I was assigned to Da Nang Hospital. For some reason, many of the personnel who happened to be outside one evening took a siren seriously and headed to a large aluminum-clad building, reinforced nearly to the top with sandbags. After surviving the initial rush of people storming into the building, my claustrophobia kicked in. I managed to get outside and braced myself against the sandbags on the side opposite of where I figured any incoming projectiles may be approaching from. After that, I subscribed to the belief that the chance of enemy fire striking me was substantially less than that of being crushed by friendly bodies crowding the entry to the shelter. There was no incoming fire that night. Nor was there on any other night while I was at Da Nang (other than the outer perimeter). There were just more false alarms. If there were attacks, they weren't near the hospital complex.

As my friend Alan later told me, there were several artillery attacks on the hospital compound during his tour. I often wondered if everybody on base was new that night or if there had been a legitimate suspicion of an attack stemming from that particular incident. From then on, I followed the lead of others who apparently shared my fear of being compressed into a small shelter whose capacity was overwhelmed and sought refuge in any space that appeared to give some protection. But never again did I enter the dreaded, packed shelters.

So, the trip to hell had begun, actually quite innocently. There was no death and destruction here at the VD clinic, and I stayed out of triage, away from death and dismemberment. Little did I know that these eight days were a preliminary run and that the fires of hell were being warmed up as the ship sailed back into Da Nang Harbor. It was then that I finally caught a relay launch to the ship and was to become an old salty sailor at last.

The small watercraft brought seven or eight of the ship's crew alongside the Great White Whore. Its red crosses were a designation that meant hostile fire was prohibited by the Geneva Convention. Yeah, right. The agreement, which we were to abide by, was one the enemy took as a joke. I soon learned that my fellow corpsmen in the field didn't wear their caducei for a similar reason. The emblem was meant to let the enemy identify a medic so as not to kill him. But it was actually the favorite target of the enemy.

Most of the crew on the small boat were already stationed on the ship and had gone into Da Nang for one reason or another. The ones with seabags were easily identified as the rookies. Since the sea was choppy and ladders didn't work, one at a time, we were sent a rope. We would hold onto the heavy seabag and onto the rope and be hoisted by crane onto the deck. Anyone who wasn't in tough physical shape would be the next victim received at the ship's triage station.

Welcome aboard! You finally made it, sailor! You are about to experience day number one aboard a United States Navy vessel. The sea was churning, and all the newcomers were turning green at the gills. The marines and new guys were puking all over the place, and things were getting messy. So, I set my mind to it that this greenhorn wasn't going to give in, even if I had to swallow my own vomit. Since I had a stomach that wouldn't let me regurgitate even when anyone else would be blowing chunks from sea to shining sea, I survived the first day ordeal with all food in place, and I was on my way to becoming a real sailor.

The rest of my first evening aboard ship was spent being assigned a rack and locker in the crowded quarters that housed enlisted corpsmen only. Nurses had their own quarters of course, as did the male officers (in the same section of the ship). The rest of the ship's crew, which took care of maintaining and guiding the ship, had separate quarters.

My rack (or bed to civilians) was at the bottom of a stack of three hammock-like devices in which each of us (except the top) had just enough room to get in and could barely turn over unless the man above you wasn't in his rack. Mine was near the shower room, which meant not getting much sleep even on nights when there was actually an opportunity to get a little shut-eye. I don't recall how many were berthed there, but it was a few hundred at least, and it was a busy place, even at night.

One thing nobody has ever heard me complain about was the living conditions. That is reserved for my fellow vets who served in the jungle and other areas of combat. As bad as conditions seemed at the time, they were like living in the Hilton compared to others who didn't have a roof over their head; seldom had square meals; and were hunted down by the, snakes, bugs, spiders, and leeches.

In fact, my first dining experience was surprising. Food aboard a US Navy ship thirteen thousand miles away from home was, under the circumstances, somewhat amazing. Compared to what I expected, it was like eating in a floating gourmet restaurant—well, to an extent.

As for privacy, there was no more privacy than boot camp had allowed. All these men had one large head (bathroom) and one large shower room that also included sinks for shaving. We made the best of it. But my most vivid memory (unfortunately) was the three hundred-pound redhead who enjoyed running around naked. He stripped when he hit the bottom of the ladder (stairs) going into the berthing complex and did not dress until he was ready to leave. This was not a pretty sight! He was a very likeable guy, but men (most of them) just failed to want to hang around with an extra-large, naked, overstuffed, redheaded sailor.

With a quick tour of the ship completed (including ward C-2, the psychiatric ward, where I would be stationed) and an incorrect expectation of what was to come implanted in my brain, I was now the new guy on the USS *Repose*. The reason I say there was an incorrect expectation is a simple one. The ship had just returned from a week of fun in Hong Kong. Therefore, almost all patients except for a few walking wounded had been released before sailing to a foreign port. The Great White Whore had returned to its destiny, and all hell was ready to break loose.

Here's a quick review of logistics for the *Repose*, as compiled by Mike Burns (who appears later in this book), starting with personnel:

- 750 hospital beds
- 25 doctors
- 29 nurses
- 3 dentists
- 315 hospital corpsmen

These numbers do not reflect ship's company (only medical personnel).

Burns also compiled the logistic of the *Repose*'s storied history:

- Commissioned in 1943 as *Marine Beaver*
- Commissioned as a US hospital ship on May 26, 1946
- Decommissioned and recommissioned several times
- Served in both the Korean War and the Vietnam War
- Sold for scrapping on April 18, 1975

Chapter 5

"I looked up and there before me was a pale horse! Its rider was named Death, and Hades was following close behind him."

—Revelation 6:8

My tour aboard the *Repose* began with things going slowly for a few days. A couple of admissions to the psychiatric ward here and there, and slowly we built up a patient status of fifteen or so. Many had "character disorders." They'd made it through boot camp and were now faced with the reality of their situation. Their coping mechanisms deteriorated quickly because they had never really coped with the serious side of life in the first place. There were those who couldn't handle authority because they saw that much of the authority came from junior officers in the field, who had no conception of what they were doing there and how to handle their authority. Then came the real cases of those whose brains just decided they weren't going to accept the reality of what was happening to the sensory organs. The body would shut down because the brain ceased trying to decipher what orders to relate to in a certain situation. This was previously considered "shell shock."

Then an increasingly alarming number of different patterns of behavior disorders became prevalent. Drug abuse was on the rise. By this time, some of the marines were chronic abusers, while others would overdose before they learned how to use the drugs in a somewhat controlled, sensible manner. Marijuana, alcohol, and just about every drug imaginable was prevalent in Vietnam. Some came from beans of plants native to the area. Yet others came from all over the globe, making it into the hands of the black marketers. It became increasingly difficult at times to differentiate between and diagnose combat stress disorder from drug-induced disorders.

In most instances, we were able to get the young men back into battle within a few days. A little bit of rest and a little counseling would usually do wonders for them. The others would be medevaced by helicopter or small boat craft to Da Nang. As far as we knew, they probably had just received their ticket back to the world. Once I escorted a patient to Da Nang, I had no idea where his final destination might be. At that time, I really wasn't concerned with where he was going. I got him where I was supposed to deliver him, and now it was up to me to get back to the ship. It didn't matter how long I stayed ashore as long as I was back for my next shift. If I left during my regular shift, I was pretty well on shore leave until the next day. However, once daylight faded, the ship seemed a much safer environment. Therefore, unless I had to find a launch or chopper headed for the *Repose* immediately, I normally spent a few hours looking for old friends or traveling throughout the large military complex, talking to soldiers and listening to their stories. It was nice to find a "sane" marine to talk to, someone who could provide a perspective on the marine experience that would balance out the stories I'd heard from marines with character disorders.

Day by day, the patient load returned to what I was told was normal until FQ (flight quarters) began to sound seemingly every few minutes. When flight quarters were piped and announced, each corpsman who was "off duty" from his regular station and was on the FQ list for that time period literally ran to the staging area just to the starboard (right) side of the helicopter landing pad, which was at the aft (rear) of the ship. Once the chopper landed, we would take turns unloading wounded marines, usually on stretchers, to triage. In the case of the walking wounded, a corpsman would escort him to triage. If there were many walking wounded, they would follow the line behind the stretcher bearers.

A typical scene would be the one captured in the *Milwaukee Journal* in 1968 of myself and another corpsman carrying a wounded marine on a stretcher, while our third buddy carried an IV bottle that was providing life-sustaining dextrose to the patient until we got him to triage on the port (left) side of the ship.

At first, flight quarters were about as routine as regular duty on the psychiatric ward. We would unload the wounded and stay with them and the doctors treating them until they were sent to their destinations, which would be surgery, medical ward, X-ray, or one of the other various units. The bad part was that this was in addition to the eight- to twelve-hour shift we had already worked at our primary assignment.

I learned to deal with a wide variety of maladies. On ward C-2, I had already dealt with character disorders, anger, and a wide variety of psychiatric disorders, real or faked. Although I was trained as a corpsman first, I hadn't actually dealt much with injuries and not with injury-related death at all. That was one of the benefits of going into a specialist rating. I had dealt with some of these things, including natural deaths during my tour at Bethesda. But this was fast becoming a brand-new experience. It was an experience that I dealt with well at the time, while having no idea how it would impact my own psyche after I left the war scene and ventured back into civilian life.

The *Repose* sat approximately three miles offshore most of the time. Spotlights shone brightly, glaring off the huge red crosses that were painted on the smokestack and sides of the ship identifying the *Repose* as one of the two hospital ships stationed there at the time. The other was the USS *Sanctuary*. They were our rivals in a sense because it seemed as though every time we were scheduled to visit a foreign port (except for repairs in the Philippines), they ended up going instead. Much of that was probably rumors; they undoubtedly felt the same about us. The one thing we did know was that we respected each other because the personnel from one ship could not have handled the massive amount of casualties sent to the two hospital ships combined.

We seldom spent more than two consecutive days in one spot. Our three stations were offshore from the areas that typically suffered the most casualties—Chu Lai; Phu Bai; and the point nearest the demilitarized zone, Dong Ha. Sitting near those areas, we received patients from all over the country, including Chu Lai, Phu Bai, and many others. After a tour of the coast, we would pull into Da Nang harbor every week or so. Here, we would pick up supplies and drop off patients returning to duty or being sent back to the world, having been injured severely enough that their fighting days were over and they would be sent to military hospitals stateside. This took a little pressure off Da Nang Hospital's efforts.

We would pick up our new shipmates at Da Nang and also say good-bye to our comrades whose tour was complete. When our tour was finished, we would depart the ship on our last scheduled stop at Da Nang. That is where all (I am sure there were a few exceptions) the arrivals and departures to and from the States originated. Except for extreme circumstances, this was the first and last base you saw even if you arrived or departed by ship, instead of by air.

Da Nang was truly the nerve center of the United States military in Vietnam. Had the North Vietnamese developed the capability to destroy this air base and hospital complex, along with its strategic command, there were only two things I could foresee happening. Either the war would be over within days, and our troops inland would be annihilated, or Hanoi and Haiphong would be nuked. More than likely, both of the above would have occurred. The one comfort of being stationed on a hospital ship was knowing that, if one was to be sunk by enemy fire, the later of the above actions might well have been a foregone conclusion, as the hospital ships were totally unarmed, being covered by the Geneva Convention as off limits to hostile fire. But then, did Lyndon Johnson even know the rules of the Geneva Convention?

The ship's staff was also defenseless when departing the ship, regardless of circumstances. We were never issued a firearm. The only weapons I ever experienced were those immediately removed from the injured and sent back to the chopper that had delivered them. The enemy was well aware of this, so instead of attacking our defenseless ship, they continued to provide us with casualties. During my tour came major battles with massive amounts of casualties. Several of those were during my first couple months aboard ship.

I could go to history sites and figure out what dates each major battle was fought between November 1, 1967, and October 31 of the following year. But providing you with a calendar of events and carefully placing them in chronological order would serve no purpose, at least for me. When you are treating a casualty, where he was wounded or what day it was held no significance. Time seemed to drift into a different, faraway dimension; a clock had no real presence. We handled events one at a time as they appeared. Sometimes, events entailed days instead of hours. We slept when we could and looked forward to another quiet, uneventful trip to Subic Bay. The location of the wound and knowing how to treat it as quickly and efficiently as time allowed was all that mattered. I will never forget that James E. Williams, Jr., was mortally wounded at Quang Tri province. Though I didn't know it then, Williams and his passing would one day play a big role in my life.

History books will reveal the dates and fact of battles. The single concern of the medical staff was "here and now." What did it matter if the patient was flown in from Khe San or from Cambodia? And yes, there were injuries and deaths in Laos and Cambodia. But at the time, it did not matter where they came from. If they died, they were just as dead as if it were somebody who died of a heart attack standing in front of you while you were brushing your teeth at your home in Montana.

Having mentioned history books, let me make something clear. I am not naive enough to think our grandchildren's history books do more than mention there was a war in a place called Vietnam—a place they couldn't find on a map within five minutes. To research information about what a friend's grandchild calls "my grandfather's war," one would have to dig much deeper than a textbook.

I would discover many years later that, in many cases, the government would list a soldier as "killed in action" at the location where the injury occurred, rather than on either of the hospital ships. That doesn't bother me though, as more often than not, those working in "graves registration" at Da Nang had no idea where the body was received from—whether directly from the field or from a hospital ship. The next chopper headed to Da Nang from the ship, if there was space, would transport bodies to the air base. The pilots, gunners, or corpsmen aboard the flight didn't discuss such pleasantries with those who removed the bodies. When identified by dog tags, marines would be then connected to documentation noting what unit they belonged to and where that unit was located at the time. That location was most often recorded as the place of death. As for the cases with which I am familiar, if the soldier was alive when reaching the ship and survived long enough for records of care to be implemented, my guess is the ship would, in that case, be listed as the location of death. To the deceased soldier's family, the geographical place of death mattered. To the government, it was just another dead soldier and a number listed in the swiftly growing list of casualties.

Although I have a lot of qualms as to how the government dispersed information, I cannot fault it in a case of a US marine dying in the field when he might have died on the helicopter on transport or immediately following arrival aboard ship. As you will understand later in this book, you might feel comforted that your son, brother, or other loved one might not have died as lonely a death as you have perceived for many years. However, as in one special case to be revealed later, you might cling to the hope that your loved one died in friendly care and that the government did not "cover up" the fact of where he died. It was just impossible to claim whether his actual death occurred in the field, in a chopper, or soon after being received at a hospital in the field or at sea. Forgive me for giving LBJ and his group of fellow asshole administrators the benefit of doubt over cover-ups in at least one situation. However, place of death in a war such as this, was, in many cases, impossible to record with certainty.

If you take offense to me calling most of our patients "marines," as opposed to "soldiers," "sailors," "airmen," or any other designation, be assured there is a reason. I am not slighting the casualties of other branches of the service. They were as important as marines, and there is certainly no slighting of any of our war dead, certainly not by yours truly. I only use the term "marines" because, by far, the largest percentage of our patients were marines. The Navy Medical Corps treated marines, as it was responsible for all those under the Department of the Navy.

For those of you not familiar with military structure, there is no department of the Marine Corps. The corps falls under the US Department of the Navy. While at times I like to joke about this, I am only stating this for the purpose of informing the reader that army and air force bases usually provided care for their own injured, and the navy provides care to marines and navy personnel. However, at times, we treated patients of any designation if we were the closest facility. This also included care for NVA and even Vietcong. Remember, we were medical professionals, and a life was a life to us. If I mentioned treating what appeared to be Chinese patients, I would probably be put on a hit list. We also treated "ROKs," as in injured from the Republic of Korea (as allies) and others whose nationality I am not absolutely sure of, so I will let it go at that. My purpose is not to argue over who was and who was not involved in the war—or whose side they fought for. Let it suffice to say we honored the motto of the USS *Repose*, "Restitutor Vitae" (Restorer of Life).

By far, most of patients we treated were United States Marines. They came in by helicopters of all types. Many came in by Hueys, which were the small, fast choppers that could get in and out quickly, as a dust off, without providing a large target like the jolly green giants, chinooks, and some of the others. One type of air force helicopter landed twice while I was on duty. Nobody appreciated having to remove the wounded from it because it was small, and its blades came down at a very low trajectory at the sides of the machine. It would decapitate the first corpsman to approach and disengage anywhere except directly from the front. We were used to unloading patients from the side. But then we would take the shortest route to triage by cutting in front of the chopper—except for this one. One corpsman got a little too close, and the suction created from the blades removed his hat from his back pocket, swept it up into the blades, and severed the bill from the cap. It taught us all very quickly to respect this funny-looking bird used by the air force. Other choppers created a backwash that blew loose objects away, rather than sucking them up.

Most recoveries from helicopters were routine as far as unloading the wounded. Several of the injured were walking wounded, and we simply escorted them to triage and then returned to help others. Usually, once you escorted or carried off a patient, there were enough men on flight quarters duty that one didn't need to return to the flight deck. Some of the larger choppers held enough wounded marines that we returned to the bird again. But the agony occurred when bird after bird arrived, and you knew the proverbial shit had hit the fan somewhere on land. This was when things got extremely hectic.

I had never been close to a helicopter in my life until my tour on the *Repose* began. Soon, I began to hope I would never see one up close again in my life. I would change my mind about twenty-two years later.

Helicopters are synonymous with different perspectives or events with different military backgrounds. For many marines and soldiers, they are synonymous with deployment or returning from the field. With some, they are linked to receiving supplies or mail. To others, they provided cover during battles. To the unfortunate, they provided evacuation. The pilots are among the bravest men (now women) I ever saw.

To the corpsmen, nurses, and doctors, helicopters meant one thing. Doctors and nurses can't relate to one specific aspect as much as the corpsmen, because, even though they treated the wounded, they did not participate in carrying them from the chopper to triage. But for us, we were the ones to poke our heads inside and see what was arriving. The scene was seldom one we anticipated. Nor were the smells. The olfactory sense sometimes beat the optical response. But we all knew the precious cargo aboard each flight was ours to deal with at the best of our ability.

I had seen one person die before I left for Vietnam. When I was about eleven years old, I saw a man we called "Buttermilk" fall from a tree he was trimming. He rode a rope down several feet. But when it let loose, he fell directly onto a pipe used as a fence post. The pipe entered just above his hips and impaled itself about two feet into his torso. That was the only time I saw the glassy eyes of a tragic death victim until I reached the age of nineteen.

Soon, reality presented itself—I hadn't come here to be just a psychiatric technician. I'd come here to deal with injury and death, as well as to treat those who couldn't deal with the psychological stress of war.

The first few shifts of flight quarters were fairly routine. A few walking wounded and those on stretchers who were carried into triage were treated quickly and sent to the ward where they would be admitted, or to surgery, X-ray, or whatever appropriate destination was applicable. Then came a few more seriously injured marines. Blood-soaked uniforms and blankets were becoming the norm, rather than the exception. The dying were catching up in numbers to those who would be quickly returned to duty. The screams of the seriously and terminally injured were often ear piercing. I still experience those audible sensations in dreams and during times when certain stressors present themselves.

Then came the smell of the result of flesh wounds caused by "Willie Peter," or white phosphorous. It ate through uniforms. It ate through skin. Then if it was a large enough piece, it ate through not only organs, but also sometimes even bones. The smell was horrific. Even today, similar smells come back to haunt me, and I'm sure many of those who were hit with the stuff and those who were with them and those who treated them still experience this phenomenon. It is a smell your brain may put away for the time being, but it never forgets it. Burnt flesh and urine are two odors that are very specific. Maybe you haven't smelled burnt flesh, but we all recognize the odor of urine, perhaps a smell we experience when we walk into nursing homes.

Not only do the sights, sounds, and smells never disappear, all the senses are locked into remembering pain and death. The taste of blood is one of the most irritating of the recalled senses. It passes our way much too often. Those working in a "regular" hospital can rinse their mouths quickly if they get blood in their mouths. With precautions taken today, it doesn't happen often. Not only did we not wear protective masks, hell, we weren't even issued latex gloves. Those were for surgeons. They were used to protect the patient in most cases, rather than today, when they are used to protect the medical staff as well.

I fail to remember washing my hands in between taking care of patients. Nor do I recall the facilities to be able to scrub down. We certainly transferred blood, dirt, and many germs from one patient to the next. Times have changed, and so have procedures. But at that time, all of us did the best we could. Our entire focus was on the patient receiving care at the moment.

We were assigned to flight quarters during about half to two-thirds of the time we were not scheduled for duty at our primary assignment. Sometimes, we were primary and sometimes, secondary, which meant the primary crew handled things until the shit hit the fan. Then it became a very long day or, more likely, a very long night.

Regular duty on the psychiatric ward (C-2) was usually fairly easy duty. Sometimes, we even played cards with patients, assuming the caseload was low. This usually happened when we were getting ready to go to Subic Bay, Philippines, for ship's maintenance. My coworker friend, Stan, and I became the reigning champions at Hearts, a game I had never even played before I landed on C-2.

The calm didn't persist very often once we hit the coastline. It seemed as though casualties had been waiting in line from the minute we left. A lot of business could accumulate in less than a week. Then all hell let loose, and the Philippine memory was left in the distant past.

Little did I know the morning after I arrived "in-country" (aka

Vietnam), what was to be the third deadliest battle as far as American casualties would begin in Dak To. It went on for a month, but I couldn't grasp the enormity of it because, when I boarded the *Repose* on November 8, it was only occupied by staff and walking wounded, who got to take the ride to Hong Kong. Even though the number of casualties ballooned quickly, I had nothing to compare those numbers to, as I was the new kid on the block. Therefore, the fact that we would soon have injured soldiers lying on stretchers on the outside decks did not tell me this was an exception. Soon, I would discover it *was* an exception that would play itself out again in about two months, from mid-January until sometime in April when the shit hit the fan in Khe Sanh. Two hundred and five Americans would die during that extended battle. Casualties included on January 31, 1968, alone, across the country totaled 246. This was the deadliest single day of the war.

Despite January 31 being the deadliest day, the month of February, which included the deadliest week, would become the deadliest month of the war, with a total of 3,895 casualties. This included the monthlong battle at Hue in which 119 troops were killed. This was the major North Vietnamese drive, which became known as the Tet Offensive. In my own humble opinion, this was when Ho Chi Minh let LBJ know who was winning the war. He had the support of his troops and his country. Johnson was facing turmoil from the streets of San Francisco to the shores of the country, where he was facing military defeat. He should have been congratulated and honored for being the only American president to taste the bitterness of losing a war.

It seemed as though we took on almost all the casualties from Hue, which, for some reason, is the time period I seem to remember most. Flight quarters was relentless. I believe it was the time period during which I unintentionally gave the others serving flight quarters one day a major shock.

Things got so bad it seemed as though, for days, we constantly went from regular ward duty to flight quarters to supply detail, unloading supplies from ship to ship. The more action we saw, the more extra supplies we needed. I went over one hundred hours at one period without any sleep, with the only exceptions being to doze off for a few minutes here and there. There was not a minute I could lay down for a short rest. I'd often wondered what happened when the body shuts down from lack of rest and says, "I'm not going to take it any longer." Well, one early afternoon, I experienced the answer to that question. Sleep became only a memory of the way things used to be—a vision from the far distant past.

Suffering from utter exhaustion, I was literally falling asleep on my feet. We had opened a makeshift morgue in a room across from triage. There were twelve gurneys in the room, and I had just carried up the eleventh and final body to be transported by chopper to Da Nang. There was one open gurney with a white sheet lying on it. It looked so tempting I couldn't resist what my body and mind were telling me to do. I lay down on the gurney, pulled the sheet completely over myself, including my head, figuring nobody would find me, and the choppers would awaken me when they came whirling in again. I dozed off. But after more than four days without sleep, no amount of noise could wake me up.

When I did wake up, I had no idea where I was or what was happening. I sat up and threw the sheet off. Then, to my surprise and dismay, I felt myself falling and landing with a terrific thud. I heard two corpsmen gasp with fright and surprise. They were two of my friends, who were carrying my "body" on the stretcher I had climbed onto, awaiting a Huey. Fortunately, the lieutenant and all the corpsmen, once they caught their collective breath, thought it was hilarious. Seeing my reaction, they realized what had happened. I'm quite sure that, although I was one of the top practical jokers aboard the ship, I would have been in deep shit had they thought I'd pulled this off as a prank, and rightfully so.

It is my story I want to tell, so I don't bother trying to remember dates. The names and times of battles and excessive casualties come more from research than memory of the exact time they occurred. I remember them from a time frame perspective simply because they all happened fairly early in my tour. I compartmentalized periods of time, rather than specific dates. Even in research, some dates tend to vary depending on an individual's research. Again, I am not attempting to be absolute as far as numbers or dates. This book is not intended to be a research project but, rather, the experiences of an individual hospital corpsman.

Sometimes several battles raged at once. It wasn't the dead that took the toll on us physically but, rather, the wounded. They were the ones who needed treatment and a lot of attention. The days we took on the most injured soldiers were the worst. The deceased needed no treatment. With them, the only difficult task was to bag them if they weren't already tagged in green government-issue body bags, at which time two of us would carry them to the morgue. We had to carry them down a very steep set of steps at times because we didn't always have access to an elevator. Oh yes, those steps led to the chow hall. The "holding refrigerators" were conveniently placed next to food storage.

Only one exact date sticks in my mind, and it wasn't until about twenty-eight years later that I would recall that exact date. Until 1995, the date of December 27, 1967, meant little to me, other than it was fifteen days past my twentieth birthday and two days after Christmas. The most significant date of the war for me personally occurred that day. In fact, it was to become one of the most significant evenings of my entire life.

I cannot recall what the weather was like on that particular day. The day and date was entirely insignificant to me at the time. Christmas was over. It would be my third and final Christmas as a sailor and, fortunately, my only Christmas in a combat zone. Two days after Christmas, December 27, 1967, the shit hit the fan that evening. We received incoming patients all evening and well into the night. I was on the second or third round of patients since the latest flight quarters had sounded. The previous patients had been either walking wounded or soldiers who were on stretchers but not severely wounded.

Then came the event that would change my personality, my life, and my entire being from that minute until they close the lid on my coffin.

Chapter 6

"This, then is how you should pray: 'Our Father who art in heaven'"

—Matthew 6:9

From the deck at the aft of the USS *Repose*, I watched as the next helicopter appeared in the evening sky. After a couple months of experience, we knew when the chopper was approaching several minutes before it arrived. Our eyes were trained to capture that small dot in the sky, coming from the west (land to sea), and our ears became extremely sensitive to the *swish, swish* of the rotor wash. The Huey had its own undeniable sound, which still haunts me today when I hear one flying overhead.

By the length of time we had been on flight quarters and the number of choppers that had been arriving, it was obvious that one of the marine units had taken a devastating hit that evening. Little did we know or even care which unit had been hit, because that wasn't important to the medical staff. All that mattered was there were lives to be saved and injuries to be dealt with. The fact that it happened to be the ninth unit of the 3rd Marine Battalion meant little to us, as did the fact they had been hit in Quang Tri province. Our brothers needed our help, no matter who they were or where they came from.

I approached the next chopper just as I did any other. Keep your head down, get the patient out of the chopper, and head to triage.

Get the wounded inside as soon as possible and onto a gurney so a doctor could check his wounds and then utter his disposition for treatment—if treatable.

This was not one of the ordinary retrievals that most ended up being. All but a few of the others faded into the hot tropical nights soon after they ended. With the exception of one other major incident, I don't recall the detailed specifics of any other patients I treated from extraction until final destination.

Carrying a wounded comrade off the chopper into triage was no easy task. I weighed only 145 pounds myself, and it felt like those we carried were several hundred pounds, even if they weighed little more than I did. I have no recollection of how heavy this particular patient was on the way from the Huey to the gurney where we set up the stretcher in triage. To that point, nothing was different about this marine or his injury.

A blanket had been placed over the torso, legs, and arms of this patient. All that was showing was his face and hands. Although he was nonresponsive, there was no obvious sign of blood or injury. The doctor at this particular station lifted the blanket to evaluate the patient. I was on the other side across from the doctor. Therefore, I was unable to see the chest wound that was evidently fatal; one look at the doctor as he placed the blanket back over the wound, and I knew the verdict beyond any doubt. Death was imminent. The verdict was sustained. Only God could overrule it, and in this particular case, he chose not to.

Then came the words that have reverberated through my mind since that evening. The sun had just faded, and evening had turned to night as we were unloading the chopper. For some reason, I remember it was particularly cool that night, but I do not recall if there was a light rain falling. It would have seemed quite appropriate for it to be raining at that time of year. But all I recall with certainty is that it wasn't raining hard, as was the case many times along the normally calm waters of the South China Sea. The weather and memories of any other stimuli or conditions at the time stayed over there. They didn't return to the world with me—at least not immediately.

But the words from the doctor haunted me forever. They haunt me often, day and night, awake and asleep, daydreaming and alert. "Take him to the corner." Those five words, in any other context, would mean very little to anyone. But in triage, aboard the USS *Repose*, they pronounced a forlorn message to those who heard them. The wound was untreatable—terminal. Death was eminent. There was no intravenous drip, as was standard operating procedure for wounded who weren't already receiving fluids upon arrival. There was no chance of survival for the one over whose body the words had been spoken. There was no substitute for the several pints of blood, which couldn't be stopped from ebbing to a traumatic chest injury— no plugging the massive hole in a young soldier's newly acquired body cavity. The grim reaper had come to claim another of our young heroes. And I had no idea that, within a very few minutes, this young marine would become a brother to me. Though we hadn't known each other in life, our paths would cross that night, into eternity, for a reason—a reason known only to God. Those paths would pass in death, rather than in life.

As another corpsman and I were removing our patient from a triage unit to "the corner," another marine, who obviously had been with our patient, approached and said, "Williams, it'll be all right. You'll soon be back in ..." (The last of his words was unclear.)

The fact that I didn't hear that last word would be crucial several years later. But for then, it was one marine's way of saying goodbye to his fallen comrade, not wanting to admit to either of them that the young man would return to wherever with an American flag draped over his coffin. The other marine walked away from "Williams," as he had said his final goodbye.

As we placed the stretcher in the far rear section or the corner, my partner headed back through triage to the flight deck to unload another helicopter. I had no idea which fellow corpsman was accompanying me.

Despite all the mental anguish I have gone through since that dark, sullen night, I thank God that some unknown force turned me around to look at Williams one last time. It would be an action, or perhaps even a reaction to some unknown force, that would change my life forever. The "forever" would seem to be a negative for many years. Throughout the next nearly forty years, I thought this was one of the most devastating mistakes I had ever made. Turning around for that one last glance seemed to be a curse that would lead to nightmares for the rest of my life.

But there would be one more significant battle to face before I was to do what God had set out for me to do that fateful night aboard the USS *Repose*. In order for me to carry out my assignment, He was going to force me to battle against all odds.

A line officer (not a doctor) approached and said, "OK, Turner, there are more choppers coming in. Go out and get another one" (patient).

Knowing that, by military rules and procedure, I was dead wrong, I refused a direct order. From the first day in medical training, I could hear the words detailing the first duty of a corpsman—"to keep as many men at as many guns for as long as possible." This was part of the hospital corpsman code of conduct, a chapter of the military bible.

"Turner, that's an order!"

I'm not proud of, nor do I believe the words that escaped my mouth after the order was barked out again in a much sterner fashion. "F—— you!" Then I wisely added one more word. "Sir!" That wasn't me. I don't say stuff like that—especially not to an officer. But that's what came out. And then perhaps the biggest and most stunning event of my military experience occurred. The lieutenant turned and walked away.

I figured a court-martial awaited me after things quieted down that night. But as our favorite saying went, "What are you going to do? Send me to Vietnam?" To my amazement, there was never any repercussion from that event. Lieutenant (whoever) and I had connected. He had a military obligation, and I had a moral and divine one. He would never remember this incident twenty-four hours later. He knew, as Kenny Rogers later would sing, "when to hold them and when to fold them." My memory of the moment is locked into eternity.

Then my attention was back with Williams. A slight motion caught my attention. Williams had managed to raise a finger ever so slightly. Despite all the morphine he had received from his field corpsman and his catatonic state, his index finger motioned for me to come back. At first, I thought it was an illusion. You have heard the old saying that dead men don't talk. Dead men don't make gestures.

But indeed, he had moved his finger at great exertion. He was asking me to return, using the strength he could not have possibly mustered on his own. So, I went back to him and his lips moved.

Dead men don't talk. Or do they?

Williams's lips puckered, and the slightest breath exited his lungs. He was attempting to tell me something. But what? All I could comprehend was that whatever he was trying to relate to me started with the letter *f* or *p*. The sound was that of a person sleeping and making a slight noise that was somewhat short of snoring. I didn't think he would have the strength or enough life force left to begin a guessing game. Therefore, I knew my guesses at what he was saying were extremely limited.

My first guess wasn't very bright. I was hearing what I thought was the beginning of a word I thought a dying young man would want to address. "Family?" My first guess was *family*. What an idiot! *Family* didn't start with the sound he was making. What a time to realize that phonetics wasn't my specialty. I would have to guess again. And I knew time was at a premium. Death waits for no man. Yet, here before me was a young man who, at death's doorstep, was bound and determined to use me—whether as a messenger or for something else, I would figure out later.

"Ppphhrrr," came the sound again.

What was it? I had to get it right. *Got to get it now*, I told myself. No more chances. I had one final shot.

Prayer. This had to be it. Either it was *prayer*, or all was lost. Did I have a religious marine? Was there such a thing? Did prayer start with the letter *p*? I had really messed up on my first try! I had to go for it. I had to be *prayer*. "Prayer?" God, let that be it, or I had failed.

I felt a squeeze on my finger.

Where did it come from?

How did he manage to be holding onto my finger?

Impossible!

I didn't realize I had been holding his hand. But obviously, I was. He squeezed my finger ever so slightly when I said the word he was so desperately trying to make me understand. Thank God, I had done it. No, not really. God gave me the ability to decipher the sound. Actually, He gave this gift, not to me, but to a dying young man who just wanted to have someone pray over him in his final seconds.

Instead of cursing God over his fate, this young marine wanted all to be well with God. Satan had failed, in all his desperation, to snuff out this life while he might have a grasp on this kid. I don't know where Williams stood with God that night. What I do know is that Satan still thought he had a chance. Oh, so close! All he had to do was close his eyes and let his drained body relax. Then it would all be over.

As the lieutenant and several others in that triage room watched and listened, I held the young marine's hand and began to fulfill his final wish on this earth. The words flowed from my mouth without effort. Although the Lord's Prayer was deeply embedded in my memory, the passages seemed to flow from a source from without, rather than from within. It was as if I was hearing a voice coming from within the depths of the South China Sea, rather than from within the room and from within myself. It was a voice I didn't recognize as my own, other than I knew my lips were moving to the words of the prayer Jesus taught His disciples to pray:

Our Father who art in heaven,

Hallowed be thy name.

Thy kingdom come,

Thy will be done, on earth as it is in heaven.

Give us this day our daily bread.

And forgive us our trespasses, as we forgive those who trespass against us.

And lead us not into temptation, but deliver us from evil.

For Thine is the kingdom, the power and the glory for ever. Amen.

As James E. Williams, Jr., passed from his war-torn life into eternity, God began what was to be a long struggle within the life of another young man. One man's earthly struggles ended when the young marine closed his eyes. The young sailor's struggles began when he opened his.

God took over that night. He took over a dying man's soul. And he took over a living man's future.

Chapter 7

"Yea though I walk through the valley of the shadow of death, I will fear no evil, for thou art with me."

—Psalm 23:4

I have no recollection whatsoever what happened during the rest of that evening. To this day, I cannot remember if I returned to the helipad, which would be my assumption, as I know how intense that evening was. I would not even recall the date until nearly thirty years later. Things happened so rapidly that what I had just experienced did not seem significant at the time. I was caught up in the whirlwind called war, where things just keep on happening. The mind fails to pause and ask, *OK, are you ready for the next chapter?*

The entire year I spent aboard the *Repose* and in and out of Da Nang seems like a blur now. I have little recollection of the infrastructure of the ship. If it still existed and I boarded it today, I could find ward C-2, the chow hall, the berthing area, and triage, of course, without taxing my memory. Memories of all other areas seem to have dissipated once I left the ship on October 31, 1968.

Each time I went to Da Nang and returned to the ship, what I do remember is seeing those red crosses on the smokestack and sides of the ship announcing that this was a United States hospital ship. The sign that didn't actually exist was, "If you want Lyndon Johnson to have an excuse to end this war, all you have to do is fire a round at these sacred crosses."

Each time I saw those crosses after I became familiar with the tragedies of war, I was reminded of those famous words of the 23rd Psalm: "Yea though I walk through the valley of the shadow of death, I will fear no evil. For thou art with me."

Yes, the great white boat and her sister ship, *Sanctuary*, were places of healing for many. But for others, they were where young men were brought to die. And of course, many died before they were received aboard and were never welcomed by the crosses that stood for comfort and lifesaving abilities.

Most people were under the impression that the hospital ships were strictly for emergency status and that patients were flown out as quickly as they were brought aboard. That was my take on the operation of the floating hospitals until my hands-on experience. Suddenly, I realized this was a state-of-the-art, modern medical facility. It was staffed by the navy's highly trained, devoted medical staff, ranging from doctors and nurses to corpsmen who were each experts in their chosen fields.

Operating rooms weren't exactly the surgical suites found at the National Naval Medical Center in Bethesda, but the major difference was the lack of space and not the quality of equipment and staffing. Patients were kept aboard until stabilized if their wounds were serious. There was no rush to send them off (except at times of heightened activity on the battlefield), as there was no facility better equipped to treat them on land. Usually, by the time they were able to be sent to Da Nang, they were ready to be flown back to the world.

For many, the hospital ships meant renewed life, but we weren't miracle workers. Unfortunately, as in any hospital, death visited frequently. The saddest part was that death came to young men here long before they even experienced visions of reaching their prime. The valley of the shadow of death sailed the coast of South Vietnam every day, awaiting the dead and dying. But it was also a haven for the injured and a last chance stop before death's door.

For many young soldiers, their final chopper flight came after death. They didn't know their bodies had been flown from the battle sight to the place that would have provided them comfort and rest. Their final flight was too late. The corpsmen who unloaded their lifeless bodies made the trip to the morgue, rather than to triage.

Most bodies were flown in during or immediately following a battle. But sometimes, the bodies were not recovered until after the area had been secured. One such instance is another source of nightmares I have dealt with since a hot, humid, sunny afternoon when my name was called over the loudspeaker to report to the officer of the day on the top deck. I wish that day could be wiped from memory. Sometimes, the brain can do that, and sometimes, it doesn't. Maybe there are some things my brain wiped out because I didn't want to remember. This day was not one of them.

"Hospitalman Turner, report to the top deck," the voice rang from the speaker. "Report to the officer of the day!"

This was something out of the ordinary. I had been called to report to my ward before but never to anywhere else. It didn't sound right. It didn't feel right. And I was soon to discover that it wasn't right. Why me? Of all the corpsmen aboard the ship, why had they called my name for something so gross, so pitiful, so deeply embedded in my mind as to provide lifelong mental torture? Why me, Lord, why me? I never received an answer to that question. All I know is that, somewhere in the mix, the Holy Spirit was involved. I have no question as to that fact.

As I arrived on the top level, I saw a couple officers, including the captain of the ship and a nurse, who were all as pale as ghosts. I could see trouble a long way off, and I knew I was right in the middle of it.

As I approached the living, I knew the path I tread was among the dead. There, in front of me, lay three body bags. There was nothing positive that could come of this situation. My assignment wasn't yet perfectly clear, but I could see that, whatever it was, it wasn't going to be pleasant.

As I approached the team I didn't even get a chance to salute my superiors. When the ship's captain approached me, I could only imagine that, somehow, he knew the contents of one of the body bags contained someone who was dear to me.

The good news was that my first thought was wrong. I wasn't in any kind of trouble. A court-martial didn't loom over my head. That wasn't why I had been called here. The ship's captain appeared like a ghost out of nowhere. His words remain as confusing to me today as they were the moment he spoke them. "Turner, we have some bodies that need to be checked and identified. Two or three other people have tried to do the job and failed."

The nurse I could see was, obviously, one of those he spoke of. She was not only pale, but also shaking almost hysterically, and the puddle of vomit behind her apparently had been the regurgitative response to her failed attempt to do what I was now being asked to do.

To this day, I have not the slightest idea who may have given anyone my name to perform such a wretched task. None of the doctors I knew were at the scene, and those who were there could hardly have had any idea who I was. As I sit here writing, it occurs to me the chief petty officer whose cigar I ate and kept down (story to come) may possibly have been the culprit.

The words the captain spoke hit me and leveled me like a ton of bricks. "Turner, I'm told you are the only one who has the stomach for what we need you to do. I need you to identify the remains of three marines who were killed in action at least three days ago and have lain in the sun until they could be retrieved." His short speech ended with the words, "If you are unable to perform this task, don't worry about it. Nobody else has been able to do it!"

I have no idea if I gave a verbal response. I unzipped the first dark green body bag. And without thinking of the condition of the body, I did not one but two things I'll live with the rest of my life.

First, I blame the officers, as well as myself, for this mistake. I inhaled without thinking. The stench from the decaying body remains embedded within my psyche today. There are times when the olfactory system recalls the horrid odor. I can't say that any particular thing sets off my recollection of the smell, but it has reconstituted itself several times over the years. There has never been an apparent source from which the smell originated. Once while squirrel hunting, the smell appeared out of nowhere. This time I expected to locate the source. I was certain there was the corpse of a deer or possibly even human remains nearby. I spent about forty-five minutes looking for a dead animal, which I never found. Fortunately, no human body existed either.

Again, I was convinced I was taken back to that day on the *Repose* by some psychological aspect, but not by reality. It is much the same as the recurrence of a smell of roses when none are present. Does it take me back to the funeral home following my father's death? I simply don't know. There are some questions that cannot be answered in this world. Having gone on to earn degrees in psychology and counseling, I can tell you that, for every question, there is not necessarily an answer. I say *necessarily* because what might be an answer by a counselor, psychologist, or psychiatrist for one person does not mean the brain functions the same in all people. Some "answers" only lead to another question.

That is enough of the psychology lesson; I'll get back to my story. The second mistake I was to make was to reach full force for the dead soldier's dog tag. I reached for the dog tag under the military-issued, green T-shirt. Only the head and upper chest area were exposed. I reached down into the body bag and lifted the T-shirt without being able to visualize what I was doing.

I was used to dealing with bodies by this point, but not with skin that had broken down under the intense heat of the unforgiving "dragon's breath" known as the Vietnam sun. Had I known better, I would have grasped the dog tag gently with two fingers and unsnapped it from its chain.

As I carelessly reached for the small silver plate, my hand went into the dead soldier's body cavity nearly to my wrist. I heard at least two of the officers cough, and one was retching uncontrollably. Why did they watch me when they themselves had failed miserably (though understandably)? I don't know if he puked his guts out or not; he was several feet away by the time I turned around.

The dog tag was enclosed in my fist, and when I pulled my hand back, it oozed with body "slime." That is the only description I can think of to describe the texture and constituency of the body fluids I experienced, and I mean no disrespect to my deceased brother.

Could one of you gutless assholes please get me a towel, a rag, or anything? Could you at least stand there with me? Would you like for me to be your personal steward and serve you some type of fancy desert over my fallen brother's body?

I stood there alone. Just me and God. And He wasn't in a comforting mood that hot afternoon on the South China Sea.

I wiped the dog tag off on my trousers and read the name. Rodriguez was the first dead soldier's name. I don't recall the first name. He looked to be of Hispanic descent. But his facial features, like the rest of his body, were distorted as the result of the searing heat—the temperatures had been well over one hundred degrees. There was more than one Rodriguez killed in action during my tour. I have often been tempted to research which one he was. But I guess, since he was already deceased, his identity wasn't as important to me as that of Williams. This marine's soul was long gone from this earth by the time of my involvement.

I zipped the bag and laid the dog tag atop it. Then I moved to the next bag. Now, I was a veteran body checker. I swore I would not make the same mistake again, and I didn't. The other two body checks went smoothly. I do not recall any details about the condition of the bodies, the manner in which I removed the dog tags, or the names on them. I can only assume all three bodies were in the same state of decay, as they had all been flown in together.

I am quite sure the second and third body checks would have been extremely traumatic had the first not have been the experience it was. I knew now what not to do, so I gently removed the tags. The only reason I know I did this was because I remember lying them on the closed bags. I turned and walked away—away from the ungrateful bastards who didn't have the guts or the courage to do the job themselves.

None of the officers thanked me. None of them acknowledged

what I had done. Screw you all. And screw the government you represent. I love my country, and I would still die for my flag—but not for Lyndon B. Johnson, the corrupt members of the government, or what they stood for. The cowardly bastards! And that includes the bunch of inept officers who stood their distance and never issued a "thank you" or a "well done" to the ending of this traumatic event.

The incident was completed, except for one thing, which I felt a strong commitment to do. I backed up and saluted my three fallen comrades. This was the only way I knew how to show my respect for three young men who I did not know. But I knew their families would now receive their bodies. They had been identified and identified correctly. I am sure their bodies were not viewed by their families due to their condition, but the bodies lie in the correct graves—no thanks to our highly trained, gutless officers, who stood there that dreaded day. Your son's and brother's bodies were returned with the US government having taken credit for correctly identifying them.

To those who worked in "graves identification" ashore, my sincere prayers go out to you. My hope is that, as much as you went through, you were trained and realized what you would experience. Hopefully, you had the tactics down pat before you actually performed body identifications.

Chapter 8

"Where have all the soldiers gone?"

—"Where Have All the Flowers Gone?" Bob Seger

Lies, lies, and more lies! This seemed to be the theme of the Johnson administration. How could an American president expect the public to be so gullible? Even the troops were catching onto the lies of the powers that be. His kingdom was crumbling under his feet, and the quake began its tremors some thirteen thousand miles away.

After my experience with the three bodies, I performed many more "unofficial" body checks, as did all the corpsmen at flight quarters and at the morgue. The fatalities piled up, and the lies became more and more apparent. While I never again encountered the impact of the body identifications I'd performed previously, we identified bodies as they arrived. The difference was that they were not received in such gross condition.

One day, I checked in seven bodies, all undoubtedly American by their uniforms and dog tags. A few weeks later, when in the Philippines, I came across a copy of the *Pacific Stars and Stripes* newspaper. There were three American casualties listed in the entire Republic of South Vietnam for the same date I had checked in seven bodies myself.

First of all, I was not the only one on the *Repose* who identified bodies from the battle that occurred that date. Second, all bodies of those killed in action that day were not flown to the *Repose*. There was a war going on all over the country, and we only received a portion of those wounded in action and killed in action for any given time period. And remember, this did not include army casualties (except in rare circumstances).

So, who does the reader believe, me or Lyndon Johnson's press corps? Personally, I don't give a shit any more now than I did then. If I was out to protest the war, I wouldn't have been there. I only know what I saw. And what I saw and what I read were not the same by any stretch of the imagination!

Also, when we read the more than 58,000 names on "the Wall," where are the rest of the figures left out of the *Stars and Stripes*?

"Where have all the soldiers gone?" Suppose someone left over from the Johnson administration comes forth before they are all gone and explains to us the discrepancies. Sadly, as I sit here writing now, there are none left to defend themselves. History records itself. I do not need to debate what I experienced against the perpetrators of lies told in order to keep the war going.

Where have all Johnson's puppets gone? Probably to hell. Every one of them! (I say that loosely, as I am not judging souls.) When will they ever learn? When will they ever learn?

Sadly, many years later, I have to guess that the answer to that question is never!

Fortunately, one of the lessons we learned in Southeast Asia was that the generals, not the president's cabinet, must be allowed to run the war. No matter which party leads us into conflict, regardless of whether war is just or unjust, politicians can only declare war. They cannot and must not ever again attempt to engineer the battles. Democrat, Republican, or otherwise, the White House cannot be the place from which war is fought.

Another thing I learned not far into my tour was that medals were handed out according to who witnessed an event, rather than what the magnitude of the deed actually was. One night, a wounded marine was brought in aboard a Huey with other wounded comrades.

I happened to be assigned to the patient, who was possibly the most potentially lethal patient ever brought aboard the ship.

Again, it was late evening, and darkness had fallen over the South China Sea. Another corpsman had carried the stretcher with me from the heliport to triage. My partner had exited triage back to flight quarter line when I was on my way out myself. I heard one of the walking wounded patients yell, "Don't move!"

Thinking the marine was yelling at me, I froze. I thought maybe he was candidate for C-2 and had "lost it." Then I turned around and saw that a walking wounded marine was referring to the doctor who was about to pull a bandage off the wounded marine's leg. Fortunately, the doctor, like me, had frozen immediately. I could have walked out of triage at that instant, but for some unknown reason, I chose not to. I remained frozen in place, other than to turn to look at the second marine who, thank God, turned out to know how to react to the peril at hand.

In a demanding voice, the experienced marine said, "I need one man to stay here with me, and I need everyone else to clear out of here, and clear out now! I need one volunteer to stay and help me disarm a grenade."

Suddenly, without question, all the doctors, nurses, and other corpsmen vanished like the blink of an eye. Or did they? My full attention was on the wounded marine, and nobody else mattered at the moment. I looked at the weathered marine. Evidently, my eye contact told him I was his volunteer. To this day, I don't know who placed the gigantic *S* on my forehead for a year. It didn't distinguish *Stupid* from *Superman*. But one more time, the *S* mark had appeared, and here I was, in the middle of another situation for which I hadn't intended to volunteer.

Heroes aren't born. They just happen to appear at the right place, at the right time. No, I'm not going to suggest I was a hero that night, but there was a hero present. Only the marine who had either been slightly injured or perhaps had just coincidentally escorted his wounded buddies on the chopper that night was equal to the task at hand.

For the first time in my several months aboard the ship, I was in triage with only two other souls—at least only two that mattered. This was an anomaly during flight quarters. But, again, VA testing has revealed that my recollection of my experiences is legitimate.

"If you're going to do this, I need you to do what I tell you to do, exactly as I tell you—or we're all dead." Those were his first words to me. He carefully gave me orders on how we were to disarm the booby trap that had been wrapped around the patient's right leg by the Vietcong. The bastards had spared his life to attack a hospital ship in a way that would enable them to pull it off under the "legal" rules of war. Of course, booby traps were against the Geneva Convention. But the tactic had probably been used from the first caveman war.

I would never have detected the rigged grenade. Obviously, the treating physician had not seen it and was about to pull on the bandage that would have sent us all back to the world in our own body bags. Those who were not working on the individual who was rigged would have been critically if not fatally wounded within seconds if the doctor had taken the next action, rather than tonight's hero.

"When I pull on the bandage, the pin will release, and the grenade will activate. Just trust me. I can't deactivate it. But I can direct you on how to dispose of it, hopefully before it hits the water." This is not an exact quote but the words as I remember them.

I was still hoping my "guide" would take the thing so I could run like hell as he did whatever it was he had in mind to dispose of our ungodly possession.

Oh shit, there's no time to think! No time to back out. All I could do was trust this marine, who was calm as a cucumber, and pray he had a reason to be so confident in himself. More than that, he actually appeared to be confident about directing a noncombatant corpsman with a live grenade in his hand.

Here we go, Lord. This is in Your hands because I can't handle it alone. I felt the pin give and push inward. Just from watching old war movies, I subconsciously counted to three and waited for the explosion that I would not hear, one way or the other.

Silence! I was still running, holding the grenade, which was wrapped by part of the bandage the marine had cut apart from the rest of the bandage.

Will you take this cup from me? That was my first thought.

"It's yours now. And you're going to do exactly as I tell you. Hold the thing just as you're holding it right now." Yet, I remember him standing by our wounded comrade. I supposed he was ready to, again, tell everyone to clear the area. But there wasn't a soul within sight, at least not in my path. All medical and support staff abandoned the area as I approached the triage door.

I remember the chopper still sitting on the pad. I didn't see it, but I heard the all-too-familiar sound of the blades going *swish, swish, swish.*

"I don't want you to let go of the handle. I just want you to throw it into the water. Don't see how far you can toss it. But don't just drop it alongside the ship."

Without hesitating, I tossed it what I Imagine was about ten feet from the railing of the ship. I knew there wasn't enough time to run before it went off, so I just sort of folded up, slid down the outside bulkhead, and covered my eyes.

Blurp was the closest way I can describe what I heard. Maybe others who have heard explosives going off underwater would describe the sound differently. I imagined it was kind of like an underwater whale fart!

The marine seemed to have disappeared when I returned. And suddenly, life aboard triage was returning to normal.

No big deal! No explosion. No casualties. No medal for heroism for a marine who saved not only a fellow injured marine and several members of the medical personnel in triage but also the triage area itself, which would have been severely incapacitated.

My friend, whoever you are, you deserve a medal for your heroics. You were at the right place at the right time, except you didn't happen to have the right witness to see that you were given a commendation for valor. Nor did I. As the old drunk in boot camp often reminded us, "War is hell, and this is war!"

Unfortunately, the heroes are the ones who had the right witnesses. Triage aboard a US Navy hospital ship isn't a place where medals are handed out. But one marine is out there who may have a chest full of medals but probably none as deserved as the one he wasn't issued.

As I was deep in thought reliving this incident many years later, I was blindsided by the revelation that I had never really sat back and reminisced about this event while in a deep thought process. I'd relived it over and over but had not strongly concentrated on exactly how the scene unfolded. I could never remember what this marine looked like—I had no recollection of a name tag or of his size, possible accent, rank, or even uniform. There was nothing specific in his tone of voice, such as panic or sense of urgency. There was absolutely nothing—as in absolutely nothing. Nothing, nothing, nothing! There was no apparent character. This didn't strike me as odd until I began thinking of my return to triage. Whose voice had I heard calling in desperation for a volunteer? I certainly did not question that at the time. Who did I think I saw who was giving me directions in a voice as calm as a cucumber?

As I sat back and concentrated on this event, I began to realize how I had remembered things. It wasn't how the events actually progressed but, rather, how my mind had processed events on that day, now fifty some years ago. When I wrote my memoirs, it was just a quick reliving of things as I saw them from a distance. But now a new window was opened, one that was revealed through a time of healing and through faith. I prayed I could recollect this event as it had actually transpired, rather than what I recalled at a time I was being torn apart from the effects of post-traumatic stress.

As I concentrated on "perception versus reality" (an issue I harped on in every one of the psych classes I taught), the actual occurrence of events was revealed to me.

I realized it was some time before I returned to triage. This made sense, as most staff were back on station, which meant at least several minutes had elapsed. I must have just sat there against the outer bulkhead of the *Repose* for an unspecified number of minutes. However long it was, enough time had gone by that the patient had been removed (to surgery, radiology, or wherever a doctor had ordered). The marine who had led me into this endeavor was also gone.

As hard as I attempt to remember his actual presence, I cannot recall it. The question is, who patted me on the shoulder as if to let me know the mission was accomplished? The answer is, I don't know! And yet, now ... I do know.

My faith has revealed this secret that was kept from me all these years and was revealed at a time God saw fit. For some reason, I accept the fact that there is a reason for everything—"a season [reason] for everything under heaven" (Ecclesiastes 3:1).

As a result of this revelation, I could have backed up and erased the part I wrote about the one who should have received a medal for this. Now, I look back and am so glad I felt the way I did. I didn't deserve a medal, which I stated in the first place. I still believe I had the right idea as to who deserved a medal and all the credit. But now I realize it wasn't a mortal soldier I saw there in battle fatigues. If you don't understand to whom all the honor and glory belong, then you wouldn't understand the whole point anyway.

At this point, I praise God for revealing something I should have understood a long time ago. But He does things in His way and in His time, not ours.

In making a long story short, I cannot thank two very good friends enough for playing their parts in this realization that, unbeknownst to them both, has led me to a peace of mind I thought I would never receive. John Looney (a VA counselor) has been a longtime friend, and Mike Burns is a man I didn't know until a couple of years ago. Both are Vietnam veterans and brothers. To both of you, I'm sure God has involved you in many lives and that you have done much for others that you have no idea about. God bless you both in the work and volunteer services you have provided our brothers and sisters. And recently, one other name has been added—Kellie Bonham, to whom I was able to relate these events at the local VA clinic.

As for the late Mike Burns's part, Mike was a Vietnam vet (army) who was searching for fellow Vietnam veterans who had experienced a "spiritual event" during their service in Vietnam. When I explained my story about Williams, he didn't seem to think this was the type of story he was considering for his book. I clearly understood his thoughts and respected them. After all, it was his book, and I didn't want to lose a friendship that had just begun. We emailed each other often. One day, I told him the story of the grenade. I'm not sure exactly how he worded his reply, but suddenly it hit me. The story of Williams and the story of the grenade were tied together. If you are not a person of faith, then skip the next sentence and proceed to the next chapter.

After all these years, I realized the disappearing soldier may well have been a guardian angel, none other than PFC James E. Williams, Jr.!

Chapter 9

"All is fair in love and war."

—1620 translation of Miguel de Cervantes's Don Quixote, by Tom Sheldon

No matter how much you believed in your government at the time, you still began to question the purpose and reality of the war. Why are we here? Who invited us? Are we serving a purpose? Is the domino theory really a legitimate concern? Of what real use is this small chunk of land to China other than the sea coast? Obviously, we are not going to maintain supremacy over people thirteen thousand miles away for a lengthy period of time.

If our battle was with North Vietnam, then why weren't we fighting them and desolating their cities, instead of the cities of the country we were supposedly defending? Of course the Vietcong were going to fight us as long as we battled on their soil. But would they be a threat if we actually took away the threat from the North and China?

These aren't questions that can be answered. They're the thoughts of those who were fighting and watching their buddies die—never knowing if they would be next to be shipped home in a body bag.

As the towns were ravaged, so were the people. One of the experiences I witnessed was brought back through counseling and questioning when I applied for a VA rating for post-traumatic stress. One of three mandatory requirements for disability acceptance was, at that time, predicated on the fact that the applicant must be able to answer yes to the question of whether or not he had experienced anyone being tortured while in Vietnam. Two examples immediately came to mind—one in which I was not directly involved but was, instead, an eyewitness.

One night, we received a real prize in triage. I happened to be in line at the right time and place to receive an incoming patient who was obviously Vietnamese. When we got him to triage and removed the blanket that covered his uniform, that uniform revealed he was an NVA (North Vietnamese Army) captain. Those of us who accompanied him knew that, for political purposes, we would need to be "extra accommodating" to any enemy soldier, especially such a high-ranking individual. This may not have been a general, but NVA soldiers were seldom flown to a hospital ship. Somehow, an exception had been made, whether on purpose or inadvertently.

The soldier had been wounded seriously and had to be prepped for surgery immediately as a result of a gunshot wound. The two of us who had carried him into triage on a stretcher then took him to the surgical prep area. The first task was to get him undressed and cleaned up so the doctors could do their part. Although there were nurses aboard the ship, there were none present at this area, which was surprising. However, if there had been mass casualties being brought in at this time, everybody did whatever they could, and all nurses may have been assisting in triage. Who knows? At times like this, rank was thrown out the window. Doctors' duties were handled by nurses, and nurses responsibilities were handled by corpsmen. Many times, corpsmen handled the responsibilities of doctors.

Our task was to prep the soldier for abdominal gunshot wound surgery. When he was cleaned up, and all the bleeding was stopped and clotted blood removed, the next task was to catheterize him. No big deal. This was a daily routine in a hospital. But this one would be a major exception.

Place yourself in a situation where you ended up in the hands of the enemy, and you could not speak their language. Now picture yourself lying there naked while several men spoke in a foreign language and held medical items you were not familiar with.

As we struggled trying to relate our intentions to the wounded man, our translator showed up. Now, we figured, things would go much more smoothly. Sam would translate for us. What was already a bad scene turned into a nightmare for everybody concerned, except for Sam.

The soldier became even more apprehensive once Sam began "translating" our intentions. Surely, he had knowledge of a catheter and its purpose as a medical tool, especially in preparation for a surgical procedure. The man screamed and fought us until we tied his arms and legs to the bed. Even at that, we had to give him a mild sedative. Since he would be receiving anesthesia, we didn't want to sedate him too deeply.

What I had been witnessing was my first experience in torture. Not only was I witnessing torture, I was unknowingly participating in it. Unbeknownst to the rest of us, Sam had a different agenda. Sam was a South Vietnamese soldier and had just returned from two weeks emergency leave, which was obvious to us. But what we didn't know was that he had returned home to move his family because the Vietcong had torched his home when they'd discovered his status in the military. He had lost everything except for his wife and two children. Now, he feared they would track his family down and kill them since he'd returned to duty. He was doubly despised since he was not only a member of the South Vietnamese Army but was also being asked to treat a member of the dreaded enemy.

Sam had "interpreted" everything we asked him to relay to the wounded soldier as a threat. Once we got the patient catheterized and sent to surgery, Sam told us he had told the soldier we were going to cut his penis off and stuff it up his ass, just as the Vietcong did to many of the South Vietnamese and American soldiers they had captured. If the captain had taken part in these rituals himself, it had to be a valid threat to him. He knew the ropes. He was a soldier in a war of torture.

At times I wondered which side could be more sadistic. There isn't any story or form of torture I had heard about whose validity I doubted for a heartbeat.

I guess I really couldn't blame Sam for what he had done. But I didn't support his actions and didn't think it was as hilarious as some of the guys did. But this was war, and war was hell!

The next morning, a marine search party came aboard the ship and was looking for the NVA captain who had been brought in and operated on the previous night. He had been admitted to the surgical ward after his surgery that night. At bed check in the morning, his rack was empty, and he was never seen again. It is very unlikely he could have walked out of the ward, let alone got to the outside deck. What most likely happened was that a couple of ambulatory patients (marines) carried him out and dumped him overboard that night.

Was that what really happened to the captain? Was his fate sealed despite being rescued and treated by the Americans? Was Sam involved in his disappearance, or was he satisfied with his verbal torture? One thing I can guarantee is that nobody who was involved ever confessed, and we will never know the answer. Would his training as an officer have led to suicide before he could be interrogated? Could he have made it outside to jump overboard? Just another chapter of the war closed without an answer. But my question is, was it ever reported that a North Vietnamese captain disappeared from the USS *Repose* that night? Or was it one of those things that can't become a political issue if it isn't reported?

The other incident of torture I witnessed was in Da Nang. I had flown in by chopper to escort a psychiatric patient to the hospital there. When I had a chance to get off the ship for a couple hours, I always made the best attempt to make a day of it. I would visit friends at the hospital or walk the streets of Da Nang, as it was my only chance to experience the Vietnamese culture firsthand.

On that particular day, I was walking alone near a high fence that either separated the compound from the city of Da Nang or maybe just separated two sections of the base. At any rate, I came upon a US Marine and a South Vietnamese woman. The woman had been walking along the fence. It appeared to me that she had been minding her own business, but I was not familiar with the policy of handling Vietnamese civilians. The marine yelled for her to stop. She obeyed his order, and he told her to get on her knees. I don't know if she didn't understand English enough to comprehend his command or if she was being defiant. From my viewpoint, I assumed the former. He hit her in the face with his M16 rifle and knocked her to the ground. I couldn't tell what information he was trying to get from her because, at that point, he began speaking Vietnamese, and I recognized very few words in their language.

Each time he asked a question and she answered, he followed by kicking her and hitting her with the butt of his M16. As I considered coming to her defense, I thought better of risking my own health or life. From witnessing the demeanor of this soldier, I was not going to have any influence on attempting to calm him down anyway. Besides that, I was defenseless without a weapon.

Repeatedly, the woman got up, only to be knocked back down. Then she tried to crawl away. It seemed like this went on for half an hour, but I'm sure it lasted only a few minutes. Finally, he pushed the woman to the ground one final time and then walked away. She managed to get to her feet once more and staggered away, covered with blood.

I would never know if that particular soldier was just having a bad day or if his interrogation was legitimate. But judging from a distance, I would call it unjust and undue punishment. I sincerely doubt the woman, who was dressed in black as a typical peasant, had any intelligence secrets that might have won the war for us if he had been able to extract them from her.

Oh, the good old streets of Da Nang. Anything you could possibly want could be found there, alongside most things you wouldn't want.

Cigarettes were sold there through the black market. Watches and all forms of jewelry were cheap. You couldn't help but wonder if the pieces of jewelry were taken from a person before or after he or she was reduced to a corpse. Decks of cards with pornographic pictures were popular, as, of course, was booze. If you drank the hooch, you were not guaranteed to live until the next firefight, which might have been a blessing in disguise.

One afternoon in Da Nang, a very young girl came up to me and said, "Hey, GI, you bang-bang my sister? Five bucks."

Having no intentions of having sex of any kind with her sister or any other disease-laden native of this venereal disease-infested city, I inquisitively asked, "How old is your sister?"

The little tyke replied, "She big girl. She ten!"

I wondered how many military personnel had done a ten-year old over there. On second thought, I probably didn't want to know, because it didn't seem to be an uncommon thing. When it came to sex, some guys would take what they could get from whomever they could get it—even with a "consenting" ten-year-old.

After seeing the film about syphilis in boot camp, I was resolved to abstain from sex over there—period. The picture on the screen with the caption "male or female" was burned into my brain forever. It was the picture of a person whose crotch was a large black area between the legs that had been totally obliterated by the dreaded disease. To this day, I have no idea if the subject was male or female, but it sure left a hell of an impression on me. I was reminded of this when I would hear pipes rattling in the head as someone stood at a urinal and held onto the plumbing while he urinated. The pain was so great at times the poor guy would convulse in agony. We all knew where the part he was holding onto had been a few days before. That's when I was very glad I had learned well from the movie. There were no condoms at that time, which left virtually no form of protection.

How wrong were the men who had sex with the Vietnamese women and girls? Well, I've often heard that is part of the spoils of war. I guess many of the females profited from prostitution, and many consider that morally and legally acceptable. But where do you draw the line between a woman and a girl? In war, does a ten-year-old who is receiving pay for providing sex constitute unethical behavior? Of course, there was rape, which was (and surely is) prevalent in any war. Is there any truth to the old adage that says, "Everything is fair in love and war"? I don't buy it. But then, as old-fashioned as I am, I don't buy into the child sex bit, even though their own families were selling their young daughters for a few moments of pleasure.

Syphilis was bad enough. But thank God, AIDS wasn't around yet. What would make it even worse was the fact that we treated so many open wounds and were constantly inundated with body fluids, yet we were not provided with latex gloves. Those were few and far between and, as I mentioned previously, were pretty well reserved for surgical procedures.

As bad as things may have seemed for the Vietnamese, they had a new form of miraculous medical insurance. It was called United States medical assistance. The natives were being treated for illness and injuries as they had never been treated by their own, by the French, or by any other government. The American medics were a savior for the people who were injured and suffering critical illness if they could get to a base hospital (including hospital ships). We treated the Vietnamese to the point I actually wrote to my congressman, Wayne L. Hayes, chairman of the Ways and Means Committee and one of the most powerful politicians of the time. I will address this in a few ensuing paragraphs.

When one of the surgical wards was overrun with casualties, I was called from the psychiatric ward to assist on postsurgical patients for a shift or two. That was where I met a six-year-old boy whose face had been entirely rebuilt by surgeons on the ship. He had been paid by the Vietcong to deliver a grenade or some sort of device, which he delivered and set off, killing six American marines and critically injuring several more. In the process, his lower face was almost entirely obliterated.

Through what was a result of a modern medical miracle, the jawbone, teeth, skin, lips, and so on had all been replaced. By the time I met him, which was approximately six weeks after his last surgery, one would have barely noticed any remaining scars. What a miracle for the youngster who was a paid murderer. At what age do we turn our heads and say he is a juvenile? At six years of age, the Vietnamese were probably considered adults in their own society. Yet, someone with a lot of gold or silver on his collar decided we would invest a lot of time and money in this little killer.

As a Christian, I could root for the kid. As a corpsman who saw the devastation these kids were capable of, I had one problem. That problem manifested itself in a personal struggle I encountered with the same dental department that played a major role in creating a new face for the "child" in question.

I had somehow managed to escape the infamous "red line" in boot camp when we went through our physicals. When you followed the red line, you were placed in a holding company until your medical problem had been processed. Before entering boot camp, I had several teeth extracted or filled so I could clear my physical exam. Although I needed more dental work, I was hoping to be cleared to go through boot camp and that I would be told I could deal with my dental issues later.

Actually, after being told to follow the red line to go to a medical holding unit, I proceeded to sneak to the other line and, indeed, dealt with dental issues later.

Thinking I could finish my tour, I ignored the aching teeth until they hurt so badly while I was aboard ship that I scheduled an appointment with the dentist to have them checked. I'd had a couple fillings taken care of earlier, but I was in desperate need of more dental care, which was denied because I might lose a day or two of flight quarters. I wrote a letter to my congressman, the Honorable Wayne L. Hayes (mentioned above). At the time, he was about fifth in line of succession to the president. It was about two weeks later when I received a note from the chief of the dental department informing me I was to see him at an appointed time.

The doctor proceeded to give me a lecture about writing to my congressman. He didn't appreciate it. However, I was about to receive the royal treatment from the department. Soon, I had all the fillings I would need, the teeth extracted that were now too far deteriorated to save, lower partials, and full upper dentures.

I assumed my congressman had requested a reply after I was taken care of, rather than a letter saying I would be given an appointment at some future date. At any rate, my mouth was finally in good shape, and a letter was on its way to the congressman's office from yours truly. I am quite sure another letter was on its way from the chief of dentistry. And by the way, I did not miss a minute of work!

One humorous note from all this was that the night I had my molars and wisdom teeth extracted, we were served steak for the first and only time I could remember aboard ship. My friends laughed at me during dinner that night, but I went to the chow hall (I had planned on skipping the meal that night until I discovered what was on the menu). And I was served my steak, which I proceeded to gum to death.

My gums were not only bleeding but also still partially numb. I swore the head of the dental department planned the steak menu to coincide with the date I was to have my teeth pulled. I wasn't about to lose any part of this battle.

In all fairness to the head of the dental department, whose name escapes me now, he was very cordial and did not do anything negative to show he resented the letter he received from my congressman.

Ironically, you may remember Mr. Hayes as the one who lost his office as head of the powerful Ways and Means Committee (which was much more powerful then than it is today) when he hired a secretary who could not type or run an office efficiently but who was quite attractive. And, well, if you can't recall the story, I'm sure you get the point. Nevertheless, Mr. Hayes was loyal to this constituents in the military, and I am living proof of that.

Chapter 10

"Your country is desolate, your cities burned with fire; your fields are being stripped by foreigners right before you, laid to waste as when overthrown by strangers."

—*Isaiah 1:7*

One of the most significant ways the land was being raped was through Agent Orange—you know, the defoliant that the American government swore did not exist until so many of our men developed debilitating symptoms that led to total disability and death. Sadly enough, the troops in the fields and jungles of Vietnam were being sprayed with the devastating liquid. But this wasn't the only way soldiers came in contact with the defoliant.

As corpsmen, we would have this strange liquid all over our hands and arms, not to mention our clothing. Then we would wipe the sweat from our face with our hands. At the time, we didn't worry about it because we didn't know what we were dealing with. Then came a point where we realized what the wet substance was. However, without protective covering, it made little difference; we were not about to refuse treatment to our fallen comrades.

Even before I left Vietnam, I knew I had received several doses of Agent Orange and God knows what other poisons. All I could do was to hope and pray I would be one of the fortunate ones and not develop symptoms. Unfortunately, this would have a profound impact on my life many years later.

I was fortunate enough not to be in the jungles of Vietnam, but we were told of the devastation caused by the defoliants. How could those in charge try to convince even an idiot that this would not have such a devastating effect on human skin? Then once it penetrated the skin, it went to the vital organs. The scientists who made the stuff knew it, and the military echelon knew it, too. Yet the military denied knowing the effects of Agent Orange, let alone the fact that it was dispersed over wide areas of the country. Again, our sincere thanks to our thirty-sixth president and his cabinet. The power-hungry mongrel was believed, by many, to be behind the assassination of then president, John F. Kennedy. I often wondered if Hubert Humphrey thought he had a chance to succeed Johnson, even though he was reigning vice president. Many events would occur before the election that was eventually won by Richard Nixon. I will not get any deeper into politics. But you must understand, we might have been young and somewhat uneducated, but we were far from stupid! The writing was already on the wall. It didn't make any difference who would be the next commander of our troops. The war was winding down. And we were losing!

As I look back many years later, the entire scenario recalls those words of Isaiah speaking of his vision of Judah and Jerusalem. "Your country is desolate, your cities burned with fire; your fields are being stripped by foreigners right before you, laid waste as when overthrown by strangers." (Isaiah 1:7).

I have always been amazed that the realization of these words of havoc and devastation are followed in the next chapter of Isaiah by the following: "He will judge between the nations and will settle disputes for many peoples. They will beat their swords into plowshares and their spears into pruning hooks. Nation will not take up sword against nation, nor will they train for war any more" ((Isaiah 2:4).

How many times have I recited these words on Memorial Day during services at church or gatherings for Disabled American Veterans, Veterans of Foreign Wars, or American Legions? How many times have other speakers quoted Isaiah, knowing the answer lies in the book of Matthew concerning the last days: "You will hear of wars and rumors of wars, but see to it that you are not alarmed. These things must happen, but the end is still to come. Nation will rise against nation, and kingdom against kingdom."

The war in Vietnam is over, but it has only been replaced. After the last wars in Iraq and Afghanistan and the fighting in most of the Middle East are terminated, what will be next? Surely, even those who are not Christians can foresee the words of Matthew as being truly prophetic.

Each following war, skirmish, or whatever word our government wishes to impose on us other than the word *war* has its own version of Agent Orange. It appears almost as a cartoon in which a general confesses, "Oops, Mr. President. We didn't realize that chemical would slowly kill our own troops and their successive generations for years to come!"

How long will our government, from generation to generation, think it is up to us to control the world?

Chapter 11

"Out of the depths have I cried unto thee, O, Lord, Lord, hear my voice: let thine ears be attentive to my cry for mercy."

Psalm 130: 1–2

Again, I was about to experience what could have been a life-ending or, at least, a life-altering event.

I went on another eventful trip to the Philippines. Dr. Sears invited the psych staff to a Christmas party off base in Olongapo. I was the last to leave the ship and really didn't want to head beyond the gates alone, but it was daylight, and I managed to find the place where the "party" was being held. I walked in, and through the billowing weed, cigarette, and cigar smoke, I could see a Filipino dancer on a small stage. Under her naked body was a long-necked bottle … and you get it. This is intended to be a book for young adults to learn lessons from. It's not about pornography.

I didn't even see my friends through the thick haze of cigarette and weed smoke. I turned away and walked back to the street where a jitney sat, awaiting passengers headed back to Olongapo and the gates to the US military base. I wasn't a fan of smoke from any of the above. I was also a Christian, whose principles were different than those of my friends and probably 99 percent of GIs. I am not judging others. I'm simply stating my own principles, which I believed were important to uphold, whether or not anyone from back home would ever know about what I did when I was away in a far-off land.

The ride was uneventful until we reached the main gate at Subic Bay. The driver pulled up well short of the designated drop-off area. When I paid him with the correct number of pesos, he demanded more money. I refused his attempt at extortion, and he pulled a switchblade and held it to my throat. I knew better than to resist, but I still held my ground as to the payment. Suddenly, a police vehicle arrived, and I was about to meet the Olongapo chief of police.

I tried to explain what had transpired, and he told me very firmly in good English, "Shut up and get in the car," which I obediently did immediately. I expected to be behind bars within seconds of entering the station, where he said, "Sit down, keep your mouth shut, and listen to me very carefully".

I did as directed, as I wasn't about to make two enemies within fifteen minutes. He proceeded to tell me that I would have been robbed and quite possibly murdered for my "bravery." He placed an unmistakably emphasis on the word *bravery*!

Then he asked me for money. But to my overwhelming surprise, he said, "Give me the exact amount you owe for the ride," which I did without question. He told me what had just happened to me wasn't at all uncommon. "But most GI's have more sense and less balls than you!"

"I'll see to it that the man gets his money after I drive you to the gate, and I'll tell you one thing. Do not ever cross the gate again because I won't save your ass a second time. I don't know why I even stopped in the first place, but I guess I just never saw a sailor do what I saw you do."

We got back in the cruiser. Not a word was said. I had questions I wanted to ask, but I just let things be as they were. A few blocks away, he said, "Get out!"

As I exited the cruiser, I looked him in the eye and said, "Thank you, sir." I gently shut the door and walked safely through the main gate—for the last time ever!

Before this occurred, I had spent several hours in the residential part of Olongapo. I soon became familiar with the reason it was called the "shithole of the world."

Houses, or rather hooches, were built on stilts over the river so waste could be deposited directly into the river, as there was no mode of sanitation whatsoever. Young kids, from about five to twelve years old, would dive into the river for coins. They would even dive in for a penny. No goggles or anything but underwear. They maybe didn't even own that much.

I am one who seldom closes my eyes underwater. Even I couldn't imagine attempting to see anything through such filth. It was sickening to think my fellow Americans could get a kick out of this. I passed out what coins I had into a couple kids' hands and walked away in disgust.

I learned another valuable lesson as to how good I'd had it in my youth, even without a father. Mom seemed even more like an angel every time I witnessed something like this.

Chapter 12

"The Bible teaches that the Christian should be law-abiding. The Bible also teaches loyalty to country. A loyalty and love of country does not mean that we cannot criticize certain unjust laws that may discriminate against special groups. The Bible says that God is no respecter of persons. All should have equal opportunities. The government of God is to be our model."

—*Billy Graham*

Republicans can blame Democrats all they want (and vice versa). But the lust for power and dominance envelops every man who takes the oath of president of the United States of America. Mr. Johnson wasn't much different than those who proceeded or succeeded him. He just had the largest ego of the bunch. He led many warriors to their deaths in the modern American history of unjustified wars.

Two generations after Vietnam, we, the prematurely gray-haired bastards of society, still can't explain why we can now listen to the songs of the Byrds or Bob Dylan—those who could have been considered protesters, whose songs were supposedly not directed at the troops. Why did we become a generation of the hated and disrespected assholes who chose to serve our country rather than go to Canada or stay home and protest?

The average American still looks back with more respect for the flower children and those who cooked their brains on drugs during that era. Their stories are more exciting than ours, as they are filled with love and lust, instead of war and blood. Their colors are psychedelic swirls and flowers, instead of green uniforms covered by flowing crimson.

We still dance to the tune of "make love, not war." Yet, those who served are expected to forget the past. As well-meaning as her statement was, my sister, not long before her death, told Linda (to whom I am now married), "I wish he would forget about Vietnam and just let it go." How typically in tune she was with the rest of the nation. Nobody could know how we wished it was that easy. Click your heels three times, Dorothy, and say, "Now we will forget!"

As much as I believe in the power of prayer, that is the one prayer we pray—asking why we can't forget those memories forever imbedded in our thoughts and minds—that God will not answer for us until the lids close on our caskets.

Yet, we Vietnam veterans seem to be classified as the figment of our own imagination. We shouldn't be critical of our own government, the one that sprayed us with Agent Orange and refused to give its generals permission to fight on our own terms. Rules of engagement were as political as anything else.

Where were we going? What would we be doing there? We figured the survivors would eventually figure that out once we returned to the world. We still don't have answers, and the connotation of "Vietnam veteran" still casts its long, dreary shadow over us day and night.

The films made about the Americans in Vietnam do not deal with the compassion that was ever-present for one another. People don't want to see the love and compassion a corpsman/medic has for his compatriots. They want to see the blood and gore of the movies that made men filthy rich—men who didn't know Vietnam from their asshole.

We were the loyal ones of the '60s and '70s who answered the call to duty. Some were drafted while the majority of us volunteered. But now we are the unjust because we question our government.

We would have been politically correct if we had questioned the government then, instead of later.

What a screwed-up nation! One that honors the protestor rather than those who gave their lives. "A loyalty and love of country does not mean that we cannot criticize certain unjust laws that may discriminate against special groups." Billy Graham hit the nail on the head with his statement. Yet we are the ones who are looked down on as being disloyal for the rules that discriminated against our very being.

We weren't even protected by our own government when we got our one well-deserved week of R & R (rest and relaxation) away from the combat zone. Although ships' crews who were stationed in the combat zone received hostile fire pay, we didn't rate R & R. We were told over and over we were going to places like Thailand. Every time we got our hopes up about going anywhere except the Philippines for ship maintenance, we were told a few days before scheduled departure that the trip had been canceled.

After a while, once the powers-that-be decided their bullshit was causing low morale, we finally were allowed to put in for R & R. If you didn't get your R & R in by the end of your tenth month in-country, you got screwed out of it altogether. So, when I got my request sheet, the places I wanted to go were booked until the end of the year. Australia and Malaysia were my two choices, but both of them and just about any other place was unavailable. Then I made one of the biggest mistakes of my life. I made the near fatal mistake of choosing Tokyo.

When September came, I left the ship and flew into Da Nang on a medevac chopper. That night, I left for Tokyo. The flight was calm compared to the flight I had taken to Vietnam ten months ago. But the one vivid memory of that flight was the landing. The pilot had just given the local time and temperature. Then he said the fog was so thick at Tokyo Airport that our landing would be guided to the tarmac by instruments. I looked out the window into the total whiteness of the heaviest fog I had ever witnessed. Suddenly, the airstrip appeared just a few feet below us, and immediately we felt the tires make contact with the tarmac.

We thought we were dead at that point. We didn't even have time to gasp between seeing the ground and feeling the initial bump. But the controller in the tower knew what he was doing, and we made a perfectly smooth landing.

I thought my worst time in Japan had come and gone as quickly as the proverbial thief in the night. But little did I know that experience would be mild, compared to what was to follow.

Other than the landing, all I can remember of that flight was the sailor who sat next to me. His name was Stone. His first name was something like Kevin or Ken. He was a black man about a year or so older than me, and we got to know each other during the flight. We disembarked and went wherever it was we needed to go to check in. Once that was accomplished, we were sent to a barracks of some sort where nobody stayed while on R & R, but it was made available to us if we wanted to stay on base. Again, the true colors of our government were flying high, as we were not told of the places to stay clear of or about the people from whom we should keep our distance.

Stone and I stayed at a high-class hotel, where speaking English was as common as if we were in New York City. During our first day in Tokyo, we took in the sights of the city and contemplated where we would spend the rest of the week. We visited the Tokyo Tower, which is a model of the Eiffel Tower in Paris. As we got to the top platform, I remember being the only one in the group who would stand in the middle of the glass floor. The floor extended high above the highway and sidewalks, where automobiles and people appeared as tiny insects scurrying about the busy city.

That afternoon, we witnessed a Buddhist wedding from across the street at a pagoda that, I imagine, served as a temple.

Each day, we traveled to different cities and saw more and more of the culture of inner Japan. Downtown Tokyo was westernized as far as the large department stores and restaurants were concerned.

One evening, two barmaids came up to Stone and me and asked us to buy them a drink. The one next to me came up from behind me. Then she slipped in front of me, took my hand, and placed it over her breast. She introduced herself as Nikki. Wanting no part of dealing with prostitutes, I removed her hand and politely told her I was tired and was going to my room. Stone agreed with me, but then made the mistake of giving them our room numbers, and they said they would be up later to see us.

Sure enough, when eight o'clock arrived, so did the two ladies. I let them knock on my door until they left. To my surprise, Stone was smart enough not to make any noise and did not let them know he was in his room, either. I was sure they hadn't run out of victims for the night and that there was lots of money to be made on American GIs.

This was pretty well forgotten about until the flight back to Da Nang. Several of the guys were talking about the whores they'd had in Tokyo. When they began discussing names, Nikki was either the biggest whore in the Orient, or it was the predominant name used by Japanese prostitutes.

One of the neatest sights I visited was the brand-new Olympic stadium in Tokyo. Although I had been to baseball and football games in Cleveland, Pittsburgh, and Columbus (Ohio State), I had never seen anything like this stadium. Somehow, we were able to get a complete tour of all the extremely modern facilities. One could stand there and picture all the greatest athletes in the world parading around the track and then competing in the various Olympic events. It was just an awesome sight.

One day, Stone and I went our separate ways for some reason, and I was walking the streets of downtown Tokyo. It was evening but not yet dusk when a young Japanese man spoke to me. He spoke, surprisingly, extremely good English. He seemed to know more about Ohio than any of the GIs I knew who weren't from my home state. He had supposedly attended Ohio State University as some type of exchange student. This was believable since he knew so much about the university and its sports teams. As an avid Ohio State fan, I affirmed he was very familiar with the university and its long athletic history.

The man was older than I was, probably in this midtwenties.

He offered to take me on a tour of the university at the outskirts of Tokyo. This was when I made one of, if not the most, regrettable mistakes of my life. At the age of twenty and having been through as much as I had experienced at such a young age, I should have known better than to accept his hospitality. It only took a few minutes into the cab ride until we passed the university. He said that anti-American sentiment was running high and that we had better not stop because there was rioting, and I would soon become a victim of the riots. At first, I fell for it because there was a protest taking place in front of one of the buildings we passed. Of course, I had no idea whether they were protesting against American policy or one of their political parties. Instead of having the cab driver turn around and head for the hotel where I was staying, we continued going in the same direction for a mile or so and then exited the cab in front of a building that ended up being a motel.

I had no choice but to follow my "guide" into the building. When I did, I finally realized what was happening. Although I knew no Japanese except for thank you, it was apparent that he was booking a room for the night. I was told that, as an American, I would never make it back to downtown Tokyo at night, that both he and I would be dragged out of the taxi and killed.

The application process for post-traumatic stress disorder through the Veterans Administration twenty-eight years later would bring back the vivid memories of the rape that occurred that night. Not knowing karate or any advanced self-defense tactics left me vulnerable, and my attacker proved to me how much he knew about martial arts. This left me knowing without any doubt that I was defenseless.

After being violated, I was told it was my turn to "return the favor." At this point I was willing to suffer any consequences for failing to reason with or cooperate with him. I could not obtain an erection with the thought of having sex with another man, and I made that clear by telling him he would have to kill me if that was going to be the penalty for refusal. To my surprise, he told me he could respect that.

My attacker refused to let me go that night because I could not make it back to Tokyo on my own. Although I did not believe him earlier that the two of us couldn't go back to the city, I knew I had absolutely no chance of survival in this zoo by myself.

So, I stayed awake all night, trying to think of any way to escape the room and get to the front desk and have the night clerk call the police. I was afraid events would repeat themselves in the morning, but there was no possible avenue of escape. I knew if he killed me and left me in the room, he would never be caught. So, I stayed awake and prayed all night that I would be released at dawn with no further injuries or experiences similar to the previous night.

In the morning as I lay there, feigning sleep, he told me to get up and get dressed. We went to the front desk, where he called a cab, gave the driver directions to my destination, and paid him in advance.

I returned to the hotel and then went to the R & R processing center and tried to report what had taken place, but to no avail. Those who were stationed there were not concerned with the welfare of those who chose to come to Tokyo on R & R. Their job was to move you through the line one day and back out seven days later. How very reminiscent of boot camp!

When I was questioned by the VA many years later why I failed to report the incident when I returned to Vietnam, I said there was no use embarrassing myself because nobody gave a shit. The only time I had ever gone to sick bay, I had been chided for complaining about back pain by the doctor. I had hurt my back while playing softball at Chu Lai, and all I wanted was something for pain, not an early ticket home.

When I returned to the ship, I waited about two weeks and then drew a vial of blood from myself. (As a corpsman, I drew blood almost daily so it was no big deal to me.) I wrote a fake name under "patient," requesting results for venereal disease and sent it to the lab. When the results returned, everybody was trying to figure out who the patient was. I looked at the results, which were negative. And we decided to throw the slip out after checking the ship's entire patient roster and finding no matching name.

Years later, that I'd failed to report this incident would come to haunt me. Although the culprit would never have been apprehended, it would have certainly aided my case when I applied for disability through the Veterans Administration. I learned a lesson from this incident too late for myself. But let this be advice for the reader who might enter the service later. Always cover your ass, even if it causes you embarrassment.

Although any injury report should be a part of your permanent record, the military still has ways of erasing incidents. When I broke a toe playing basketball at Bethesda (this was a service-connected injury that got me started with the Disabled American Veterans), I sent for a copy of the injury report. All such records were supposedly kept in St. Louis. However, in some cases, such as the aforementioned injury, a fire in the '70s had supposedly wiped out some records. Although I was told in a letter that mine was not among those lost, it could not be found. Ironically, the report for a slight injury in a softball game that took place in-country had also disappeared. For those who may need to verify medical records in the future, be sure to obtain a record of any medical problem, injury, or any other situation when it occurs. Keep a copy of that record!

Knowing I hadn't caught any type of venereal disease from the incident was imperative. Just before I left the ship, I put through another ghost slip after drawing another lab specimen. I was afraid I might have done the first test too early to get actual results.

The rest of my time on R & R was spent walking around Tokyo and taking some tours on other parts of the main island. I was never alone without another American in my company. I guess by today's standards, one would say how stupid I was to have gotten myself into such a predicament. However, the world was different then. At least my part of the world had been different, until I was introduced to the rest of it. Little towns in Ohio were much different than the largest city on earth. It was just one of those minor things that Uncle Sam forgot to warn us about.

What happened to me on their watch reaffirmed my lack of trust in the government and Lyndon Johnson, who, in my humble opinion, was so focused on winning the war, he'd forgotten the troops. We were robots for whom the government had no feeling. There was no remorse from the higher-ups for the families back home. It was a day-to-day thing by now, bringing back the flag-draped coffins. A navy chaplain or other officer would knock on the door, seemingly with great remorse, and tell a mother or widow her son or husband was dead, and she would be notified of when his body would arrive. No offense to the one visiting the deceased's relative. But after the first few notifications, remorse wasn't a true factor.

Death was no longer honorable, except to family and friends who mourned their young heroes. In the grand offices in the nation's capital, the only concern was to extend the war day by day. For what? Unfortunately, we never received an official answer. LBJ took the war out of the hands of the Joint Chiefs of Staff and those who were supposedly in control of the situation thirteen thousand miles from Washington.

To this day, I continue to repeat my words, "I would still die for my flag and my country, but not for the government of the United States of America." How many lives of our young men and women are worth the price of whatever was the underlying cause of the war? Oh, that's right. I forgot. It was the infamous "domino theory" we were fighting against! Or was it?

How many times could officials lie about the number of casualties and think the people couldn't add them up? How many deaths could a small town like Beallsville, Ohio, sustain when seven of its young men were killed in battle in Vietnam, the most per capita of any city or town in the nation?

How many sons, daughters, or close relatives of the top brass in the government were carried off the hospital ships or directly from the battlefield? While the answer isn't zero, it surely is minuscule compared to the number of those from poor, average-income, or median-income families.

How will my brothers and sisters ever shake the stigma attached to the Vietnam veteran? We still, today, live with the labels of "baby killer," "rapist," "cold-blooded killer," and on and on. In every war, there are those who defy the rules of engagement. Dating from the first war fought thousands of years ago, there have been those who pillage and rape. That will never cease. But in the war in Vietnam, every incident, whether true or not, was brought to the forefront and scrutinized by the press.

None of us will deny the torture tactics that occurred over there. But they weren't learned there. They were learned in previous wars.

I can and will swear that I never touched a Vietnamese woman, let alone a child, in a sexual manner. As repelling as rape is to me, it isn't anything new in war. I know it happened there. Prostitution ran rampant, but it was no different than what went on in the backdrop of wars that preceded it—be that World War I, World War II, the Korean War, the Inquisition, or the invasion led by William the Conqueror.

Children have been killed in war from day one. In fact, we are told in the Bible of Herod's killing of all infant males two years of age or under. Having killed all those innocent babies, Herod was unable to kill the one he targeted. They were the victims of that "war."

That atrocities have been going on since the invention of war doesn't make it right for soldiers to commit them today. But they have, indeed, forever been a part of war. Yet, still today I am reminded that, as a Vietnam veteran, I am a "baby killer." The fact that I was there saving lives, including those of the enemy, doesn't matter. The label is for all of us. And because of a few, we will take it to our graves.

Has our government ever attempted to alleviate the permanently attached stigmas we returned home with? Hell no. But we don't dare slip and call a foreigner a slang term, or we will be sent to classes to become "sensitized" to political correctness. I am not condoning that type of slander, only repeating that it is a double standard.

One morning, at a clergy association meeting, one of the pastors delved into politics, a subject we supposedly forbade. When he discovered I was a registered voter of a certain party, he began calling me "baby killer." This is the same man who, when he introduced me to an individual or a group, always said, "This is Kurt Turner. He was a navy corpsman in Vietnam. He saved people's lives."

I asked Randy to take back what he'd called me. He kept it up, and I told him I took offense, as that was a label given to Vietnam vets. He was already aware of that. Yet, he repeated it. I asked him once more to shut up and take it back, since he was now, surely, aware of why it was so offensive to me. He repeated it a third time.

There were two long, narrow tables where we sat. We were directly across from each other. Randy outweighed me by probably 125 pounds. For the first time since Vietnam, I found myself in a physical battle. I reached across both tables. I was actually laying on one table and stretched across the other. I managed to grab Randy by the throat. Another member of the group was able to grab my hand, but I wouldn't let go. I don't remember intentionally letting go of his throat. It must have been the Holy Spirit that protected Randy because, suddenly, my hand let go.

Randy called me several times that week, but I was in no mood to answer the phone. A few days later, the pastor who had broken up the fight called and told me Randy was in the hospital. They feared he was the victim of a severe heart attack.

To go or not to go—that was the question only I could answer. I walked into the hospital room, where Randy was sitting up in his bed. When I walked in, he put this arms out. When I embraced him, his first words were, "Please forgive me, Kurt." The incident had evidently worn heavily on his mind. It was a moment I knew God was smiling. Hatred had turned to love, just as Jesus had demanded.

We are to show no anger toward our government or to those who would crucify us because we are the veterans of the "wrongful war." Fifty years later, we are still the bastards of society. Everything that goes wrong in any military function is compared to Vietnam. We set the standards of screwing up a war. Why? Because we weren't permitted to fight a war. We were only permitted to engage in "conflict." Yes, we are still the "baby killers" and the traitors who left our "free love" society!

I know, I know. Many will come up to us now when we wear a hat or pin showing we are a Vietnam vet and thank us for our service. That is great, and we are honored by this. But we cannot forget the past and how we were treated like a dog turd being kicked alongside a sidewalk into the street, awaiting the pending street sweeper.

Conflict is fought battle by battle. War is fought by knocking the shit out of your enemy and sending the troops home.

We are still reminded today about the Vietnam "conflict." How do more than 58,000 troops die in a "conflict"? Maybe that's because they were sacrificed, instead of killed in action. Our soldiers fired their weapons when they were permitted, and they sat as targets much too often.

Maybe we would have been blessed if General Westmoreland and the Joint Chiefs of Staff would have had the balls to stand Johnson down. Maybe we were led by a bunch of cowards who wouldn't support the troops the way they could have. Maybe we should take a look at our troops in Afghanistan and Iraq today, many of whom have insufficient flak jackets because the government won't give the Department of Defense enough money to cover the cost. But yet a proposal of $87 million to rebuild Iraq is the primary concern of the president. To hell with the safety of the troops! They are expendable, while oil isn't.

Chapter 13

"If your cause is just, if your principles are pure, and if your conduct is prudent, you need not fear the multitude of opposing hosts."

—John Witherspoon, signer of the Declaration of Independence

After six days of supposed rest and relaxation, it was back onto the big bird for the trip southwest. Several hours later, we touched down on familiar territory. This time, Da Nang Air Base sprawled across the shore in a way I hadn't seen in daylight. Nothing I had ever seen compared to it. There were no flares or flashes of enemy fire in the distance.

There would be no waiting for the ship to return this time. She sat majestically in the harbor as if to say, "Welcome home, sailor." I was so glad to get out of Japan and back to my "home away from home." I don't remember how I got back to the ship. It might have been by chopper, or it might have been by boat. This is one of the many memories that have failed me since my return.

All I know was that I was now a "short-timer" and was down to leaving this part of the world forever within five or six weeks. I had seen many other corpsmen come and go. A few would return for another stint. This was something I would not consider. For me, as it was for many of my compatriots, I was leaving here to be discharged.

I would soon have my year in as Halloween neared again. It was the magical day.

How appropriate for a day to set my sights on. Halloween, of all days! The day when the spirits arise and the dead come back to life. But unfortunately, the dead I had dealt with for the past almost eleven months wouldn't arise that night. Death here was permanent.

It was, though, the day the Great Pumpkin would again arise from the pumpkin patch. At least Charlie Brown hoped so.

The words of John Witherspoon rang clear—so clear they would be the basis of our cry. Our cause was just! Our principles were pure.

We were the pawns of the war. The top brass in Washington couldn't use our slogan. They didn't even attempt to come up with their own.

Our conduct was prudent. That statement would be challenged forever in the annals of war. Those opposing hosts would come from near and far. They would eventually come from home—from within, let alone abroad. We would be labeled the scourge of the American military for all time, past and present. We would be criticized all over the world. But the part we were forced to deal with that we couldn't successfully apprehend was dealing with it at home.

But for now, I would deal with the lies and the stress for another month or two without letting it get to the point where I would function at less than 100 percent capacity. That happened to too many men, especially those in the field. How many marines had we admitted to the psych ward because they were short-timers, and the closer they got to discharge date, the more the fear set in? The skies became darker, and the roads longer. The winds of war whispered, "You are next."

Soldiers experienced many fears during that last month or so. There was the fear of leaving those who had become like brothers to them. In combat situations, the term *brother* takes on a whole new meaning. It has nothing to do with two male siblings who share a common bloodline. There was that fear of leaving their brothers to fend for themselves, just as others had feared for your safety when they left. A good friend once told me of the guilt he experienced when he discovered the general he had guarded for a year was killed not long after his tour ended. It was a very normal psychological state, but nobody had explained this to us.

Then came the fear of being a "normal" soldier, marine, airman, or sailor back in the world. What did the word *normal* mean? We hadn't been "normal" for what seemed like a lifetime! There was no enemy to fight. Would we kill our own if we got into a fight? Could we endure normal everyday stress? We were no longer trained to do that. People feared us. We were no longer normal. Nor were we the people we had been before we'd deployed.

Many were trained to kill during times of tumultuous stress. We, as corpsmen, were trained to respond when help was needed. We didn't look at our watches and say we were off duty. We responded to save our brothers' lives or at least to give them a fighting chance of survival. We aboard the hospital ships may not have died alongside them (though many of the field corpsmen died with them in the jungles). However, we fought for their lives when their arteries bled and they puked blood all over us.

We took it to heart when a brother died. Yes, we often just moved on to the next patient because to stall over a dead comrade would leave another in peril. But we weren't coldhearted. We felt their pain. We were dedicated to them, just as they were dedicated in battle. Their cause was just, and so was ours.

Seldom did a dying victim see tears in our eyes. But when the time was past and night came, so came the tears and the sobs. We were only human. We weren't gods of some sort who could produce healing when the body was so ravaged by a land mine that the dog tags were the only source of identification.

Others died in our arms while we stood helpless and knew we couldn't stop the massive hemorrhaging. We couldn't plug a hole in a heart or stuff intestines back into place. But against all hope and reasoning, we tried!

Some asked during this time, "Where is God?" God was right there with us and with the fallen heroes we attended to. He knew they gave the supreme sacrifice. Their cause was just. It was admirable. They gave their lives to their country. They gave their lives so that others might live. They gave their lives so that you and I could continue to live as a free people in a free nation. War is hell, and this was war. Those who didn't return gave us what we have today. Although their sacrifice didn't help me place any trust in my government, it allowed me to continue to have faith in my country, my flag, and my God.

By the way, where was God? He was right where He is today. He shed a tear with the passing of each who had given his soul to Jesus Christ. He experienced it before we did. He watched his own son suffer and die on a cross so that our brothers would live with Him in paradise. Paradise was a place we could not imagine. From the battlefield to a place where there was no more death; no pain, hunger, or thirst; and no emotional stress or sorrow was an unfathomable distance. That, my friend, is the answer to that age-old question, Where was God?

When I came down to my last few days on the ship, the short-timer syndrome finally hit home. I had seen it so much in others that I thought this would make me exempt from it. But as others before me, I awaited the impending disaster that seemed to happen to so many who were in their last few days of their tour.

Stories abound of those who were down to their last few days when disaster struck. James Serena, who graduated from Bellaire High School a year behind me, was being flown from the field to go on R & R when the chopper carrying him and other troops exploded. Many soldiers would die on what was to be their last day of combat before heading home.

Was it a psychological condition that made some soldiers reckless because they knew they were just about to leave? Were they too cautious? I don't know if any research was done on this phenomenon. Of course, you were in the same amount of danger on the last day of your tour as the first day, or day 113 or day 267. Maybe it was just more pronounced when a soldier was killed on the last day of his tour. Maybe that was coincidence and nothing more. I do not believe in coincidence.

At any rate, I began to have fears that the ship or a chopper I was aboard would be hit by a rocket, or maybe another patient would enter triage with a booby trap strapped to him. But I had already decided I wouldn't do anything different. Life would endure as usual.

Then came the "ship over" talk, as we called it. Those who were to be discharged from active duty, upon return to the world, would be called individually to the master chief assigned to that task. I immediately let the chief know I wasn't interested in anything except returning to civilian life. He asked me why I seemed so bitter.

"I am still an E-3, even though I passed the E-4 test three times and was in, at least, the ninety-seventh percentile of grades each time."

"Give me a week, and I will find out where the problem lies."

Several days passed, and I received the return call from the chief. "Some drippy yeoman at Bethesda forgot to check off one of your practical factors." (We were required to complete several tasks before we were permitted to begin our class B school.)

"So, I've received E-3 pay for over a year and had all the work details and extra flight quarters as an NCO (noncommissioned officer) because of someone else's mistake. If that was true, I shouldn't have been allowed to take the test, and it would have been taken care of then."

"You will come back as E-5 because I know some of the things you did that weren't officially noted on your record." No explanation was given. "I'll see, personally, that you will be eligible for the E-6 test in two years. And if you pass, you'll be one of the youngest E-6s in the navy."

"Thank you, Chief. I appreciate you finding out where the problem occurred and for being so kind. But I'm not interested in shipping over."

What would it take for you to stay in the navy, son?"

"Rear admiral!"

"Well, I don't think I could quite pull that off!"

(Jokingly and very respectfully), I quipped, "Now it's up to vice admiral!"

"Good luck, son. And I wish you well in civilian life."

He then reached out, and we shook hands. Whether he agreed with my decision or not, he showed respect. And I never forgot it.

We each have to make many important decisions in life. We are responsible for our decisions whether they end up being good or bad. Later in life, I would revisit that moment aboard the *Repose* and wonder if I made the right decision. I might have had a very successful career in the military. At the same time, I could have been signing my death warrant. I might not have ended up with a broken marriage and a daughter who would never speak to me again. On the other hand, I will share later about the successful careers I have endured.

We each have critical decisions to make. I made mine, and I will live with them and accept them.

Did I have a short-timer attitude? One day my replacement and I got into a fistfight in Dr. Sears's office. I have no idea what it was about, but I do remember when the chief nurse heard us, opened the door, and put us "on report." She went to Dr. Sears and told him, "Turner is short-timer and needs to be punished."

I acted like I was really concerned but knew what was coming up. I bit my tongue as Dr. Sears listened to her politely and then (although she outranked him by a stripe) verbally laid into her. He reminded her that we NP techs were under his command, and we would answer to him and him only. He dressed her down and then excused her from the discussion and from the scene. George, the other corpsman involved, was shaking. I didn't blame him since he was a rookie and had not yet experienced Dr. Sears's loyalty to his NP techs. Besides, he had just received an ass whoopin'! The doctor looked at us sternly and said something like, "If you guys get caught doing this again, I'll write you up and send your asses back to the chief nurse!"

George was ready to shit himself when I burst out laughing, along with Dr. Sears. I think he would have issued me a medal for holding it back if there was such a medal in the repertoire of the United States Navy!

I had continued to fly into Da Nang accompanying the injured, the dying, and the dead, though it was seldom mandatory. I did it out of respect for my fallen brothers. Each excursion would be a round trip. But on day 364, that changed.

Handshakes with the staff I had worked with were in order, and I was off the ship as soon as we sailed into Da Nang harbor on the evening of October 30, 1968. It was just turning dark, which usually meant no launch would be allowed to leave the ship until daylight. However, there was a miraculous exception that particular evening. I don't remember why an exception was made; maybe a senior officer had business on shore. What I do remember was that, somehow, I ended up on that launch, one day earlier than I was supposed to and was homeward bound. It was the first step—only a baby step. But I was on my way, ever fearful fate would cross my path before I could no longer view the shore of Da Nang when my plane left the next morning.

I checked into the airport, knowing I had eight to twelve hours before my scheduled flight to Alaska and then to Atlanta, Georgia. That was plenty of time to be killed or injured if there was an attack on the airport that night.

My first thought was to head for the hospital and stay there for the night in somewhat familiar surroundings. It certainly wasn't for safety reasons because the hospital had been hit several times in the past.

My next idea was to go back to the desk and inquire about any flights leaving before morning. I didn't care where a flight was destined or how long I might spend waiting for a flight out to another foreign land. Getting back to the world was not my primary concern. Getting out of this hellhole called Vietnam was my only concern at the moment. I would worry about the rest of the trip once I was out of country.

I decided it couldn't hurt anything to, at least, ask if there was a way out of here any earlier. I knew this was a common occurrence, and I would probably do nothing more than piss off some tired clerk. But what did I have to lose?

When the clerk at the flight desk saw the caduceus on my uniform sleeve, he asked if I was willing to take a medevac flight and help take care of injured patients on the flight. I told him I had been doing that for a year, so one more night wouldn't bother me a bit and that it would actually be an honor.

When another corpsman appeared behind me, I asked if he could be afforded the same offer. That actually made three of us, because when we boarded the enormous MAC transport for wherever we were going, another corpsman joined us in the spacious body of the plane.

Something seemed terribly wrong here. We were on a plane that appeared to be so large we could have set up a football field, but there were no patients. There were no stretchers, no wheelchairs, and no medical equipment. There was nothing here, including seats. It was just a gigantic empty fuselage. Had we entered the Twilight Zone?

At this point, I figured we would be carrying patients in on stretchers all night from somewhere inside the complex to fill this arena.

One of the air force pilots came back and greeted us. When we stood to salute him, he smiled. "Knock off the military shit and relax," he told us, adding, "You will be in the air for eight or nine hours if we aren't diverted."

We had already figured out how to pull three single seats out of their hideaway spaces in the bulkhead. Before we returned to our seats, we asked where we were going. To our surprise, the major wouldn't tell us. At first, we thought he was kidding us, as he was smiling and had already told us we need not use military manners.

"We are leaving hostile airspace and headed for a friendly area. So, relax. And once we are in flight for about three hours, our destination will not be subject to change. At that point, I will tell you where we are headed."

It wasn't until about three hours later that we were graced by his presence. He was true to his word and announced where we were headed. Up to that time, it was almost as if we had been captured. We were told to buckle up upon takeoff. This was announced over the PA system, which echoed throughout the cavernous space where we would spend the next eight or so hours. The voice wasn't the sexy voice of a young stewardess. But three young corpsmen weren't too disappointed!

Sometime later, another announcement was made that we could remove our seat belts. I thought we were going to float around the body of the gigantic plane in weightlessness. There wasn't a single window in the fuselage. The fact that we were flying at night was bad enough when you are claustrophobic, but not being able to at least look at the stars and see if you are actually moving was almost enough to make me wish I had waited for morning to catch my scheduled flight. But not quite enough! All I needed was to recall my haste to get the hell out of country at the first available minute. By midnight, it was actually October 31—Halloween. The Peanuts gang was celebrating the day in my honor!

It happened that the major who had spoken to us previously was the copilot. He had returned to notify us that the flight had reached the point of no return, and our destination was Tokyo, Japan. This announcement sent a chill through me. I had no desire to return to that place. I did calm down, realizing I would be at the airport and not out in the jungles of the city as before.

Next, we were told that, once we arrived in Tokyo, we were more or less on our own. However, we would be taken to the terminal that handles military personnel. "We will not be responsible for you from that point on. However, you will be under military privilege." That amounted to saying we wouldn't be flying aboard a military plane, that it would be a civilian flight reserved for military personnel—just like the Flying Tiger Airlines one year previous.

That was fine with me, except we didn't know when we would be leaving or where we would be headed. But we were out of the hellhole we knew as Vietnam and had concluded the first leg of our journey home.

At the counter, we were told our flight was scheduled to leave in about three hours and we would be flying nonstop to Seattle-Tacoma Airport in Washington. I had hoped to at least make a stop in Alaska, as I would have if I had kept my scheduled flight. From there, the flight would have ended up in Atlanta. But I was out of Vietnam. And in the end, I was headed for someplace in the States. It didn't really matter exactly where in the United States. I was on my way back to the world!

I don't remember any of the particulars of the flight from Tokyo to Seattle except that it was a very long trip, and the weather was good, unlike my trip two months prior. We touched down in Seattle, and all of us couldn't wait to touch American soil. But first things first. We had to wait for customs officials to check our baggage and ask if we were transporting this or that contraband.

Of course, all of us were carrying some type of military clothing that we were supposed to have turned in. Some had specifically-issued gear confiscated, such as knives and parts of guns. Nobody, as far as I knew, had anything major enough to cause them to be escorted off the plane. Contraband was confiscated, and that was the end of it.

Some of us were a little more fortunate. We had items such as steel-plated combat boots in the right place in our seabags. After all, we had worn them as part of our uniform and didn't believe they would be sent back to Nam. We knew damn well where they would end up, and we might as well have them for keepsakes, rather than knowing they'd be sold on the black market by way of the employees of customs.

So, finally, here we were on American soil for the first time in over a year. As for most marines, it was the first time in thirteen months they had seen the world. The date was November 1, 1968.

When I disembarked, I was told I would have to secure my own transportation to the naval station, which was several miles from the airport. Imagine that! Uncle Sam got us back to the States and dumped us off at an airport in a city that was just about as foreign as Tokyo to most of us. Having no real choice of mode of transportation, I hailed a cab, and off we went.

As I was sitting there in the back seat of the cab, I was listening to the newscast on the radio when I started yelling and screaming, "The son of a bitch just killed the rest of us."

The cab driver stopped the vehicle and told me to get out. "You're one of those crazy sons of bitches who just came back from Nam, aren't you?"

It was obvious to me the cabbie hadn't heard what was just announced on the news. I told him Johnson had just declared a cease to the bombing. It was a death warrant to those in the fields and jungles of the land I had just left behind. The commander and chief of the world's greatest army had just given orders to give the enemy permission to massacre our own troops. No wonder the asshole had announced he wasn't running for office again. He had shamed this nation and was now doing the same to the very troops he had vowed to defend and protect. This was one sick, power-hungry bastard. Judas Iscariot seemed like a good guy today!

The head of the free world had just announced he had decided not to run for president again several months earlier. I never saw so many sober marines and sailors celebrating like they had that evening aboard ship. We were all glad the war would be winding down, but Johnson didn't get anything else right. So why believe he would get it right by telling Ho Chi Minh he was pulling troops out, yet still fighting a war?

The cabbie at least showed some comprehension of my concern and drove on to the naval station. I don't recall what he said when I paid him, but I could see a glitter of remorse in his eyes. I doubt he would have had any idea what Johnson's statement meant if I hadn't been in his cab at the moment of the great betrayer's proclamation.

I checked into the naval station at Tacoma to await discharge. This would be my last temporary duty station. I thought I would be discharged immediately, since I'd had my discharge physical completed aboard the *Repose*. To my surprise, I would be held there exactly two weeks. I have no idea why I couldn't be processed any faster, but it wasn't in the cards. I was assigned a gravy job, taking temperatures, heart rates, and blood pressure (TPRs) of other sailors being discharged at the naval base.

I only worked whatever hours I felt like working and did some sightseeing around Seattle and Mt. Rainier. Again, my status of hospital corpsman gave me the freedom to do pretty well whatever I wanted to do, except get the hell out of the state of Washington and head for home. The chief petty officer I reported to had great compassion for the returning troops. If we did what little he asked of us, he would, in turn, give us plenty of time to tour the area and lounge around except for the few hours he actually needed us to work. He gave us no reason to express short-timer attitudes.

The greatest thing here was *no flight quarters*—no being called out of a restless sleep in the middle of the night. I can honestly say I would have gladly worked twelve-hour shifts and not complained.

I came back home, remembering there had been good times aboard the *Repose*, including eating cigars as a dare and dumping a case of beer, one bottle, at a time after it was found in the nursing station in C-2. Someone brought beer aboard, and I have no idea how it happened to be discovered or exactly who discovered it, but it was. Each of us took turns emptying bottles over the fantail. I was the only one who wasn't saddened to perform the punishment because I didn't drink. What long faces existed on C-2 that day!

Then there was the chief who'd tried to teach me how to use a push broom. The stub of a cigar seemed to be permanently planted in the corner of his mouth. He was a good old fellow and very well-liked. As I was sweeping a ramp between decks one evening, he approached me and told me I was doing it wrong. I was dragging the broom toward me instead of pushing it. Kiddingly, I asked him to show me how to do it his way. When he finished, I took the broom, swept an area the same size in half the time, and asked the guys hanging around the area to judge who did the better job. When the vote was tabulated the chief turned to me and said, "Where did you learn that, Turner?"

"My mama taught me how to do that, Chief. She told me there's the navy way of doing things, and there's Mama's way!"

"Damn you, Turner. I should have known you knew what you were doing, or you wouldn't have challenged me!"

Everyone had a good laugh, including the chief, as he walked away chewing on his ever-present cigar.

Sometime later, when a couple guys dared me to eat a cigar and had made their bets, I was down to the stub. Little did they know that my friends who knew I didn't puke over raunchy cigars or anything else had set them up. Along came the chief and asked what was going on. I turned around, cocked my hat like an old salty sailor (mimicking the way he wore his hat), cigar stub in the corner of my mouth, and asked the chief if he wanted to get in on the betting. He wasn't going to turn us in for this, but he didn't dare get caught betting on it himself.

One of the guys explained to him the ten-minute rule. If I threw up within ten minutes, I lost the bet. I had never lost one yet and wasn't about to lose this one either. He turned his back as the debts were collected. Then he turned around and said. "OK, Turner, I can't make a bet and lose a stripe. But I'll make a friendly bet you can't keep one of these down, and I'll make it five minutes instead of ten!"

Of course, several of the guys took the bet. I had five minutes to consume the raunchiest cigar I had ever encountered and then five minutes to hold it down.

"I'll be damned!" were his famous last words as he walked away after losing the bet. I didn't even get to tell him, "Mama also said don't take a bet you might lose!"

The first time I disembarked the ship at Subic Bay in the Philippines, Ray, Stan, and I were walking through the streets of Olongapo. Two young men about our age came up to us. Unexpectedly, one walked right up to me and said, "You are very good-looking!"

Whoa there! Nobody ever accused me of being good-looking. I don't even remember anyone in my family so much as eluding to that. I drew my fist back, with visions of this wiseass lying flat on his back with a bloody nose.

Either Ray or Stan grabbed me and said, "This guy was only trying to tell you you seem like a nice person." He also advised me to thank the guy and keep walking. Walk away, I did. But thanking him for the compliment, no way!

Although this incident ended up seeming hilarious to me, I had just learned a very, very important lesson. Remember, sailor, you are not on your own turf. You must honor traditions and customs of the land you are visiting.

If I could find the gentleman today who offended me, I would certainly apologize to him and tell him he had taught me a very valuable lesson. I realized I had learned the easy way and not the hard way. Fortunately, this wasn't the first trip to this foreign country for my two friends.

Another memorable trip was to the capital of the Philippines with the same two friends. We managed to get a few days off the ship, which was in Subic Bay for supplies and repairs. On the way to Manilla, Ray, Stan, and I visited the site of the infamous WWII Bataan Death March. We walked about two miles down the road on which the troops had been led by the Japanese, many to their death. As usual, it was very hot and muggy in near junglelike conditions. As we traversed the narrow, dusty road, approaching a small village, we were halted by our guide.

Along came the totally unexpected. Several yards in front of us, stretched completely across the road was a boa constrictor. In its midsection was a huge lump. The guide informed us that the giant reptile had evidently swallowed a full-size pig from a farm near the village. We were delayed almost a half hour waiting for the snake to cross the road. We could just as easily have stepped over it because it wasn't in attack mode, but we did as the guide instructed.

The entire time we followed the beaten path around Bataan, a city of about seven hundred thousand, was a psychological torture. I spent the two hours or so visualizing those soldiers who had traversed this path a generation before me. As I read an account of the march written many years ago by one of the brave souls who walked this road before me, I wondered who the lucky ones were in the end. The story of the Bataan Death March is one of the saddest in the annals of war.

Were the ones who died at the beginning of the road actually the fortunate souls? Or were the survivors the fortunate ones? Not even history can give the answer. Only those who survived had the answer. The first thing I think of is the phenomenon known as survivor's guilt. It eats at you and tells you over and over that someone else could have possibly lived, if only you would have sacrificed your own life.

Of course, each survivor could answer that question only for himself. When I consider the psychological pain from post-traumatic stress, I look at these men and realize few of them received treatment to help ease the emotional pain and agony. Certainly, they received the best medical attention available at the time they were rescued. But there was no treatment that even scratched the surface of what's available today for psychological intervention.

Then came the end of the march—the final destination for most of those soldiers. If you have never been there, the road ends at the caves. Yes, caves, carved out of stone by the sea since time immemorial. The formation of the landscape is altered by never-ending waves, creating large open spaces where you can walk inside and envision those men entering at low tide. When I first laid eyes upon it, it gave the immediate impression that only the hand of God could create something so beautiful but only mankind could make so deadly.

If you listen, your own inner soul will experience the anguished cries of those poor souls when the tide came in. Those voices were now silenced in death, death by drowning. Then came the dead silence. History would list them as KIA (killed in action). Many of the bodies were swept out to sea and never recovered. They were listed as MIA (missing in action).

Those were the brave men of the Greatest Generation. I'm not so sure that "generation" was any greater than any other, but those who served and gave their lives are the greatest, no matter which generation they belonged to. Half a century later, I still hear those voices when I sit in silence. And remember.

The next day, we visited Manila, the capital city. Memory fails me when I try to remember how we managed to join a tour of the Pink House, the residency of then President Ferdinand Marcos. A

Philippine soldier approached the three of us and signaled us to leave the group and join him.

Oh shit, this cannot be good! I thought. *What did we get into now?* At least we were kept together and not separated. He led us to an office, which was plush but not exactly as fancy as I would have expected once we were told what it was.

This was the office of President Marcos. The soldier told us to follow and directed us one by one to take a seat in the president's chair! We weren't in uniform, but I'm sure we stuck out in the crowd as being members of the US military. Why did this man pick us? We didn't have time to ask. He hustled us out of the room, and in decent English told us something to the effect of, "Get the hell out of here before we all get shot!"

Certainly, this was an unexpected honor here. I was the same guy who had challenged this country's custom of receiving a compliment.

Each of us had our moments. While most of our stories are gut-wrenching and full of horror, those of us who were fortunate enough to return to the world have to admit there were some good memories also. Those who were injured early in their tour were robbed of those type memories. I sincerely feel for those in any war who came home without a positive story to tell, especially those not experiencing some type of humor.

And of course, there are those who did not return. Those who survived long enough would have made loved ones smile with some of their stories. However, those events are lost for eternity.

PART THREE

Chapter 14

"How does it feel to be on your own, with no direction home, a complete unknown, like a rolling stone?"

—*Bob Dylan, "Like a Rolling Stone"*

I t didn't take long for me to realize that things in the world would be very different than I had expected. We hadn't been told things would never be the same. Before we crossed the pond, we thought we would arrive home, not heroes, but neither as the scourge of the earth. One would have surmised that we were Lyndon Johnson's personal bitches.

There was no debriefing offered. There was no warning as to what we would face. We were twenty-year-old kids who had left home as children and returned (as adults) as the assholes of the country. We didn't ask to be loved or even accepted. We only wanted to filter back into society. We just wanted to be left alone as if we had never left.

But we did leave. And those who came back in body bags were honored to an extent. But as time wore on and arrival of body bags became the norm, even the dead were no longer heroes. They were just casualties that were expected to arrive daily. This was no big deal. They shouldn't have gone over there in the first place. They had no business being there. The only difference between the dead and the rest of us was that they were dead assholes, while we were living assholes.

Maybe our government had no business sending us there. But to those who went, our cause was just. We to defend freedom, whether that was the real purpose of the war or not. I am proud that I went to Vietnam instead of Canada. And if I had come home in a body bag, I would have expected my family to accept the fact that I served when and where I was called and that I wasn't a coward. Those who ran to Canada were cowards. The yellow streak they wore remains on their back. We can smell them a mile away. Yes, they lived, and they may not have suffered the consequences we suffered, but they were cowards. And each of those who served, whether they saw Vietnam or not, were heroes. Not everybody could serve in one area, and those who served at home did what they were called to do.

Of course, there were politically protected sons of politicians who served in the reserves to get out of active duty. I am talking about the type of politicians who would see to it their sons would fly enough hours in the reserves to qualify as "veterans" but would get out of serving in a war.

Regardless of my political affiliation or views, I will never accept the actions that have been documented about one man who would later become president of the United States. He became a certified pilot and then subsequently was rejected by the University of Texas Law School. After being commissioned as a fighter pilot, he missed eight months of duty between May 1972 and May 1973. He then was granted an early discharge to attend Harvard Business School. His actions nearly caused him to lose the 2000 election to Al Gore in one of the (if not the) most controversial presidential elections prior to 2020. This isn't a commentary about his time in office but, rather, about how he became listed as a "veteran." The story was told as a TV documentary. These were the basis of the documentary, not facts I claim to have verified on my own.

Meanwhile, back to the '60s, my stay of exactly two weeks in Seattle seemed to cover months rather than days. I can't recall much of what went on there. I don't remember what kind of barracks I stayed in, only that things were rather relaxed, and strict military procedures were not in place. Each day, I awaited my orders to fly to Pittsburgh. There was no reason to keep me there. I had already passed my physical exam. Plus, it was costing the government to house and feed me for no good reason.

Finally, the day came that my orders were set. I was to leave Seattle on November 15. I was being discharged, as in getting the hell out of the navy and never being a sailor again! I would never again be a corpsman again (which was the only part I would miss). But little did I know that my medical training would help me save two or maybe three lives later on in civilian life.

Again, I flew over the Rockies at night and still hadn't seen much of the United States from the air. However, the glowing lights of the airport at Pittsburgh were a welcoming sight this time. Now, they were growing brighter by the second, instead of becoming dimmer, fading away as they had a year ago.

The first thunderstorm I experienced after returning brought me back to the storms I remembered as a kid. I had gotten used to the flash of lightning and then the bang of thunder during storms at my duty stations. Briefly forgotten were the storms of home, where the thunder would rumble up and down the hills of the Ohio River valley, reverberating like the bombs dropped by the B-52 bombers. The roaring thunder brought back the ghosts of a land far away but not forgotten by the echoes of my mind.

My DD-214 would show eleven months and twenty-four days in combat zone for hostile fire pay. It doesn't reflect a week of hell in Japan. But the most amazing thing it holds is verification that I passed the E-4 exam on my first attempt—a raise in rank and pay, which I never received. Even with this proof, I was unable to receive back pay because … well, because that isn't the military way to do things. Sorry for your luck, Mr. Turner. You are a civilian now, and we don't discuss military matters with civilians.

The best part of my DD-214 was that I even passed military requirements for petty officer 2 (E-5). Go figure!

Several years later, I was reading over my comp and pen exam (compensation and pension). It was noted that I was discharged as E-5 (Hospitalman Second Class). I went back to my DD-214 and studied it thoroughly; there, on the bottom, was noted my advancement to E-5. When the master chief had told me I would "come back as an E-5," I had taken for granted that came with the stipulation that I reupped for four years. In a sense, that meant very little. But at the same time, not many sailors make E-5 in just thirty-eight months. He had kept his promise, the result of which I discovered, most likely, years after his death.

On May 11, 1971, I was issued an honorable discharge, giving me six years of active and inactive duty. I guess that meant I was officially out of Uncle Sam's military confines and a civilian forevermore—unless things got so ugly veterans were recalled.

Speaking of the above date, soon after that, I received my draft notice in the mail. This was one time I had a good laugh on Uncle Sam. I figured I was one who could legally burn my draft notice. But I had too much pride to do that even as a joke. I took the notification to the county courthouse, and they did whatever they had to do. In the meantime, several employees had a good laugh along with me. For once, Uncle Sam provided me with some humor!

My first and last naval reserve meeting in Warwood, West Virginia, was mandatory. I met the commander prior to the meeting and informed him I would like to sign any necessary papers immediately because I had put my time in and was not interested in remaining a member of the United States (active) military in any way. He told me I had to attend one meeting but that he would let me sign the papers and skip out of the meeting.

The commander did have one question for me before I signed the release. I will never forget his question or my answer.

"What would it take to get you to stay in the Navy Reserve?"

"I'll come back when all the draft dodgers have been rounded up and sent where I was. When they each do a tour, I'll not only join the reserves, but I'll do another active tour!"

End of discussion. The remark was not intended personally toward the commander. He was a very mild-mannered gentleman, who had probably heard many other disgruntled sailors make similar remarks. He shook hands with me and wished me good luck in my future.

But luck would not be much of a factor in my future. Like the average Vietnam vet, I faced a future that would be marred by the experiences of a past life. I didn't have the memories of my buddy being blown apart with his blood all over me. As I said before, the "grunts" in the jungle were the heroes. They were the ones we expected to have problems dealing with the past later on. What I failed to realize was how my experiences built from day to day, how they became cumulative. I had been so busy I didn't even realize how much death and suffering I had witnessed. Later, as I spoke to Ray, my ship comrade, I guess I must have just hit the wrong times to have flight quarters. I know everybody had terrible experiences, but evidently most others had a little bit more luck than I did in experiencing those with mortal wounds. Many patients were already dead on arrival. Those weren't as difficult to deal with because they were usually covered with a blanket or sheet and were "only" a body and not a living, suffering person.

I seemed to have the luck of the draw in receiving the mortally wounded but still living category. I had the ones I prayed with at their moment of death. I had the one with the booby trap strapped to his leg. I was called, for some unknown reason, when neither the nurse nor anyone else could handle identifying the decaying corpses after three days in the unforgiving tropical sun.

I even had the master sergeant who walked on the ward one day looking for a corpsman named Turner. I have no idea where he got my name or to whom he talked. He had been bitten by a dog and was told to go to the ship. (We were harbored in Da Nang at the time.) He needed a series of three rabies shots. He brought the hypodermic, filled with the vaccine with him, and handed it to me. I asked who had told him to tell me to give the injections, and he refused to tell me. I had never done this before, and it wasn't part of my training. He lifted his shirt, exposed his muscular body and asked if I knew where the shot went. I had always heard of rabies shots being given in the belly. So, in went the needle, and I slowly injected the serum. I had heard it burned badly, but he didn't flinch. He tucked his shirt in and said, "Same time tomorrow!"

Two days later, we finished up. He did thank me but still refused to tell me who had sent him to me specifically.

I began to think there was a note somewhere that said, "If you don't know who to assign it to, give the job to Turner." I'm sure many other corpsmen have their own oddball stories to tell also. It isn't like I think I'm the only one who had these types of experiences.

To the young men like Williams and Rodriguez, your deaths have taken a toll over the years. Yet, I was the fortunate one. I lived, and you didn't. I'll never regret being there for you. For everything, there is a season. Your families mourned, and mine received a living veteran safely returned home with stories to tell about you. For every season, there is a reason. Had timing not worked out as it did, I would not have met Shep Chase. Therefore, he would not have seen to it that I got treatment for the post-traumatic stress disorder. In turn, I wouldn't have been there for him when he gave his soul to Jesus Christ shortly before his death. And so, even as my past haunts me, yet, during, and since Vietnam, I have been a caregiver for so many people. I feel it's not anything to brag about but, rather, something to take a personal pride in—pride, as in the Holy Spirit was my guide.

I didn't always feel so good about myself though. Upon my return, I felt like a misfit. Many of my close friends had opted to go to college rather than enlist. One or two had gone to Canada, and I had no desire to recognize their existence once they returned. College and an education was one thing, and being a coward and running away was another. Years later, I would discover that two of my good friends had joined the military. After their subsequent deaths, I would learn they had each served a tour of combat duty. To Bob and John, thank you!

At any rate, I was a loner and the odd man out. I had done what I thought was honorable and served my country. I didn't want a hero's welcome because I wasn't a hero. But I didn't expect to be treated like a worthless piece of shit after giving nearly three and a half years of my life so that others could enjoy their lives back at home.

When I filed for unemployment compensation, I was told I had to wait because I had been paid several days leave upon discharge. For some odd reason, I didn't happen to use up my allotted leave over there. Imagine that! By the time I would have been eligible for benefits, I figured I didn't want anything else from the government. So, I said the hell with it.

By January, I went to work for a loan company in Wheeling, West Virginia. The manager and assistant manager gave me the accounts they wanted no part of. My first home collection was in a shady part of the Wheeling area, and a woman tried to get me to help her pay off her debt by offering sexual favors. "Goodbye ma'am. I'll have the manager give you a call and see if he is willing to give you some financial assistance!"

A few days later, I was bitten by a German shepherd. The assistant manager saw it as a laughing matter. I didn't. So, I told him to shove the job and send me my check. I received a call from the district manager the following day and was given an apology. He wasn't the one who owed me an apology. I politely told him to send the assistant manager to see the lady and the dog owner because I wouldn't be returning. I guess you could chalk another one up to a returning vet who was taken for granted.

Soon, I got "temporary" employment only a mile and a half from home at a concrete block plant where my future father-in-law was employed. I worked my butt off tearing down a concrete block wall, a job that was to last a week. By noon the second day, I was finished with the job. I must have impressed the boss because, the next day, I was hired full-time as a regular employee.

All the employees there were much older than I was, so I wasn't very well accepted. I wasn't there to take anyone's job. But some of the older men didn't want to work overtime and saw me as a challenge because I was willing to work hard and often worked eighty hours a week. The work was hard, and it was dirty. But it was a job and I was able to make double payments on my car and got way ahead on house payments. Years later, after open-heart surgery, I was told I had white lung disease from working in the cement and fly ash bins at Arrow Block Company.

Not long after this, I got married. I began attending Ohio University Eastern campus, taking one class at a time, since I was working long hours and six days a week. It wasn't easy. I fell asleep several times on my way home from class because it was a twenty-mile drive, and by 10:00 p.m., I was totally exhausted. I would stick my head out the window and turn the radio on full blast to keep myself awake. Fortunately, during the times I dozed off, I never actually fell sound asleep at the wheel.

I started with economics classes and didn't do well. After my first few classes, I had a C average. That was an improvement from high school, but it wasn't good enough. I knew I had to get my grades up, and I knew economics wasn't my bag. So, I switched to history and political science without actually declaring a major.

In January 1972, my son, Ryan, was born. It was the best thing that had ever happened in my life and would be equaled only when my daughter, Carrie, was born in October 1976.

Work was hard but steady. I was only laid off one week. When I went back to the employment office, I was asked if I would quit school if they found a job placement for me. I explained that I was attending night classes and would be returning to my job as soon as the weather warmed up. My application was denied. I returned to the office and demanded to see the veteran's representative, with whom I immediately set things straight. After all the hassle, I was called back to work the following week, and the waiting period had not expired. Therefore, I was ineligible for benefits anyway. Yet, I was pleased to see that the State of Ohio was taking care of its veterans.

In the meantime, I would be the victim of a back injury in 1973. I was lifting a metal pallet the blocks were pressed onto. It probably weighed fifteen pounds, at most. I don't know if I turned wrong or what happened, but a severe pain, like a bolt of lightning, shot up my back and down my leg. I managed to work for three years in severe pain. Lifting ninety-four-pound bags of cement and seventy-two-pound bags of mortar was a significant part of my job. Cleaning the concrete mixer every day would take its toll, until I was bent over as if I was ninety years old and began missing work because of the pain. We had no sick leave and one week of vacation per year, which had to be taken all at one time. Much to my dismay, I went to the manager and told him I would go on workers' compensation until I could get something done for my back. By this time, I had ruptured a second disc in my lumbar spine, and in November 1976, I had no choice but to go through surgery.

Those who have had lower back surgery in recent years have no idea what the surgery was like in those days. They cut through the muscle and scraped nerves, which took months to heal.

Sections of some nerves never healed completely. The surgeon told me one of the disks was in a hundred fragments and had almost severed the sciatic nerve. Being a very fast healer, I was only off less than six months. But after returning to work, I was injured again about nine months later. On March 17, 1977, I was hit in the head by a piece of machinery that had performed out of sequence for months. I had filed reports concerning the problem and turned them into management repeatedly. There was nobody to blame but one person.

A new foreman had been hired, and we accused the secondary company of hiring him to run the company into bankruptcy. It wasn't long before one co-owner bought his partner out. The foreman had dropped a metal bar on my father-in-law's head from a height of about eighty feet. Fortunately, we had been issued hard hats about a year prior to the incident. I found Ron lying unconscious with the bar lying beside him. The foreman had walked away, thinking nobody would suspect him as the culprit. He expected us to take careless chances like he did. He didn't seem to care who got injured, as long as it wasn't him.

As I noted, my second injury occurred nine months after my return to work. One Thursday, the machine that loaded the fresh blocks onto a rack to be dried in the kilns was once more jumping out of sequence. This was nothing new. Again, I had complained about this very problem time after time. On that day, it flew back and hit me in the head. After sitting in the office for about half an hour, I drove to the nearby hospital myself. After ordering X-rays, the doctor told me not to return to work until Monday. He said I would either be able to return then, or else I would never go back to work. The second part of the "either" won out. I had one cervical disc removed soon afterward. That was the beginning of the neck situation. More on that soon. Ironically, I have no problem remembering the date the injury occurred. It happened on March 17, St. Patrick's Day. So much for the luck of the Irish.

A few years later, I discovered that Amos (the foreman hired by the primary company involved, who we believed was hired to break the secondary company financially, by which I was employed) had tried to outrun a slow-moving train in his Jeep, crossing the railroad tracks behind the block plant. The train couldn't stop in time, and Amos was dead. This was one of the few people I could not force myself to feel sorry for. I didn't hate him; I despised him. I would never have wished this on him, but he died as he had lived, taking chances and trying to see how far he could push others.

Amos had once suspended a driver three days without pay for forgetting to turn his truck engine off one evening. This happened right after Amos forgot to deploy the wheels of his private aircraft when he landed on a flight to Cleveland. He was incensed when he knew I had found out about his near-deadly experience. I refused to tell him my source of information, which irked him even more. The man always talked about being a Christian. He was among the meanest, most vicious persons I have known who professed to be very close to God. On that autumn afternoon, he was much closer to his maker than he presumed.

It was the head and neck injury that eventually did me in. After having the third fusion, I attended school full-time. I got my grades up and switched my major back to my roots from the navy, returning to psychology. I had all the credits I needed in psychology and only needed a few courses in other subjects. When I enrolled, nobody told me that, under a new policy, foreign language had been added to all degrees. I was stuck, big-time, because the school didn't offer foreign language except on campus in Athens, Ohio.

I was able to bypass the foreign language requirements at Wheeling College (formerly known as Wheeling Jesuit University, now known as Wheeling University), but I had to declare another major and complete the entire program for criminal justice. I did this in less than nine months. By the time I graduated, I had brought my GPA up to 3.6 overall and 4.0 at WJU.

I would subsequently enroll at the University of Dayton, where I managed a 3.95 GPA, completing my graduate study degrees in education and counseling in less than a year and a half.

During this time, I had begun coaching Little League baseball. Ryan developed into quite a pitcher, and I worked with him at the ball field and in the yard every minute I could spare. I also helped coach basketball and was head football coach for one season since St. John grade school couldn't find a full-time coach. Later, I would coach Carrie's softball team for a season until the school could find someone to take my place. Carrie's high school team was in its first year, and they usually took a pretty good beating. Once she came along with her pitching, she was the first pitcher in her school to get credit for a win. By the next year, she would pitch a one-hitter against one of the top teams in the valley. Ryan had also pitched back-to-back no-hitters in Colt league.

The only games I can remember missing was when both kids played at the same time. I also missed a few of Ryan's football games his freshman year when I was in graduate school. Even at that, I had a great professor who allowed me to come in late after home games, which were played about five minutes from the school.

I had returned to work before graduate school and was hired as a fraud investigator for the county welfare department.

During all this time, it may have appeared that things were going well for me. But in actuality, my life was beginning to crumble around me. Chris and I began to argue about anything there was to argue about. I began to sit and stare out the living room window for hours at a time. I was depressed, and there seemed to be no legitimate reason for the depression. But there were factors others couldn't see or understand. I would later realize that suppression, not to mention repression, does not take a back seat to an education in psychology.

This book isn't meant to be the story of my married life. Nor is it about my problems dealing with my marriage. Chris's father was like the father I didn't have, and he treated me like a son. Her mother treated me well. They were good to me and helped us out in many situations. But it wasn't one-sided. I cut their grass and spent a lot of time working around their house and property. Their son and other daughter moved away from the area, and I was left alone helping them out, along with working eighty hours a week until my second injury, going to school, coaching, and spending every possible minute with my children.

As I said, this is not a story about my marriage. And it would be only one side of the story, even if it was about that. The only thing I will say about the issue is that, if I had been number four in her life, I doubt that things would have gone downhill as they did. I didn't mind being behind God and the kids. But being behind them and her parents got to be a burden I couldn't bear any longer, especially when she treated my mother and sister as if they were strangers.

In due respect to her, I had my own problems I was trying to cope with since my return from Vietnam. She was the one who noticed how I went through weeks of depression after watching movies like *Hamburger Hill*, *Full Metal Jacket*, and the like.

Repression is an unconscious act of pushing back old memories before they can surface into the conscious level. Suppression is an intentional attempt to push them back into the level of unconsciousness after they have begun to leak out. It is a state of being aware that the memories exist, where there is no awareness in repression. It is one point I hammered on all my students when I began teaching psychology.

Chris told me I had "changed" when I graduated from college. No, it wasn't college that changed me. I never took the attitude that I was any smarter than someone without a college degree at all. I always said that college made me a little bit wiser in some ways, but it didn't make me smarter than anyone else. The diplomas, however, were essential in obtaining employment.

If only she had realized it wasn't my education that changed my demeanor, things might have worked out differently. It wasn't Ohio University. It wasn't Wheeling College. It had nothing to do with the University of Dayton. It had nothing to do with my educational experiences in school. It was all about my time served in Vietnam. Call me weak. Call me whatever you want. I wasn't prepared to see the things I saw over there. And the worst part of it is that there were many who saw much more than I did. Most of them have gone through what I have encountered many times over. What has society blamed for their downfall? Probably their inability to cope with their war experience!

Many veterans turned to drugs and alcohol. Many became thieves because they couldn't hold a job. They hurt people because they were trained to hurt people.

Jay Teacoach, my first VA counselor, told me, instead of a druggie or an alcoholic, I became a workaholic. I continued to function in the corpsman mode. I have never given it up.

I helped people. I helped save the lives of three people long after I returned from the service, because I was trained as to what to do when someone went into a grand mal seizure or fell and cracked their skull open. I knew more than the medical squad (only the particular one involved) when I held a woman's head together and kept her grey matter from oozing out of the open wound. But each of these events took me back to that white room on the ship known as triage. I didn't visualize the little old lady I was actually working on. Instead, I visualized a young marine in his combat green fatigues, pleading to live. And then I was pissed off because of the ineptness of the squad member who asked me what I was doing to her. Maybe I should have stayed in the medical field because I cared for people. I could have let go of the woman's skull and showed the medic who questioned my expertise and let her brains gush out. I didn't have blood all over me because I wanted to prove to some shit head that blood and guts didn't make me sick, while people around me were running around puking their guts out and I was trying to get them to obtain towels and supplies for me.

One afternoon, I walked into the lobby of the Department of Human Services where I was employed. A very large man (probably 325 to 350 pounds) was sitting with his mother. He was about thirty-five years old and, because of health problems, was continuously under his mother's care.

As I walked into the lobby, he got up, and his mother followed him outside. He had a blank stare as if he was fifty miles away from reality, and I knew something was amiss. I stepped outside just in time to witness him going into a seizure. As he began falling to the sidewalk, I knew I couldn't hold his weight, so I cushioned his fall, and he landed on top of me. I was able to get from under him in time for his mother to hand me a homemade "seizure stick" to help keep him from swallowing this tongue. Then she ran around the side of the building in horror and disappeared.

I was able to get one of my fellow workers to call the emergency squad. She followed my request and asked for a "silent approach." However, the squad came rolling in from only a block away with the siren screaming and the horn blaring. The man went into a grand mal seizure. Fortunately, I was able to literally sit on him and keep him from swallowing his tongue until the squad arrived.

As soon as the squad left for the hospital, the man's mother came back and told me she was usually the one who kept him from swallowing his tongue. But if anyone else was around to take charge, she would panic and flee. At least I knew what to do. And whether or not I helped save his life, he made it and lived for at least a few more years.

The US Navy taught me well. It trained me well. I could talk a psychiatric patient into handing me his weapon, or I could take it away from him. I stood down several men who could easily have killed me or others if I had used the wrong approach. What I wasn't taught was that things would come back to me later on in life. I wasn't told I would never be the same. I wasn't told the war would never end. I wasn't even told that the liquid I got all over my skin in triage might cause me the heart disease and cancer I was to experience later in life. The government knew I may even eventually die from it, but we were expendable once we were done serving. No wonder the Veterans Administration is overwhelmed and overburdened. And I don't relate this specifically to Vietnam veterans. I can feel for veterans of other wars. I just can't relate to their individual experiences.

When I'd first returned home after being discharged, I had applied for employment at the psychiatric wing of a local hospital. Despite all my training, the only thing I qualified for was an orderly, with no responsibility other than cleaning up messes and performing minor tasks everyone else was "overqualified" to perform.

I asked, if I took the job, would the employer help with my educational costs? No deal! I asked if there was any room for advancement during the time I attended college. No deal!

I couldn't imagine going from being a hospital corpsman in a triage situation and on psychiatric wards, where, in an emergency, I could even order medications and be backed by a doctor who would sign off on whatever I did to being a ward custodian. Needless to say, that's how I ended up working at a concrete block plant so I would have enough wages to survive until I could complete my bachelor's degree.

Oh, by the way, I was never notified I could obtain government assistance through the VA for my education until after my injuries!

Chapter 15

"Hear my prayer, O Lord; let my cry for help come to you.
Do not hide your face from me when I am in distress. Turn
your ear to me; when I call, answer me quickly. For my days
vanish like smoke; my bones burn like glowing embers."

—*Psalm 102:1–3*

The cervical spine situation would worsen over the years, eventually leading to three additional discs being removed and my spine fused into one solid mass from C3 through C7 beginning in 1989 and culminating in 1993. An additional lower back surgery came in 2010, when the lowest disk (aka the tailbone) gave out. Several screws now stabilize the area.

I had migraine headaches constantly, which was finally relieved with the removal of the C6–7 disc. My power to concentrate was deeply affected. Yet, I managed to complete my master's degree through the University of Dayton in 1988 with a 3.95 average. I wasn't that smart. The classes were easy for me. It was the subject and career goal I was interested in, which made it much easier than working on my bachelor's degree.

The cervical spine injury would lead to several additional diagnoses and surgeries. I had carpal tunnel surgery performed on my left wrist. I was also diagnosed with the same problem in the right wrist but have not had surgery for it. While in rehabilitation for my neck and lower back problems in Columbus, Ohio, in 1996, I was forced to lift more weight above my head than I should have and injured my right shoulder. This injury would eventually lead to three surgeries for adhesive capsulitis and rotator cuff tear. The shoulder surgeries were done in 2002 and 2003.

My list of allowances by workers' compensation reads like a medical journal log:

> Post laminectomy syndrome cervical
> Sprain of neck
> Superficial injury—neck, face, scalp
> Carpal tunnel syndrome, left
> Cervical spinal stenosis
> Cervical disc displacement
> Disc displacement, nonspecific
> Cervical disc degeneration
> Cubital tunnel syndrome, bilateral
> Trigger thumb, left
> Lateral epicondylitis, left
> Tendonitis shoulder, right
> Synovitis shoulder, right

And so on and so forth!

That was beyond the second (cervical) spinal injury. In addition to the lower back surgery, eventually came scar tissue buildup, which has led to several bouts of intense pain, in turn, leading to months of physical therapy.

Since that time, I have been diagnosed with neuropathy and myofascial myalgia in both legs. As noted by a VA specialist, this is not from injuries. So, what does that tell you? No admission of Agent Orange, exposure to which very commonly results in these symptoms. Now, I am kept awake at night because of intense pain in my toes, again caused by the neuropathy. A VA podiatrist told me there is nothing that can be done about the pain, and I just have to live with it. Unfortunately, it is exacerbated by lying down, rather than standing. I have unsuccessfully attempted to sleep in a standing position. I cannot sleep on a recliner due to the fact that I cannot sleep on my back (or stomach). I toss from side to side all night, rotating positions constantly.

Along with these injuries have come a quadruple bypass. I had gall bladder surgery, in which two stones were released into the common duct, one finding its way to the liver. Because of this, I had a tube hanging from my belly for four months beginning in December 2002. During a follow-up surgery, one stone was removed that had embedded itself in my liver, and the other had disappeared. Disappeared to where? Don't know, don't care, as long as it is gone! In November 2022, I had another gall stone appear, this one blocking my pancreas. After all those years, it was identified by a CT scan. When the surgeon went in with a scope, it had miraculously disappeared. It wasn't the first time for that. Thank you, Lord!

Less painful were colon polyps, which were removed, and corrective surgery for trigger thumb. Then came removal of a subglottal web in my throat, which was first believed to include a tumor.

I went to see an eye, ear, nose, and throat specialist. While inserting a tube down my nose and into my throat, he found the subglottal web and a growth, which, a few weeks later, he would diagnose as a tumor. To my dismay, he inserted the tube again to show Linda the size and positioning of the tumor. In the end, that would provide proof that God would grant me with another miracle.

The doctor removed the web by laser. This was something that needed to be done because it was causing breathing difficulties and had forced one trip to the emergency room by ambulance. I hadn't been sure I would survive that specific attack. The laser surgery for the web was not much to be concerned about according to the doctor. That specific growth was a nonmalignant type, so it was removed and, to this point, has never been an issue again.

It was the second part of the surgery that was of more concern.

He didn't believe the tumor was malignant, but the status would be diagnosed by the lab after removal.

Upon awakening, I was told of the miracle. Despite photographs from the scoping and Linda earlier being shown the tumor through a scope, there was no tumor to be found! I have had no issues connected to this ever since.

Was this caused by Agent Orange? I will never know for sure. But after receiving this miracle, I was spending much more time on thanking God than on blaming the government.

This was followed by two years of miserable stomach problems caused by acid reflux, concluded by Nissen fundoplication surgery, in which the back of the stomach muscle is wrapped around the esophagus and sewn to the front side of the stomach to stop the reflux. The surgery was so risky I was unable to locate a surgeon to perform it. Even the Pittsburgh VA refused to perform the surgery. One would think a hospital whose surgeons performed all kinds of transplants, including heart transplants, would have one among them willing to perform the surgery.

After a long, drawn-out ordeal, I found a local doctor who was willing to perform the surgery. He was not a renowned surgeon like many of those at the VA, but he was willing to perform the surgery. But first, he wanted a signed letter from my gastroenterologist that the surgery was absolutely necessary. He got the letter and performed the surgery. Dr. William Bailer was a lifesaver. He is also one of the friendliest and most patient-attentive surgeons I have met. Unfortunately, I have met my share of surgeons of various specialists, not to mention general surgeons. Dr. Bailer owns cattle and runs his farm himself. His patients are not surprised to see him come in late at night wearing jeans and work boots. He fits into the category of someone who might not look like a surgeon but is, in my humble opinion, one of the best.

Again, the question is, was this condition caused by Agent Orange? I can't say it was or even that it probably was. But the many, many medical issues build the case that, at least from my perspective, many were caused by the defoliant. Various medical issues and diseases have been approved under Agent Orange. Others will never be confirmed.

Since those surgeries, I endured even more after I began writing this book. The worst was the S5 level disc (previously mentioned), where the pain became intolerable. The VA doctors in Pittsburgh gave me stronger and stronger medications. They even prescribed methadone. But it is a personality-affecting medication, which I cannot tolerate. It finally got to the point that doctors were convinced I needed the surgery. The result was unbelievable. Though healing would take time and physical therapy, the pain had diminished overnight, to a point where I considered myself nearly pain-free, at least at that site.

Other surgeries included another trigger release, this time on my right thumb. Plus, I suffered the same affliction on fingers two separate times. The fingers were treated with two injections each, three weeks apart, which were very successful, and surgeries were avoided. I won't go into all the others, except for a few more major ones.

My uncle had seven hernia surgeries throughout his lifetime. I was getting close to his record when he passed away. (I had the honor of officiating his funeral service.) I had hoped, if I ever passed his seven hernias, it would be during his lifetime. The latter didn't happen, but I did later surpass his record with hernia surgeries with my eighth. In all, I had thirteen hernias repaired during the eight surgeries. Several times, I had multiple hernias repaired during a single trip to the operating room. The umbilical hernia was the worst as far as recovery time. It was one where several were located within about a twelve-inch length and were taken down during a three-hour surgery. I continue to cut firewood, which involves a lot of lifting. I try to be just a little more careful, but I refuse to sit back and take it easy and allow my body to grow flabby. I have endured too much to let pain control me and cause me to go to waste, like I have seen too many people do.

My prostate-specific antigen was climbing, and my civilian urologist didn't seem to think it was suspicious enough to perform a biopsy. I went to the VA and asked for a biopsy, which was granted. It showed six out of twelve positive hits. They wanted me to "wait and see." I wanted something done immediately, before the cancer would spread to other organs. Things didn't go well after the surgery. The surgeon had pierced the bladder. Linda drove me eighty miles to Pittsburgh several times in the middle of the night. One night, Ryan drove when stool appeared in my catheter, and I needed to get to the hospital immediately. The surgeon then performed an ileostomy. During the nearly six-month period I dealt with this, I also had a Foley catheter. The catheter wasn't changed until five months later. And then it was only changed during a scope to check on the healing process.

Not long after that came the news that the doctors wanted to close down the ileostomy and perform a colostomy. My answer was an adamant, "No!"

The doctor's reaction was firm. "You will probably die if we don't do this soon."

My reaction was too. "I would rather die than live like this."

I got my wish, as no colostomy was performed, and the ileostomy was closed. Again, God gets the credit here. I had prayed long and hard about this decision. The surgeons were stunned by the results, and God was smiling for me. The effects of the catheter led to a leaky bladder. After three more surgeries, I have an "artificial urethral sphincter." It's unpleasant but effective. It's something I can live with, compared to a colostomy.

However, the result of the surgery came back to haunt me again. It began in the form of an eighty-mile trip to the emergency room at 2:00 a.m. The pain began low in the abdomen and gradually worked upward into the lower chest area. Then came the dry heaves. Because of my stomach surgery, I cannot throw up. I can only think of two times in my life that I was able to upchuck when I was ill. But now, it was impossible. Therefore, the next step to be carried out in each instance was to insert an NG tube through the nasal passage into the stomach. Because my cervical disk surgeries went through my throat, the insertion was extremely painful. The pain meds and anti-nausea meds would help until my gut was sucked out, but they weren't ordered until a diagnosis was confirmed. This meant a CT scan had to be done before any treatment could be ordered.

During the first occurrence, I was told I could go to a local emergency room. The doctor at that hospital would treat the symptoms and then call the VA in Pittsburgh and talk to a doctor there. If there was an available bed, I could either remain in Wheeling and pay whatever my private insurance wouldn't cover, or I could go to Pittsburgh. If there wasn't a room available, the VA would cover the entire expense, including the emergency room and hospital bill. This occurred about six times. Five of the six times, the VA had room for me, so I was transported to Pittsburgh.

It took a few hours to diagnose the problem during the first occurrence. From then on, the CT scan would be done immediately to verify the bowel blockage. After the last occurrence, there was no room for me at Pittsburgh for two days. On the second evening, the doctor had spoken to his counterpart in Pittsburgh, and they were going to send a squad to transport me the following morning. I told the doc there was no use for this because he was going to discharge me in the morning. That was news to him. But eventually, he would make it happen. He knew I was experienced in this malady. So, he agreed to make the call and tell the VA I would be discharged.

Just a note to those who think the VA covers all medical expenses, it bills any insurance provider you may have. For veterans with less than 100 percent service-connected disability, I would suggest, if you are interested, obtaining a free *Federal Benefits for Veterans, Dependents and Survivors* booklet.

After each bout of the obstruction, I would go to Pittsburgh for a follow-up exam. Each time, I would ask what I could do to avoid a reoccurrence. Was there something I should be eating? Was there something I shouldn't be eating? Was there some medicine that will help prevent this?

No, no, no. The answer was always a resounding no! That was, until my last occurrence of the problem on June 6, 2016. I was discharged with the promise of seeing a surgeon on my follow-up appointment. At that appointment, the doctor and I discussed surgical intervention. However, surgery was well out of the question. The surgeon told me the procedure would take two shifts (eleven to thirteen hours). And the risk would outweigh the benefit; my body had been through so much in the past three years, I might not survive such a lengthy surgery.

Then came what I considered another miracle in my life. It might not seem like a miracle to anyone else, but the surgeon said she knew what might help to, at least, reduce the reoccurrences of the attacks. I had been experiencing these on the average of about every five months. Her goal was to stretch them out to twelve to eighteen months. I hated to agree with her, but at least it was some kind of goal that was possibly attainable. Docusate! Yes, docusate, the stool softener one can purchase over the counter. I would take four a day for the rest of my life. What the heck. The VA would pay for it. So, as crazy as this sounded to me, it wouldn't cost me a cent to give it a try.

Honestly, this isn't a paid commercial. Whatever drug company that manufactures this medicine knows nothing about me. All I know is that God led me to the right doctor at the right time. Some doctors (especially at training hospitals, such as all VA hospitals) would jump at the chance to perform the type of surgery it would take to possibly (and I underscore the word *possibly*) correct my condition. This surgeon wanted to try an over-the-counter medicine. I honestly felt she was just trying to pacify me to get me on my way so she could proceed to her next patient. What a blessing she ended up being!

As I sit here nearly seven years later without a reoccurrence, I consider that to be a miracle! Of all the clinics and all the doctors I had experienced, here a surgeon took a shot at something that sounded ridiculous. I've had several episodes when I thought I was in the early stages of an obstruction, but taking another medication when needed, which she also prescribed, has done the trick. If I am even blessed at this reoccurring only every few years, I cannot complain.

At times, I came close to losing my faith due to the pain and mental anguish I endured because of nightmares and flashbacks.

But I did not turn away from that faith because I firmly believe there is a reason for everything. The reason would not be clear to me for several years.

As I said, those last surgeries came later on. Life went on. My wife and I couldn't agree on anything. I admit I was always moody and not pleasant to be around, but everything I did was wrong. I previously mentioned some of the problems, which I will not dwell on.

But one medical issue has played a very significant negative effect since about 1980. I began developing spots on my arm that first appeared as very small skin tags. Knowing I should just leave them alone, I did what just about anyone else would do and scratched them off. They tended to itch a good bit where the skin was raw and I had scratched them. The spots began to grow larger over the next year, or so. I was due for a physical exam with my family doctor. I showed him what were now becoming lesions. He immediately referred me to a local dermatologist.

The doctor was a pleasant, elderly gentleman who would sit and listen, which seems to be something that's becoming rare. He even told me about playing poker with my referring physician and some other local doctors. While his storytelling was no big deal one way or the other, I felt very relaxed and trusted him because he was so down-to-earth. My initial assessment of a physician includes her or his bedside manners. It matters to me how a doctor interacts with patients.

I had once been hospitalized due to my lower back injury and had managed to get an appointment with one of the most renowned neurosurgeons in the country. He was employed by a major professional sports team in Pittsburgh. I ended up telling him, "You are probably the best neurosurgeon in the country, if not the world. But you are the worst when it comes to bedside manners. And being at the Belmont County Country Club, when you promised you would see me at a certain time, which was about six hours ago, is further evidence."

His response was, "That's what most of my patients tell me."

I guess when you are that famous, you act like everything is a compliment and walk away.

So, back to the dermatologist who seemed to have the exact opposite personality to that of the neurosurgeon, he diagnosed me with psoriasis. I was to begin treating the lesions with a prescription topical ointment. Over the next several months, the lesions began to grow in number and size. The itching became worse and affected what little sleep I was getting. Next began PUVA treatments, which uses ultraviolet light. This seemed to help somewhat but took a toll on my skin from head to toe. The treatments provided a nice year-round tan but were beginning to cause more skin damage than prevention or healing.

Now was the time to ask the question I wanted to put to the dermatologist. (I'll paraphrase the conversation.) Are you familiar with Agent Orange?

I know about it, but I won't make a diagnosis using it. If I do, I'll end up in court and lose two days of work, battling the government over something I am unable to prove.

So much for that. But it did provide the answer I was looking for. He had seen many Vietnam vets presenting the same symptoms as mine. He had just provided me with an "unofficial diagnosis." But I would continue under his care because at least he was treating me as best he could. Still, my deductibles were piling up, and the problem with which the US government had provided me was costing me dearly.

It wouldn't be until I began treatment at the Pittsburgh VA for PTSD that I would get into the VA health-care system. Then I began my quest for treatment where doctors would be familiar with the symptoms of Agent Orange, even though Uncle Sam continued to fight the suggestion that the defoliant was the cause of those symptoms.

At the point I discovered I was eligible for VA health care, which was a well-kept secret at least in my area, I obtained an appointment with dermatology. I was prescribed two different topical ointments and given my own UVA machine, which was set up in my home. The difference between the PUVA and UVA machines has something to do with intensity. At least, that's my interpretation. I'm no expert in this field, so I guess I should just say they are somewhat different and somewhat identical. I saw little benefit in this treatment and stopped using it. There was no use causing further damage to my skin. The dermatologist agreed with my decision. There seemed to be nothing to stop the constant itching, and open sores or lesions now appeared all over my body, whereas before, it had mostly been limited to my extremities. Nothing was giving me relief from the itching and now burning sensation. The lesions were ugly. I began wearing long-sleeve shirts in public as much as possible. This was uncomfortable for me because I usually don't wear a jacket unless the temperature is below 40 or it's raining.

I was also told I should wear long sleeves because the sun was further damaging my skin. Much to my surprise, one dermatologist, in her write-up, stated that I had been a "sun worshiper" in my younger days.

In 2018, it got to the point that I needed more than appointments where the doctor would just monitor my skin. The "psoriasis," or whatever it was, would flare up every night when I went to bed. Not that it wasn't bad enough during the day, but it got progressively worse during the night. I would get up and walk around the house most of the night. I finally told the dermatologist I was at the point where something else had to be done.

Now, to combine health problems, I had suffered from neuropathy for several years. Numerous EMGs would prove this diagnosis. I call it "restless leg syndrome" because it feels like millions of tiny ants crawling up and down my legs inside the skin. Now, I was facing dermal and subdermal itching. There had been several nights when I got up, unable to sleep. I stayed up all night, spending most of those hours walking around the house. I would try to work on sermons or do anything to get my mind off this. But seldom did anything help.

One night—after having already taken my mirtazapine (for PTSD-induced restlessness), plus several hydroxyzine pills (antihistamine taken for itching)—I did something I had never done before (nor have I done so since). I had a bottle of rum that had been in the cupboard for many years, and I began drinking from it. I drank about a third of the bottle (a fifth), thinking, surely, I would fall asleep. You have to understand that I am not, nor have I ever been, a consumer of alcohol. I drink a beer about once every six weeks or so with pizza or when I grill outdoors in the summer. One beer, and that's my limit. It is a limit for several reasons, including the fact that I won't let a drug (and yes, alcohol is a drug) control me. Another reason is that beer bloats me to the point that I feel like I'm ready to explode if I start on a second one. Two is the most beers I have been able to, or wanted to, get down. Also, with my volunteer position as critical incident stress management / county chaplain coordinator, I would not consider pulling out of my garage if I thought there was any chance at all I would be near the 0.08 breathalyzer test limit in Ohio.

I couldn't believe I didn't experience my first hangover or any other side effects from the "night before." I awakened with only the normal amount of itching and neuropathy I usually contend with in the mornings—an amount I could live with. It was at night that the severity usually flared up.

Next were appointments with dermatology and the pain clinic at the VA. This was where I was going when I wrote about doctor/patient relations previously. The dermatologist I had seen the past two visits switched clinic hours. And because I take government transportation to Pittsburgh, I have to schedule morning appointments if at all possible.

I say "doctor"; it is often a fourth-year medical student enrolled in one of the many colleges in Pittsburgh, which is known for its several medical schools. The VA hospital is practically (physically) part of the University of Pittsburgh campus. More likely, the provider I saw was a physician's assistant. To make it easier, I will call them all doctor.

I needed to make some kind of impression on my new doctor, as I was now desperate. Fortunately for me, she got the message loud and clear. She asked me if I would consider having her prescribe methotrexate. Yes, we've all seen the commercials for just about any of the medications associated with adverse effects advertised on TV. If you suffer from this ... or this ... or that, you may be ..." You get the point. I didn't care about any of those warnings. I was all in!

The next appointment was on the same morning—pain clinic. I was greeted by a very experienced doctor (MD), who I had seen about two years prior. She had diagnosed me with myofascial myalgia, severe nerve damage resulting from my spinal surgeries, and neuropathy. She stayed away from Agent Orange like everyone else. The acupuncture she prescribed ended up being a fiasco. The doctor was Chinese, which was why the pain specialist wanted me to go to her specifically. After the first two sessions, she embarked on her yearly trip home to celebrate Chinese New Year. By the time she returned, the time allotted for my treatment had expired, and I was left out in the cold again. I called the VA and explained what had happened. I never heard from them again concerning the request for additional treatments.

During the next visit to the pain clinic doctor, I was offered acupuncture once more. But she knew I would not be willing to go that route again. At that point, she offered to prescribe pregabalin (Lyrica). Again, I had the vision of all the commercials that seemed to take up more time than the program itself. I was also offered a prescription for medical marijuana, which the VA would not supply. But I could have it filled at a licensed distributor.

"No thanks. I appreciate the offer. But for multiple reasons, I don't want to go that route."

She was not persistent and let me know she was only offering the drug and not trying coax me into trying it.

But there was a potential problem. The main reason for switching medications was the foot pain, which was something new. At night, I would be kept up or awakened by pain shooting from the end of my feet through my toes. At first, I thought the source was the sciatic nerve. But from prior experience, I knew something was amiss, since both feet were affected equally, and it was different toes receiving the pain each time. Painkillers were out of the question because, although the pain was severe as it shot through my toes and although it was repetitive, it only lasted less than a second at a time. It was now beginning to appear in the daytime. Then it began to occur even when I was standing or walking, which I hadn't experienced previously. Then it began to last several minutes—and then hours. The only remedy would be to get out of bed and walk around. This helped, but the pain was more than likely to resume when I returned to bed.

I had been on Neurontin for the nerve damage for many years. It had helped, but its effectiveness was diminishing rapidly. I had to come off it slowly. At a certain daily dose, I would begin taking the pregabalin, titrating to the desired dose. Then came the question of combining the pregabalin and methotrexate, which was another nightmare in the making. If I had to stop the methotrexate, immediately, the skin problems worsened. It had seemed like a miracle drug. The scaly surface of my hands had cleared to a point I didn't think I would ever witness again!

Back to dermatology. I had to make a very tough decision. I was battling Agent Orange on two fronts. Which should I choose? The dermatologist was willing to put me back on methotrexate once the Neurontin was out of my system, and I had been on pregabalin long enough to tell that, if a problem arose at that point, it would clearly be as a result of combining the two new prescriptions. Both doctors worked together on resolving the issue. The worsening of the psoriasis began to clear up once again. The methotrexate did not resolve the issue of the dry, itchy skin. But the open sores I had for years are no longer as prevalent and have become much more limited in quantity and severity.

The pain specialist offered to up the dosage of pregabalin, but the pain has lessened to the point that I can endure and would rather hold back on a higher dosage. If the condition warrants eventually due to increased symptoms, then I would be placed on the maximum dose of pregabalin.

So, an A+ to the two specialists for working together and coming up with a solution that confronts both issues. Truthfully, I have not been 100 percent satisfied with the VA health care I have received. However, and a huge however, the quality of service has vastly improved since Uncle Sam has cracked down on the Department of Veterans Affairs.

Pittsburgh VA was involved in a situation where, supposedly, some patients died of something similar to what we know as Legionnaires' disease. Drinking water was limited to bottled water for well over a year until the source was identified and eliminated. I don't profess to know enough about the incident to delve into it, but veterans were made aware of it when the story finally hit the national news. Supposedly, more than one veteran died from the issue. That is according to TV reports, so I cannot state that to be definitely true. But keeping abreast of the situation, I have every reason to believe the validity of the reports.

Chapter 16

"Be strong and courageous, and do the work. Do not be afraid or discouraged, for the Lord God, my God, is with you. He will not fail you or forsake you until all the work for the service of the temple of the Lord is finished."

—*1 Chronicles 28:20*

I know it wasn't one-sided. I was often in a bad mood and wanted to be left alone. I finally realized, as I mentioned previously that I was dealing with the past experiences in Vietnam. After watching some of the movies about the war, Chris confronted me, pointing out that these types of movies were deeply affecting me. I quit watching war movies. I knew what I was dealing with, but it was easier to suppress it than to deal with it.

When I taught about post-traumatic stress in college, I talked about disasters as the manifesting precipitant. When I left out the obvious (which was war), a student asked if I was a Vietnam veteran. That told me I wasn't dealing with the truth. But even then, I still wasn't ready to deal with the issue.

I am not sure what the last war movie was that I watched. It has been many years. It might have been *Full Metal Jacket*. I took Ryan with me that night. He was probably about nine years old. I remember the final scene depicting American troops walking through a village that had been torched. They were singing "Mickey Mouse." That precipitated the only question Ryan asked me on the way home. "Why were they singing that?"

One evening, I rented *Born on the Fourth of July*. Carrie was young then and was in bed. The three of us began watching it. I got up and went into the bedroom and read a book after the first half hour or so. It really hit home seeing all the men who had returned with one, two, three, or even all their limbs missing. I hadn't thought of how they might be mistreated when they got back to the States. It was a bitter wake-up call to reality for me. Things from the war were bothering me, but I suppressed them as much as possible. Many people would make the argument that I repressed them, but there is a major difference.

That's when it dawned on me that people had no idea what we Vietnam veterans were talking about most of the time. Nobody else even bothered asking questions like the one my son had asked, because they assumed it didn't really mean anything at all. Maybe they surmised all the troops were so shot up with dope they couldn't remember the words to any other song. It took a nine-year-old to admit he didn't understand what went on over there. Everyone else thought they could identify with us.

For those who ask the same question, it was a Mickey Mouse war—a fantasy war for the powers that be. They didn't have to deal with the staunch reality of death and destruction. They were half a world away from the blood and the suffering of young soldiers lying in the fields of South Vietnam, awaiting a chopper that might make it there in time before they bled to death.

That was the end of watching war movies for me, especially Vietnam War movies. The scenes involving a corpsman or medic especially tore me up and started the VCR tape in my mind running full force. (I know, we have now progressed to DVDs and streaming services.) That would bring flashbacks faster than anything else. I knew those corpsmen in the field were preparing the wounded or dead to fly out to us.

The 2001 miniseries *Band of Brothers* was just one in a string of many, such as *Saving Private Ryan*, that so many people told me I should watch. The temptation isn't even there any longer. I finally learned a lesson and learned it well.

So, the days and years lingered on. My coping mechanisms were shot. I would sit on the couch for hours at a time and stare off into space or out of the living room window. I would replay the injuries and deaths aboard the ship, along with my experiences in the morgue and on the flights to Da Nang. The anger would dwell within me over the fact that I was not promoted as I should have been.

My entire life was in turmoil. But I did everything I could not to show it publicly. Then came the three weeks from hell. I walked out the door for the last time. I could not deal with the issues between me and my wife. This cost me dearly—resulting in a permanent estrangement with Carrie and five years of Ryan having no part of my life. Unfortunately, I saw only two ways out. One was to leave Chris (which, unfortunately, meant leaving my children too). The other was suicide. As a Christian, I decided against taking my own life. I thought maybe, after time, I could reconcile with my family.

I had been staying with Mom due to her illness. The breast cancer had metastasized, and the cancer was now in her bones. She was in and out of the hospital. The cancer was taking a terrible toll on her body, but her mind was still as sharp as a tack. She would carry on intelligent conversations with me until the day she died. However, she would constantly wake me up when I dozed off during the day. I sat next to her, waiting for the angel of mercy to appear. She prayed for death. It was inevitable, yet it was slow in coming.

I had taken an early retirement due to my health issues (spinal injuries). Then my court date came and went, and my divorce was finalized. Dealing with this and not seeing my children had torn me apart. I had told Chris several times that, if we were to get back together, it would have to be through the kids. But she did everything to spite me and keep the kids away. I agreed to go to Parent's Day ceremony for Carrie's last home football game with the band. All went for naught, and the divorce was finalized three weeks before Mom died.

By Easter, Mom was so weak we were sure she would die on Easter Sunday. But she perked up just enough to go on for three more days. My sister had to get back to her job and was to leave Thursday.

Wednesday, the nurse from hospice told me, if I wanted to go to my apartment to get my mail and take a walk, I should go and not be gone more than six hours or so. I left early in the evening and took a walk over the hill and picked some wildflowers for Mom. When I got back to my apartment, I had a phone message. It was my sister, who was frantic. I didn't even listen to the entire message. I took off for Mom's, knowing there was no use rushing. But I did drive as quickly as was safely possible for Edith Ann's sake. I didn't even bother bringing the flowers with me.

Edith Ann was sitting on the porch crying. She didn't even speak. I went into the living room. My sister didn't want to be there when Mom passed, and I did want to be with her. Several people told me they think Mom purposely waited until I left because she had already put me through enough. As a counselor, I agreed with that assessment, but I guess we'll never know for sure.

Few people not connected to the Murrah Building bombing in Oklahoma City will remember the date of the bombing. But it is easy for me to remember—April 19, 1995, the day my mother died.

I had been so busy with Mom that the other memories had temporarily faded. As soon as I dealt with the funeral arrangements; the funeral itself; and getting Edith Ann's possessions back to Columbus and her apartment taken care of and so on, all hell let loose. The only reprieve I had was doing small repairs and painting jobs to get Mom's house ready to sell. It would all be on me because my sister had to return to work.

The Sunday morning before Edith Ann went home, she started leaving me notes on things she wanted of Mom's. We had already discussed and agreed on who would get what. I told her she could have anything of Mom's she wanted except a few things I had given her that I had sent or brought back from overseas.

That went well until, after deciding what all she wanted, she began leaving notes to sell certain things and send her half the money, which was my plan in the first place. I had promised Mom there would be no problems between me and my sister, so I gave Edith Ann the deed to the house and told her I would rather her take everything, including selling the house and keeping all the money. The house was our inheritance. Mom had paid cash for the house and had very few assets other than the house and a few dollars in the bank. I wanted no part of arguing over anything, so I gave her the deed, walked out crying, and wouldn't answer my phone for three days. I wasn't as angry as I was hurt. I was going to keep my promise to Mom no matter what I lost.

A few days later, Edith Ann and I talked and straightened things out. But a new problem arose. Mom had signed the car over to me. My sister didn't drive, so Mom told me to keep the car, and everything else was to be divided evenly. But when Edith Ann and my aunt got to talking, all of a sudden, the car became an issue. The house went in my name, only to make it easier to sell, as Edith Ann's required signature would delay the process once we had a buyer, since that would involve sending forms back and forth in the mail.

When I agreed to give her half of what the car was worth, she got back with me and said she was told it was worth considerably more. I told her I would put a for sale sign on it for whatever she wanted. If I was offered that amount, I would give her half. If I didn't get an offer, I would keep on using it until I did.

Knowing she had been given bad advice, she agreed to have me take it to the dealership that had sold it to Mom and get a fair assessment of the value. I told the salesman the situation and that I didn't want it appraised at one cent less than what he would sell it for himself. That way, I was as honest as I could be, and Edith Ann was satisfied she'd gotten a fair deal. Actually, she got $4,225 more than a fair deal because the car was left to me, since I would actually use it.

If other people would stay out of family business, settling things would be much easier. To this day, it offends me that I was accused of keeping something from my sister that Mom had intended for me only and not for her. Mom knew I couldn't afford to buy half the car from her before she died and that my sister couldn't use half a car, let alone a whole one. She had never obtained a driver's license and wasn't about to at this stage of her life. She, too, was dealing with breast cancer.

It wouldn't be until a week or so before Edith Ann died that she said she forgave me for what I had done after Mom's death. I let it go but couldn't help but be amazed that she still thought I was the one who was wrong. I had forgiven her long ago, but I knew she was still angry over the whole affair.

It was some time after my sister's death that I realized the cancer had affected her brain for quite some time, and I no longer held her responsible for many of her thoughts and actions. I realized she'd had many problems at work over the past two years. She was angry with coworkers constantly and was told she wasn't performing her work correctly. Her entire personality had taken a negative change. She had always been very well-liked and taken care of by those she worked with, and her performance at work had never been an issue. I had thought it was all over Mom's illness and death. But the more I learned about the past couple years of her life, the more I realized the doctors had not seen this change and related any changes to the breast cancer and not that it had metastasized to her brain.

The year prior to this, I was enrolled in a workers' compensation rehabilitation program in Columbus to attempt to help my back and neck problems. It ended up being disastrous, as a physical therapist caused an injury to my right shoulder. Seven years later, I would undergo three surgeries to partially correct the injury.

I got to see my sister every weekend during my eight weeks in Columbus. I would go home on Friday evenings. On Sunday, I would leave home in the afternoon and stop at her place and spend the evening. Little did I know that, soon, I would be taking care of her, just as I had taken care of Mom.

When I returned home from a seminar in Charleston, South Carolina, I had a message from Edith Ann that she had spent the evening in an emergency room in Columbus and that the doctor had released her and told her to go to her oncologist. I called her, and she was a nervous wreck. The doctor failed to tell her why he had suggested she go to the oncologist. I had her call for an appointment the next day, with the assurance I would take her to the appointment.

The oncologist was very blunt, but in a positive way, about the progression of her breast cancer. It had spread to the liver. I knew this was to be fatal, and while she went to the lab, I stayed to talk to the doctor. He didn't recommend a bone marrow transplant because she was overweight and her health, even other than the cancer, was not conducive to the procedure being successful. He told me she could live up to six months.

When we got back to her apartment, we discussed chemotherapy. She had undergone chemo previously and had been able to put up with the many side effects, which included loss of hair, blisters in her mouth, dry mouth, and others.

She knew nothing was going to stop the progression of the cancer this time and that chemo would only possibly prolong life for a few weeks. Although I was against it, I couldn't tell her that. It was her body and her life. She had to decide whatever she thought was best for her. She had decided against chemotherapy. But while talking to the doctor, suddenly, she decided she would attempt it. I came back to Columbus to take her to her first treatment. About twenty-four hours after that first treatment, we both knew she had made a mistake. Her mouth was filled with blisters. She couldn't eat and could barely swallow liquids. I had hoped to keep from calling hospice for a few weeks, but I knew it was time. They supplied medication and helped me with deciding what she could eat until her throat healed.

When the time arrived for her next chemo, her throat was doing much better but wasn't completely healed. The day before the scheduled appointment, she had me call and cancel it.

We were able to go shopping after that, and she got out of the apartment as much as I could get her out. She kept telling me she wanted to see the changing leaves one more time before she died. We had gone for a ride one day in Columbus, but there just weren't enough trees in the Columbus area to be able to see the brightly colored leaves, except for a few here and there.

She came home with me for a weekend in October. I had

convinced her to come with me. She was hesitant but finally agreed. In eastern Ohio, there are so many different species of trees that it is a beautiful area, especially when the foliage is changing in October. This was probably the best therapy she could have asked for. She sat on both the front and back porches at my apartment for hours at a time looking at the leaves and watching birds, raccoons, deer, and any of God's other creatures she missed since she had left the area in the late 1960s.

One night, I woke up around 2:00 a.m. and checked on her. She wasn't in bed, the bathroom, or the kitchen. I didn't hear the television or any other noises. I finally checked the back porch, and there she was. I went out and sat with her. It was a chilly autumn night (temperatures in the low forties), and she was wrapped up in a blanket staring at the sky.

I'll never forget that early morning. She said, "You know, there aren't any stars in Columbus." It had never dawned on me that she had spent so many starless nights in the big city away from her home where we grew up. She was right. There were no stars where she lived. Of course, she knew they existed but went unseen because of all the bright lights from the city glaring for miles, making the sky and its contents invisible.

If I hadn't learned anything from my sister while she was living, I learned a very valuable lesson from her as she was dying. Never take for granted the beauty God surrounds us with. The leaves and the stars are a gift from God. Yet, we don't appreciate them. Don't wait until you are dying to appreciate them. Don't take them for granted. Appreciate them while you are alive and healthy. I do. At least I do now! I have never looked at the stars and the fall foliage the same since the fall of 1997, and I will never take it for granted again, as long as I live.

When Edith Ann was still at my apartment, I took her to lunch at a restaurant that overlooks the St. Clairsville, Ohio, area. For miles upon miles, all you can see is rolling hills, trees, and fields. She asked me why I wouldn't move to Columbus. I replied, "Look over my shoulder and explain to me what you see compared to what you would see in Columbus."

All she said was, "I understand!"

Once Edith Ann's health began failing, I stayed with her for her last six months or so. I hated living in Columbus. I was used to taking my daily walk through the fields and woods. There was no place to walk in her area. There was intersection after intersection, making it extremely difficult to walk in that area. I didn't want to drive to a park because I didn't want to be that far away from her. The only time I could enjoy walking was the two times she came home with me.

She had decided to come home with me for Thanksgiving week. It gave her one last chance to get out of her apartment, and it would give me one last break because I knew, and she knew, this was her last trip "back home."

On Thanksgiving morning, I asked her if she minded if I went rabbit hunting for an hour or so. She was fine with that. I had a pager, so she could page me if she needed me, and I could be back at the apartment within minutes. I was only gone about fifteen minutes. When I returned, she said she heard my shotgun blast about ten minutes after I left.

It's amazing to me that was the day that I shot the rabbit I had been chasing for the past three years. He was a monster, as the rabbits go in Ohio. About a hundred yards below my apartment was a long, extremely thick area of brush. I had seen the rabbit several times, but he never wandered out far enough for me to get a shot at him, as he was always where he could quickly jump back deep into the brush. That Thanksgiving morning, he made a fatal mistake and had wandered out just a little too far.

I knew Edith Ann wouldn't eat wild meat but I told her that would be her Thanksgiving dinner. I cooked it and served it on the largest platter I could find. It was so large, part of its body, let alone the legs, hung out over the platter. This was a prize. It was, by far, the largest rabbit I had ever shot. We call them "woods rabbits" because they were much larger than the typical "Missouri rabbits" that are prevalent in this area.

I waited for my beloved sister to throw a fit before I told her I had cooked her a separate meal. That was probably the last practical joke I got to play on her. We then sat and ate our last Thanksgiving meal together.

Once we returned to Columbus, the cancer began kicking in with full force. Thankfully, as the doctor had promised, cancer of the liver wouldn't cause the severe pain Mom's cancer had put her through after it metastasized to the liver and bones.

Edith Ann's demeanor changed. She became angry with the world. My training in psychology and familiarity with Elisabeth Kübler-Ross's steps of dealing with death and dying kicked in. She thought everybody was going to fight over what little bit of money she had. Though she had very little money in the bank, it was all she had, and it was a lot from her perspective. I had to concede this belief because I often taught about the power of "perspective."

Ryan was to be the executor for her will. Edith Ann realized I knew all her wishes and business affairs because I had been staying with her and taking care of her, so she asked me if I would take over the assignment. Since Ryan wasn't on speaking terms with me, I was afraid this was going to present a problem. I told her, if she talked to him and he was in agreement, it would be fine with me. There were papers to be signed in Franklin County, as well as in Belmont County. I had the experience and time to do the running around. Ryan agreed and things were turned over to me. There was never a problem. Only Ryan, Carrie, and I were listed in the will. The few things that were left specifically to individuals had already been taken care of, and her "fortune" was to be split three ways.

That was all easy enough, except that some of her assets were tied to her employer and took months to receive. In the end, everything worked out to where everybody would get exactly what Edith Ann had intended them to receive, and despite paperwork delaying some transactions, everything would quickly fall into place.

In the meantime, Edith Ann had become very ill but was still ambulatory. She asked me to promise her, just as Mom had asked, that I would take care of her and keep her out of a nursing home. My reply, as with Mom, was that I would do my best. Edith Ann was much heavier than Mom though, and I could not begin to lift her. Sleeping in Edith Ann's living room on an inflatable mattress was a nightmare for me because of my back and neck. But one night, in particular, the nightmare became worse.

As in any large city there was obviously much crime. Larger cities had helicopters to search for suspects after a robbery or other crimes. One night around midnight, a helicopter flew repeatedly over her apartment building with its searchlight probing the area. When it hovered just outside the window, it really got to me. It caused me to flash back to Vietnam. For days, my mental state was about as bad as my sister's physical state. I tried to explain what had happened. But she couldn't comprehend it because I had been back from Nam since 1968.

Linda had talked to her once about my PTSD. And her reply was, "I don't understand why he doesn't just forget about Vietnam!"

I guess that's the way it is with Vietnam veterans. We're just supposed to "forget about it." As much as I feel for veterans of all wars, at least those who served during other wars had some sympathy for their nightmares and symptoms of post-traumatic stress. We weren't supposed to be there. Therefore, it was our fault that we suffered. It wasn't a "war." It shouldn't have been fought. Therefore, whatever we suffered from wasn't anyone's fault except our own. We, the "baby killers" and the target of the protesters, deserved whatever we got from the war because we had no business being over there in the first place.

Oh, of course, I forgot again; the protesters were protesting against the war, not the troops. That's bullshit! You know to use that excuse now because of us. Now you treat those returning from war, either as survivors or in caskets, as heroes. Don't try to go back and say that, in the 1960s and '70s, you supported the troops, just not the government. It is a lie that cannot be corrected. When the troops came back from the first war in Iraq, we heard speech after speech that the Vietnam veterans had finally been appeased because we were mentioned often when current troops arrived home and when the war ended.

Forget it, America! You did not welcome us home. You didn't even respect our fallen brothers. Don't think you appeased us by honoring troops who served later. But even then, some protestors lined the streets during funeral processions and motorcades in honor of those fallen heroes who served in Iraq and Afghanistan. We can feel for those families more than anyone. Some people are professionals and will show up anywhere for a few bucks and a chance to have their mug on TV.

I think I can speak for the majority of Vietnam vets (at least the ones with whom I am familiar) when I thank you for honoring and caring for those who served in battle after us. We are not bitter toward you. We are happy for you that you returned home as heroes. But America can never say we were welcomed home or that we are a welcomed part of society today. Over the years, things have evolved. But to some, we are still the bastards of society. We are the only ones who fought for our country and then came home to battle the citizens of this same country.

Wouldn't it be nice if, when we returned, we had our pictures in the papers and the media had welcoming committees as they do every few months when aliens are given permanent citizenship status? We honor those who come here and take our jobs, welfare checks, and free education (and yes, I realize all foreigners don't do that). To them, you say, "Give me your tired, your poor, your huddled masses" and all that stuff. But to the Vietnam vet, it is, "What the hell did you come back for?"

So, to hear those words from my sister set off my anger. Why don't we just forget about it? Unfortunately, it isn't that easy, America. It's like turning your television on and not being able to turn it off. It just keeps on playing the movie over and over. There is no stopping it.

On the morning of February 5, 1998, Edith Ann got up and asked me what I had done with the key for her metal box in which she kept her important papers. I told her I had never touched that key. I knew what it was for, and I always respected her privacy. I had heard her jingling keys before she went to bed the night before. I knew she had been checking or reviewing contents of the metal box and figured she didn't remember doing it. I finally told her about having heard her with the keys. She had placed them under her pillow. That's exactly where she found them.

She asked me to come in and go through her papers with her. She had never shown me her will or any of the contents of that box. She'd only told me that it existed and where I would find it when she died. Honoring her wishes, I had no desire to go near it until she asked me to.

She went over her will with me and gave me directions for a few items she hadn't previously discussed with me. Then, early the next morning at a little after midnight, she lay down and fell asleep forever, into the arms of our Lord.

Just before she fell asleep I hugged her, gave her a kiss, and told her I loved her. Even though I continuously spoke to her over the next thirteen hours or so, those were the last words she acknowledged. She fell into a coma and was nonresponsive, although, once in a while, she would moan. When she did, I would place a few drops of morphine in her mouth, which would settle her down.

That night, we had a severe ice storm. It was one of the worst ice storms I had or have ever experienced, before or since then. It covered most of the state of Ohio. My aunt had come over, but it had started snowing, and because of the forecast, I advised her to leave before the roads got worse.

Late in the evening, the death rattles set in. I knew the end was near for Edith Ann. I called the nurse at hospice. She said she didn't believe in death rattles and that my sister was only snoring. She had me hold the phone to Edith Ann's face while she listened. Again, she diagnosed the noise as snoring.

Now I was severely pissed off! When you have heard the sounds of death rattles as often as I have, you begin to wonder if this person can possibly be a nurse. The last thing I needed that night was someone questioning my medical integrity. Lady, if only you had heard death rattles like I had, you would have told me, "I know exactly what you're talking about."

At 12:15 a.m. on February 5, I called hospice and told them Edith Ann had passed away, and I didn't want anyone questioning me as to how I was sure she had expired. I told the lady what I had gone through with the nurse. She apologized profusely and began telling me the nurse had been on duty extra hours, and the ice storm had caused her a great deal of stress. I told her that was no excuse for a lack of professionalism and that I wanted a different representative from hospice other than that nurse, or I would take care of calling the funeral home myself. She assured me that someone else would be there but would be delayed because of the storm. I could accept that, as we were now under a level 3 alert as far as roads were concerned.

Another nurse showed up. Amazingly, it took her less than a half hour to get to Edith Ann's apartment. She checked to make sure Edith Ann was, in fact, deceased and then called the funeral home, which was directly across the parking lot from the apartment. We took care of counting and disposing of all medications and whatever else she was assigned to do.

It took the undertaker over an hour and a half to arrive. After preparing the body, he asked if I could help carry my sister down the long flight of stairs to the back door. My response was that I had a bad back and couldn't carry the weight. I had done my share over the past six months and wasn't about to do any more and risk a flare-up with my back problems, especially considering all I had ahead of me for the next few weeks. I tried to state this in a nice way, and he accepted it as such. He called his father, who, like himself, had dragged himself out of bed during an ice storm but showed up in a suit and tie at that time of the morning. I considered this a sign of true professionalism.

I made the phone calls I needed to make and, despite the ice, left for home at around 4:00 a.m., hoping I could keep awake, not to mention drive through the ice.

I called Father Paul Welton on my way home. Even though Edith Ann and I were both Protestant, Paul was a good friend of mine and had talked with Edith Ann earlier when she had concerns about what happened after death, such as, how soon the soul would be resurrected.

Due to the ice storm, Edith Ann's body didn't arrive in Bellaire until the late the following afternoon. I knew the funeral would be awkward for family members because Chris, Ryan, and Carrie weren't speaking to me. However, they were cordial when I had to talk to them about certain things. I asked them to sit up front during the funeral, and they did.

By then, Linda and I had become good friends. But she asked me to have the family sit up front with me, saying she would sit with some of my aunts and uncles who she had come to know. So, a potentially disastrous situation had been alleviated. None of the immediate family showed up for the dinner at church afterward. Another issue that may have prevented them from coming, but it would serve no purpose to go there.

Edith Ann had been buried next to Mom and Dad's gravesite. Fortunately, since she had prepaid her funeral expenses, I had caught the mistake that had been made. Her tombstone was in the wrong place. The cemetery association wanted to keep it as it was and sell the other lot. It would have meant her being buried next to Dad, instead of Mom. Although, this wouldn't have been a terrible ordeal, I balked at the offer. Knowing she had expected to be buried in a certain spot, I thought it was only proper she would be at rest where she had expected to be buried, which was next to Mom.

Finally, it was all over. I had no family left, at least nobody who claimed me. My Uncle Bill (on Dad's side) was the only one who kept in contact with me. I felt like an orphan. But fortunately, at my age, I realized how tough it must be on somebody who was truly an orphan at an early age. There is always something to be thankful for, no matter how bad things seemed to be. I had always believed in the old adage, "There's always someone hurting worse."

As tough as things were, I was also cognizant of Friedrich Nietzsche's quote, "What doesn't kill you will make you stronger."

Earlier, I alluded to the fact that I was angry with God. I had lost two very good jobs (administrator and teaching) because of my health. I'd lost my mother, and I'd gone through a divorce. And now, I had endured the loss of my only sibling. My body was racked with pain. (Through all of this, I took only a couple pain pills a month, if that.)

Then one day, God opened my eyes, and I realized why all this had come about. It wasn't a curse but, rather, a blessing! He revealed to me that I would not have been able to keep both my mother and then sister out of a nursing home if I had still been working, especially while holding two jobs. This was the only request each had made of me. "Please keep me out of a nursing home if at all possible." Neither could have functioned at a level of being competent to stay home alone. Both needed care they could not provide for themselves.

As we read in Deuteronomy 3:16, "I will never leave you or forsake you." I need say no more!

Chapter 17

**"Don't you understand what I'm tryin' to say?
Can't you feel the fear I'm feelin' today?"**

—"Eve of Destruction," Barry McGuire

fter Mom's death, Shep Chase had come down from Maine on a Greyhound bus to find out what was happening to his long-time friend who had left his family. He stayed the first two days with Chris and the kids. During this time, he told me he had already figured out what was going on and talked me into going to the vet center in Wheeling, West Virginia.

I talked with a counselor for a few minutes. Jay was just about to leave his office when Shep and I appeared, but he gave us a few minutes despite running late for an appointment. I made an appointment to see him at his earliest convenience. Although I really didn't want to talk about Vietnam, Shep and Jay convinced me I needed to open up to someone.

Before going to the vet center, we went to the county service officer, who thought I was planning on applying for Agent Orange-based disability. Even though I had no thoughts of Agent Orange, Larry said I didn't have any symptoms of the dreaded defoliant. In anger, I pulled both pants legs up and showed him a pair of raw, bloody legs. He backed off and listened to me, advising me I needed to go to the vet center, if for no other reason than because he saw the anger that he had drawn from me when he'd challenged me. Larry became a good friend and was very instrumental in helping me obtain my disability through the Veterans Administration, along with Jay and Paul Hughes, service officers at the Bellaire Disabled American Veterans. All three men were perfect examples of veterans helping other veterans.

After several counseling sessions with Jay and Dan Ziff, who was a PTSD specialist at the VA Hospital in Pittsburgh, Paul made an appointment for me to see a psychiatrist in Mt. Vernon, Ohio, after applying for disability due to post-traumatic stress disorder.

The visit to Dr. X (I will not use his name so as to avoid possible legal ramifications) was a fiasco. Another doctor with the same last name had, many years earlier, misdiagnosed my lower back injury. Things were really ominous when I entered the building that housed his office and walked up the stairs of the old building. The worn, faded walls took me right back to the *Repose*. The paint was an off-color white that needed a fresh coat. The walls and decks appeared to be bowed and ready to cave in. The paint was chipped in places, kind of what you would expect at the beginning of a nightmare. Maybe this was a false perception, but I was ill at ease with this situation before even seeing this man, who claimed to be a psychiatrist who understood the minds of human beings, especially American combat veterans. My post-traumatic stress kicked in full force immediately, as the surroundings seemed almost the same as those of the *Repose*. This was not going to go well! But even at that, I hadn't foreseen what was to follow.

After half an hour or so in the waiting room, I was ushered into his office, where the doctor sat with my file in front of his face. I didn't say a word since he obviously had made no preparation in advance of his interview. He rudely sat there for several minutes, dropped the papers on his desk, and said, "You've been here for ten minutes and have not said a word about Vietnam."

Whether or not he was trying to piss me off, he did a great job of doing just that. I told him I wasn't rude enough to interrupt his reading and that he "should have been prepared, in advance, for this interview."

Things went straight to hell from there. Here was a foreigner who was supposed to be instrumental in my future. He spoke such poor English I had a terrible time understanding him. Oh yes, that's right, as an American veteran, I'm not supposed to use the "F" word—foreigner.

He finally remembered to introduce himself and said he was a (what was pronounced as /sycee-at-trist/ (otherwise known as psychiatrist). He asked me what a corpsman did in the service and wanted to know what a psychiatric technician was. After deducing that he visited his patients on a psych ward and not only at the office, I figured two pissed-off people were better than one. So I let him know I didn't appreciate that someone who had never served in the military (of any country, let alone the United States) had ended up in this position if he couldn't relate to the subject at hand (PTSD).

I left his office after a very short interview, calling him (under my breath) everything but a red-blooded, American veteran who could speak the English language and have any idea what the hell the effects of war were on men who had gone through shit he couldn't even imagine.

One more cheer for politically correct America, land of the free and home of the foreigners, who have now gotten their claws into the destination of our own veterans. I knew I'd lost any chance for a favorable report when I asked him if he had ever fought for his native India.

Sure enough, a couple weeks later, I received a letter from the VA stating that Dr. X had established there was no presence of PTSD. Once more, I want to be clear that I am not against foreigners coming here to make a living. However, my complaint is that our VA hires people such as this who cannot grasp the essence of our involvement. The fact that he practices psychiatry in private practice here draws no particular complaint on my part.

I talked to Paul Hughes, a very knowledgeable officer at the Bellaire chapter of DAV, and he told me he would assist me in filing an appeal. He asked that my case be transferred out of Ohio and into the Pittsburgh system, since I was much closer to Pittsburgh than Mt. Vernon and Cleveland. It didn't take long to realize just about everyone was doing this because Dr. X was so well known for collecting our taxpayers' money and writing off veterans.

The next step was to be interviewed by a psychiatrist at Highland Drive VA Medical Center in Pittsburgh. I can't remember her name, but I felt much more comfortable with a psychiatrist who at least showed signs of compassion and spoke clear English. When I entered her office, she told me she had already reviewed my case, including Dr. X's remarks. I told her about going into Dr. X's office and having to wait for him to review my case while I sat there.

Although she was careful not to say anything negative about the quack in Mt. Vernon, she said I deserved better than what I had gotten there. Then she floored me. Her appointments were set at increments of one hour. She had someone coming in at 10:00 a.m. (my appointment was at 9:00 a.m.), but he had come in early. She said, if I would be willing to let her interview him first, it would give her up to two hours to talk to me, as she knew she would be dealing not only with the issue at hand but also with my experience with Dr. X. It was a wise decision to be patient and wait. At least I went into the interview knowing I would be able to express myself and have someone actually listen to me.

This doctor didn't just listen to me; she also talked to me. She warned me that, because of the extra time she had allotted for me, it would give her more time to ask questions in different ways that could be detrimental to my case if I answered the same question in two different ways. I didn't care. I had come there, as was true with every interview I went to, to tell the truth, regardless of whether it helped or hurt my case.

She grilled me over and over. I realized she was asking repetitive questions but wording them differently. I was glad of this, as it only helped my credibility and destroyed any trace of lack of credibility Dr. X had noted in his attempts to ambush me. I came out of the interview mentally and emotionally exhausted. I had cried. I had gone into a shell temporarily. I had shouted. I had pounded my fist. And I am sure I'd used some language I didn't usually use. But it wasn't directed at her, and she never felt threatened.

I left Pittsburgh that day knowing someone had, at least, listened to me. Whether she believed me or not was a different issue. But I knew she had listened. She'd even brought out some of the good times I'd had in Vietnam. I drove home with a bagful of mixed emotions. Then I simply prayed that God would take things into His hands and let be whatever was to be.

A few weeks later, I received a letter from the VA. It stated that, after reviewing the write-up of the psychiatrist, there was reason to overturn Dr. X's recommendation. I had been awarded 30 percent disability for post-traumatic stress disorder.

The psychiatrists or other doctors treating or testing patients for injuries, diseases, and so on do not approve or rate disability. Their report goes to an individual or a board for review and rating percentage. I thought the 30 percent was low, but I knew it was a major step. The next time I was at Highland Drive, I made a point to look up the doctor and thank her for listening to me and for getting me a start with my claim.

Neither Paul nor Larry was satisfied with the 30 percent rating after reading the statements made by the doctor who had gotten me this far. I was convinced I could get 50 percent, while they were already talking about 70 percent. So, Paul appealed the rating of 30 percent. This led to more testing and another visit with a different psychiatrist.

By the time my next letter arrived from the VA, I had won the appeal and was granted 70 percent disability for delayed post-traumatic stress disorder. It meant more benefits, including better medical benefits than at the 30 percent level.

I was satisfied with the increased rating and had no intention of filing for 100 percent, until Shep, Larry, Jay, and Paul told me I should press on. But now I was taking a chance. The next hearing would be in Washington, DC. There was no cause for my presence there because my case would be reviewed, but I would not be a part of the proceedings. If during this review, the board decided I should be rated 100 percent, they would recommend it. However, if they felt that 70 percent was more than I deserved, they could recommend I get less than the amount I had been rated. It was a major decision to make, but I went for the appeal.

Then, the VA system decided to fight me and came out swinging with both fists! The head VA psychiatrist at Pittsburgh was the next man up. He did everything but call me a liar and let me know he would stand between me and a 100 percent rating. And fight me, he did. He didn't seem to understand the men who had served in a war several years ago while he was probably protesting along with fellow students. (Oh, excuse me, that wasn't labeled as a "war.")

His problem? His problem was my story about a grenade strapped to an injured marine's leg and my ensuing actions. He refused to believe me, saying he would either suggest to the review board a drop to a 30 percent rating if I failed a further test to determine the level at which I was experiencing the effects of PTSD or 100 percent if I passed. I accepted the challenge immediately.

In the end, that test would become a final challenge that would go a long way in determining my future. I accepted the challenge to take the new psychiatric exam. It was the Mississippi Scale for Post-traumatic Stress. The head psychiatrist had thrown the gauntlet at me, telling me I had administered and studied the other tests, and so I could possibly have swayed the results in my favor. That was bullshit. But it was true that I had been involved in testing others during my time as an NP tech. I accepted the challenge. If I scored high enough, he would agree to recommend 100 percent, but if not, I agreed to accept a final rating of 30 percent. I doubt that this was legal on his part. But I wanted to show him and the VA system he went to bat for that I was fighting for myself and for my brothers and sisters who would follow me.

The Mississippi Scale was a very short test, and within a few minutes, I walked from the secluded testing room and laid the finished test on his desk. I was told to go back to the other room and wait. I think it took him longer to grade the test than it had taken me to read it. He appeared at the door and announced that not only had passed the test, I was in an exceptionally high percentile for PTSD. I'll leave it to your imagination what I wanted to say. But as difficult as it was to do, I went back to my military days and treated him with the utmost respect, as if he had not disrespected me.

Before I left, however, I told him what the previous psychiatrist told me about the department. This upset him. Not only did I know that a study had been conducted under false pretenses. It had looked at vets who may or may not have suffered from PTSD in order to determine whether or not they were, in fact, suffering from this malady. Moreover, in the end, I had turned into the counselor, and the psychiatrist was the counsel. Now, I had his goat, as he knew everything I said was true.

The issue in question involved friends of those in the psychiatric division being brought in and tested for PTSD. Those friends had never experienced combat. If you understand research, you understand he was aiming for a negative hypothesis. The results were skewed as planned, for whatever purpose they were used. This is why I don't pay much attention to studies performed by hospitals, clinics, and the like. As my boss at the welfare department once told me, "I can make numbers say whatever I want them to say without lying. I just don't have to be honest about how I came up with the statistic I wanted to prove or disprove."

The next time I visited the unit, the doctor was no longer employed there. Again, I suffered through the long wait for the letter to come from the VA. This time, it would come from Washington, DC. When it came, I wasn't sure I wanted to open the envelope. Of course, I did open it, and the 70 percent was overturned in favor of a 100 percent rating. But the ordeal wasn't over yet. This was a recommendation, not an order.

Now, I had to go to the federal building in downtown Pittsburgh for one more hearing. A VA representative (who was assigned to my case and who I had never heard of), the hearing officer, and I went through the proceedings. While I was clueless as to exactly how the decision would be accomplished, the VA representative told me he knew the hearing officer well enough that he was sure he was going to approve the recommendation handed down from Washington, DC.

When I finally believed I could tell the story of my encounter with Williams without a tear, I discovered my belief was inaccurate. As tears rolled down my cheeks, the hearing officer suddenly stopped and said he had heard enough and had caused me enough stress. His quote was, "I've been here long enough to know real tears when I see them."

But it was another long wait for the letter to arrive. After the long wait that seemingly lasted for months (but was actually weeks), the letter arrived. He was right. I would finally be a 100 percent disabled American veteran.

This also meant another increase in medical benefits. Eye and dental care would be free, but only if I traveled to Pittsburgh each time. The problem with the VA setup was that there were services they didn't provide, such as treatment for psoriasis. So, despite the medical care offered by long distance, I continued to go to local physicians and pay what my insurance didn't cover. At least my prescriptions were free, and I got a checkup and lab work annually at the local VA clinic. But anything else provided was a four-hour round trip, plus waiting for the other vets to finish their appointments. Most trips accounted for eight hours total. Some things were worth not having to pay for. As time went on, I was able to receive all treatment at the Pittsburgh VA Hospital.

One of the drawbacks of the 100 percent rating was the write-up from the last psychiatrist who evaluated me and all my tests. While I didn't feel I was suicidal, it is difficult to disagree with the opinion he presented. When I read the results, I wanted to deny it was myself about whom he was writing and, instead, a fictitious character one might be introduced to in a novel. I didn't want to confess to being the subject of the report, but then I looked back at the changes in my life. I looked at how my life was affected by my experiences in Vietnam and Japan. I just wanted to say, "Give me my life back and keep your benefits."

I look at how my children were affected by a father who dealt with PTSD and their mother, who couldn't understand what was changing him.

Shep would never tell me what he discussed with my children when he visited them (and rightfully so) and later when they visited him in Maine. He died believing they would understand what had happened to me. He believed they would believe their father loved them when he told them it came down to two choices and that he took the one that allowed him to live. Maybe it was the right one. And maybe not. Maybe some of the family would have thought they understood why I'd committed suicide.

In 2001, Ryan and I got back together. I'm blessed not only with a son, who I had never thought would speak to me again, but also a granddaughter, grandson, and daughter-in law. There is nothing in life that compares to a loving family. You don't know that unless you've been without that relationship and are able to reestablish it at some point.

I've often preached the message of the prodigal son. Each time, I come from a different perspective. I try not to make it obvious that I am I'm telling this story from my own heart and that it is about me as much as the subjects of the parable. You see, the son wasn't the bad guy as most people interpret the story, at least not in my message and my theory. The father made the mistake of letting the son go. But then he sat and waited for him to return. He wasn't angry. He didn't question or condemn his son. He welcomed him home, and they renewed their relationship and forgave each other. Their love had never ceased. There was just a long pause in their relationship, which was caused when they both made a mistake. But he prayed, and he waited for the son to appear. In case you didn't realize, Jesus didn't call the boy the "prodigal son." That was later added as a caption for the parable. My sermon is entitled "The Prodigal Father."

As for Carrie, I have attempted to make contact with her, but not direct contact. She has the right to hate me and follow her mother's wishes. I was told by her mother that I would never walk Carrie down the aisle. She made threats about Ryan also. But he was man enough to make up his own mind. I did not get invited to Carrie's wedding. She now has two children I have never met, one of whom I have never seen.

Being a believer in one part and one aspect only of existentialism (I believe in free choice, and the other parts I do not ascribe to), I always make the argument that we each make our own choices, and we must live with those choices. Each of my children had to decide what choice they would make. Choices can be undone and changed, but at some point in the future it will be too late to change that choice. I could live with my daughter's decision if she made up her own mind, but I do not believe that was the case. Her mother made the threats, and they were carried out. No matter the events of the past, I love each member of my family and always will.

As time rolled on, I lost two very dear friends. Shep's wife, Faye, called from Maine and told me that Shep had been hospitalized. His liver was failing quickly, and he might not last twenty-four hours. I hopped in the Explorer before dawn the next morning and headed for Togus Veterans Administration Hospital in Augusta, Maine. Making four stops to fill up the vehicle, I made it there by about 11:00 p.m. I continue to pray for them every night and I always will.

I expected to hear that Shep had already passed or that he would be in a coma and unable to realize I had come to see him. However, much to my amazement, he was sitting up in bed, and I surprised him one more time. I had surprised him by walking in the house on his fiftieth birthday. We'd talked about everything we could think of in our younger years at Bethesda and on the weekend trips we made to Bellaire, alluding to the prankster I was.

Shep lasted two more days, and what wonderful days those were. We reminisced about the old days, and I teased him that I would hold back on some of the stories since his wife and kids were present. But we took a trip back more than thirty years, and it is one of the fondest memories of my life.

I told his kids about us walking through the woods one evening and swinging on monkey vines from branch to branch like a couple of monkeys. When Shep went flying off the side of a ravine, grabbing at a branch to swing to the other side, I pulled on the branch and broke it, and he went sailing through midair and got all cut up on the rocks below. The girls laughed, and I ran like hell!

Shep was deathly afraid of thunderstorms. One evening during a severe thunderstorm at the barracks at Bethesda, I poured lighter fluid on his legs and lit it. He had buried his head under a blanket and didn't see who had pulled the dirty trick on him. He jumped up and yelled, "I'll kill the dirty son of a bitch if I catch whoever did this."

All these years, I thought I'd told him later that it was me who had done it. So, here, on his death bed, Shep finally discovered before he died that I was the "dirty son-of-a-bitch" who had set him on fire in 1966. He told me, "If I could get up out of this bed right now, I would do it, and I would kick your ass!"

Memories such as this are priceless. We could have sat there that night and cried (which we did for a while). But for the most part, we made the best of it. And Shep died how he lived, one of the orneriest bastards I have ever known or will ever know! That was Shep. Never a dull moment, not even in the face of death itself. He had survived in the jungles of Vietnam. He had survived two days in a culvert with Vietcong all around him. He wasn't going to go out crying about death when he had already cheated it several times. He was as brave now as he had been when he won his medals for bravery.

He asked me that night if I would be willing to officiate his funeral. I knew this would be very difficult for me. I had never performed a funeral service since entering the ministry. I was a rookie at serving in ministry. What a way to begin!

Shep asked me how much I would charge to do his funeral. "Oh, about $2,000", I jokingly replied.

"See Faye about it," he said, and the subject was dropped.

Later that night, I was standing outside while Faye and the kids were having a smoke break. She asked me about officiating the funeral. I told her I hadn't mentioned that Shep had discussed it with me, in fear she had already made plans. So, I officially agreed to it this time.

Just before this, I had been called into the ministry, which led me to me being able to officiate Shep's funeral. That story will come in a later chapter.

Faye knew there was no way I would have accepted anything for the service. But I intentionally failed to tell her about the discussion about the $2,000 with Shep—that is until the middle of the funeral service. I did exactly what Shep would have expected me to do. I added some humor. I was going to get in my one last shot.

As I was talking about some of the great times I had with Shep, I told everyone about the $2,000. I looked directly at Faye and said, "Faye, you owe me big-time."

Everyone roared. Shep was definitely happy. People were laughing instead of crying at his funeral. My plan had worked, and it helped me through the rest of the funeral. Earlier, when I had spoken about the many of us there who were Vietnam veterans, the mood had become very somber.

But there had been one very solemn minute at the hospital. Shep's brother had been alone in the room talking to Shep. He stepped out and told me Shep wanted to talk to me alone. I was praying it was the moment I was waiting for. I felt Shep had been granted those extra two days for a reason, and God was about to confirm that. He told me, "I know I've been a rotten son of a bitch all my life, and I know I haven't been a Christian since I joined the service." As we talked, I discovered that Shep had worn his uniform to church one Sunday when he was on leave before his upcoming tour in Vietnam. He had been asked to leave the church and either change clothes or not come back at all. Isn't it funny how, even in the twentieth century, people were still making the same judgmental mistakes the early disciples made?

I asked Shep several questions about his faith and if he would remain in Christ if by some miracle he survived this ordeal. When I was convinced he was truly sincere, we prayed. Then I asked his family to come back in. We prayed again, and I anointed Shep.

The following morning after Shep passed, I spent several hours at the lighthouse at Pemaquid Point in the cold, windy, misty weather so the family could have some time to themselves. What a beautiful, peaceful place to be. The weather was bad enough that nobody else was willing to spend an afternoon there in the cold and mist, so it provided the solitude I was seeking.

It was a tough goodbye to my best friend. We had only visited each other four times since we'd parted at Bethesda in 1967. Yet, during all those years, if anyone had asked me who my best friend was, it could have invoked only one answer. Shep was the one who got me into counseling with the VA and the one who cared enough to make the trip by bus, despite his health problems and his shrapnel-filled legs, which were causing him so much intense pain at the time. I know how my own legs cramp in the tight seating area on a bus. I could only imagine the relief Shep felt when he got off that bus in Portland.

With goodbyes said to Faye, Heather, Lee, and friends, I headed home. I took the long route home because the only northeastern state I had not visited was Vermont. I had to take back roads simply because there were no main highways from southern Maine or northern New Hampshire through Vermont. The trip through the mountains would have been beautiful in the daytime. But in early November, it was dark before I could get out of New Hampshire.

After descending the mountains of Vermont, I came into a small town. I have no idea what the name of the town was, but I will never forget my trip through it. The car in front of me traveling the opposite direction must have blown a tire. It came suddenly screeching sideways toward me. All I knew was that it was a large green, older model vehicle and that I shut my eyes, expecting to wake up in some hospital in this seemingly foreign land. The vehicle was headed right at me. The next thing I knew, I saw its headlights in my rearview mirror. Not only had it missed me. It had also missed the car behind me and, apparently, everything else that had appeared to be directly in its line as it skidded into oblivion, out of control.

Somewhere in Pennsylvania at about eight o'clock the next morning, I pulled over and slept for about two hours at a roadside rest area. From there, I drove straight through. And finally, after what seemed like days, I arrived home from the trip, exhausted but extremely thankful I could be with Shep and his wonderful family and now back home in one piece.

Other than having preached at a couple of services in different churches, my ministry had just begun with Shep. At this time, I thought maybe that was the sole purpose of my calling. In fact, when I left Maine, I felt that maybe my ministry was meant to be short. Maybe, having accomplished the one thing God had sent me out to accomplish, I wouldn't even make it home. When I survived the potential accident in Vermont, I realized God had more in mind for me than anointing Shep and officiating at his funeral.

One thing I want to be clear about is that I did not save Shep's soul. Only God can take credit for that. But I am honored that he used me as a tool in the process. The chaplain at the hospital had visited Shep twice the entire time he was there. He did not appear to be concerned with patients' souls but only about where the next drink would come from. Those who are supposed to be men and women of God sometimes are actually paid to walk the halls of hospitals, sit around and chitchat, and completely ignore the fact that the salvation of a soul is at stake. At least, in His infinite wisdom, God saw this situation coming and called me.

It is to His glory that I answered the call, not to my credit in any way, shape, or form.

I can assure you that the chaplains at the Pittsburgh VA hospital are very caring and very sincere in their duties. They don't care what faith you profess if any at all. They will pray for you. And they visit each patient often unless they are turned away.

PART
FOUR

Chapter 18

"For many are called, but few are chosen."

—Matthew 22:14

November 11, 1998, was one of the most important days of my life. Little did I know what that day would bring about that would have a profound effect on me the rest of my life.

Once previously, I had been to "the Wall," as it is best known (the Vietnam Veterans Memorial), in Washington, DC. When Chris and the kids arrived with me, we walked to the information booth. A few steps more, and we were at the point where I could see the very top of the Wall. I couldn't do it! I couldn't muster up the courage to walk any further. I sat on a bench facing away from the monster of granite, while, at my insistence, the three of them walked down to the Wall and paid their respects to those who had died either in-country or later from their injuries after returning "home," or maybe only to another hospital out of harm's way. I was glad all three were able to go on without me. I was afraid they might think I would be upset if they didn't stay there with me, fearing I would think they had abandoned me. It was very important to me that they were able, for the first time, to experience any connection between me and the haunting of my nightmares.

They returned in due time, and I walked away from the tens of thousands of names, several of which I would have recognized had I traversed those last fifty yards or so to the Wall.

I can't really relay to anyone what my feelings were that evening, having, in a sense, betrayed all those comrades because I had lacked the courage to complete the three hundred-mile journey. But maybe there would be another day, another time.

Then on that chilly November day, I returned to the Wall with my old service buddy, Alan Wallace. He served as a volunteer ranger at the Wall for several years. The previous year, he had received an award for "volunteer of the year." I spent the weekend with Alan, who, at that time, resided in Reston, Virginia. We had a great time revisiting our time in Hospital Corps School at Bethesda, Maryland, at the National Naval Medical Center, plus during our two meetings at Da Nang Hospital in Vietnam.

Alan was a great host, and we had a great time together. It took me an hour to track down his apartment once I found the complex. If I had stopped the car, gotten out, and yelled his name when I first arrived, I would have saved sixty minutes of time and a whole lot of gas, as I was within several yards of his apartment. Anyway, I arrived safely. After reminiscing for hours, we called it a day and then got up a few hours later. After breakfast, we went to Fort Myer, where he was employed as a federal fireman.

Next, we took the subway (which was not even in the planning stages when we were stationed there) to Bethesda Naval Hospital. It was rather disappointing to see the changes that had taken place since October 1967, when I'd left there for the last time. Of course, the infamous tower remained as the focal point of the surrounding skyline. Actually, looking in most directions, it accounted for almost the entire skyline. It is now the new site of the Walter Reed Army Hospital.

There were no more wards 7-A through 7-F where I had worked. In fact, it was now more of a clinic and research facility than a hospital. The old Barracks 12, where I'd bunked down for almost a year and a half, was gone and had been replaced by a much more modern building.

We went to the main tower, where Alan had worked as a surgical technician, and he got a chance to reminisce with a couple chief petty officers, who graciously took the time to talk to us and go over the changes that had taken place.

Alan told them several stories that had happened during his tenure on that particular floor, including one about a retired admiral who had coughed up a lung and died on Alan's shift. Then I told them the story about James E. Williams, Jr., and pulled his obituary from my wallet. Then the most wonderful thing happened. The female chief petty officer, who had done 90 percent of the talking, excused herself, telling us not to leave until she returned. I don't know if the fact that Williams was black and my being white impressed her, but she returned with two medallions that had been given to all chief petty officers and commissioned officers who were stationed at Bethesda on the hundredth anniversary of the Navy Medical Corps. There were very few of the medallions left, and I believe she was sincere when she said they were to be given out only in rare situations. I guess we were a "rare situation." We each stood in awe and disbelief that we, as old-timers who hadn't served their country for nearly thirty years, became the latest recipients of the medallions.

I'll never forget what Alan did with his medallion. When we got to his apartment that night, he gave it to me and told me to give it to Shep when I got to Maine. I eventually made it there and honored his request.

Then we left for the Wall. I had no idea if I could do it this time or if I would turn around and go home feeling empty for the second time.

As we arrived at the information booth, Alan began talking to some of his fellow volunteers. So I just hung around, trying to muster up more courage than I had the previous trip. Finally, Alan left his friends, and we started toward the Wall. But some people, who seemed bewildered about some issue or other, caught Alan's attention, and he headed with them away from the Wall. I sucked it up and said to myself, "It's now or never." And off I went, down the sidewalk toward the black granite monster that had eluded me in the past.

The trip seemed to take at least half an hour. I remember struggling with each step, wondering if I should turn around, go to the car, and wait for Alan. I knew, if I altered one step, that would be it, and I would never go back. I seemed to be enveloped in a cloud and out of touch with reality. Those voices of the past called out and begged me to visit them one more time. I have never, ever been on nonprescription drugs, but at that moment, I had an idea what it must be like. I knew the voices weren't real. Yet, I also knew they were very real. Maybe I experienced a sort of transference from the Native American Indians who do their ceremonial dances in honoring their dead at the Wall.

I managed the courage to do what I thought, for me, was impossible. Not only did I go to the Wall, I looked up the name of James E. Williams, Jr. I have no Idea how long I stared at the engraved name in the granite, but I stood transfixed for what seemed a lifetime.

I turned around, and a young lady was standing there. She said something about me having psychologically returned to Vietnam while I was standing there and that I must have been remembering some bad times. She introduced herself. She was from Canada and was on a mission from a small college to get stories from Vietnam veterans at the Wall.

I pointed to Williams's name and agreed to tell her my story. When I finished, she gave me a hug and thanked me, tears rolling down her cheeks. Her parting words were something like, "I know I have the best story to write about, and I'm sure I just secured an A for the class."

Maybe she got her A, and maybe not. But what I am sure she received was a lesson in the horrors of war and the experiences of war that last forever, embedded in the minds of those who lived those times, whether bad, good, or both.

That evening, Alan and I said our goodbyes, and I left Virginia and headed back toward Ohio. It was a calm, bright evening and was still daylight once I was clear of the DC/Virginia area. I was back into familiar territory, which I had traveled often while stationed in Bethesda a few decades earlier. About forty-five minutes to an hour later, I would again have a life-altering experience.

Before I go on, let me fast-forward momentarily to an experience at a youth group meeting at the church I pastor. I was speaking about hearing the voice of God when I was called into the ministry when a young man asked, "What does the voice of God sound like?" It was a very good question—one that isn't easy to answer even once you have experienced it.

My answer: "It is a still, silent voice—one your ears don't hear, but your heart does." That is still my answer today. It may not be a perfect answer. And maybe nobody can relate to it if they haven't heard that calm, gentle voice embedded in their heart. It is very subtle and calm, yet extremely persuasive at the same time.

I want you to go into the ministry to help spread the gospel to those around you.

Period! No more … no less … no coaxing … no threatening. End of speech!

When I was a youngster, I talked often about wanting to become a preacher. But growing up, we all have ambitions that seldom come to fruition unless it is a family-oriented profession. I did have two uncles who were Methodist ministers, and Mom was a Sunday school teacher. But there was no real bond that placed me in a position where I was expected to carry out that profession.

Dad's death and my near-failing grades led me to the desire to serve in the military, as at least four uncles and an aunt had served before me. I didn't believe it was God calling me to serve my country though. "Country and God" put the two in the reverse order from what we are used to hearing. "God and Country" is the saying. It was my story but in reverse order!

This time, I realized God was making a serious call, and I knew it would be the last. However, my initial reaction to the shock was to tell God, "I think you meant to speak to the guy in the red Explorer that just passed me going the other way." Of course, there was no such vehicle in sight.

"Yes Lord, you have led me through the waters to this point for a reason. You took a grenade from my hand and disposed of it. You led me beside still waters, but also through the deep valleys, including the valley of the shadow of death more than once."

Linda and I weren't engaged, but we were very good friends at this time. Being that there was nothing that bonded us together at this point (such as a ring), my first step was to talk to her the next day once she arrived home from work. I did love her very much and would have been deeply disappointed if she backed out. But it was a decision she had to make, and we both had to live with.

I cut right to the point. "I was called into the ministry last night on my way home, and I accepted the call. I hope you are OK with it. And if not, I understand. But I'm telling, not asking. Now you have a choice to make!"

I honestly didn't know what her answer would be. But an answer in the negative would not have swayed my decision. My commitment had been made—Linda or no Linda. I could only hope she would stay beside me. I told her she could take her time, and I didn't need an immediate answer.

But to my surprise, she blurted out her answer. What was the exact wording of her answer? I honestly don't recall. I was just happy it was a positive one. That's all that mattered. We were good! We were going to take this trip together.

I mentioned that I had lost two of my best friends. Paul Welton was the other. Paul was a priest who served at a nearby parish. He applied for and was awarded a job with the county. He was not in my department but sat only a few offices away from mine. We had talked now and then, but I didn't consider him a particularly close friend at the time.

One day, Paul walked into my office and said he understood I had done some tax returns. This was true, in a sense, although they had been limited to family. He said he had some investments, and the man who had done his returns previously had ripped him off. So, he asked if I would work on his taxes if he provided me with at least two previous years' returns so I could figure out how to proceed with the investment parts. I agreed to take a shot at it. He promised to pay me well, but I told him I had never been in the habit of charging friends for helping them. This is a characteristic I assume was handed down from my father.

Things went well. We sat in his office at lunchtime for about three days, and we were both satisfied we had it down pat. A few weeks later, Paul told me he got the check from the IRS he was expecting. He gave me a handful of bills, which I was sure weren't one dollar bills. I refused it and walked away. Well, I soon learned that Paul was just like me. When he wanted to do something for you, he was going to do it if it took forever. Knowing I had a small coin collection, he talked me into accepting two gold coins that had been graded by Numismatic Guaranty Company. I won't go into grading coins, but if they are graded by one of a few specific companies, it is much easier to sell them because quality is everything. I only took the coins because he told me he didn't really want them in his possession but wasn't willing to sell them because they were a gift given by a good friend (most likely left to him by someone for whom he had done a favor).

A few weeks later, Paul called me on a Saturday and told me the IRS notified him that a mistake had been made on his return. Immediately, I told him I would make up for the difference. To my surprise, he began laughing and said he had received another check and that the mistake was in his favor.

Once Paul resigned his job at the welfare department and I had left work due to my disability, he was transferred to a parish in Shadyside about twenty miles away. This was the area hit hard in the 1990 flood. I would drive down about once a month, and we would go to a restaurant for breakfast. Afterward, we would go back to his office at the church and talk for an hour or two.

Being new to the ministry, I was having problems with some of the things being presented in class. Although all lay pastors in training or beyond are assigned a mentor, I soon considered Paul as my main mentor. He answered some questions on several issues with which I was having difficulty. Amazingly, he took a Presbyterian approach in his answers, knowing I wasn't asking where the Catholic Church stood on the issues.

I felt free to tell him where I disagreed with the Catholic Church on certain things. He actually agreed with me on some and explained the others so that I learned something, whether or not I agreed with it.

Paul, Linda, and I established a true friendship. He was there for me at Edith Ann's death and took part in her funeral. While a Presbyterian minister who was also close to Linda and I would perform our wedding ceremony on August 5, 2000, we asked Paul to take part in the ceremony. The offer brought tears to his eyes. His wedding gift was to rent the basement of his church and cater a meal to all in attendance (which consisted of Linda's three children and their spouses, grandchildren; my uncle, who was my best man; our very close friends, Les and his wife, and Bobbi who was the minister that performed the wedding ceremony).

It was so difficult to enter Paul's church that Saturday afternoon and eat the food he had provided. Paul had passed away of a massive coronary just nine days earlier.

He had previously asked me to be the executor of his will. As he'd named eleven people or charities as beneficiaries, I had a lot of running around to do. Paul had graciously left more than enough money to cover any of my personal expenses.

One enlightening event happened the day his attorney, with whom I was familiar to an extent, introduced me to one of his associates, saying, "Paul is the only person I ever knew who was a Catholic priest, had an executor who was a Protestant minister, and a Jewish attorney who was the father of a female rabbi!"

Yes, Stan. You hit it on the nose. Paul Welton was one of a kind!

Here's just a quick note on how we tended to "get even" with one another. When we sent Christmas cards, birthday cards, or whatever, I got into the habit of addressing his envelopes to "Monsignor Paul Welton" and then "Bishop" and so on up the chain until I reached

"Pope Paul Welton." The next card I received from him was addressed to "God," with my address below.

Another "man of the cloth" would soon enter my life as a mentor in my ministry. Lester Frank served as pastor at my home church for a short time in the mid-1990s. We became friends, but at that time, I wouldn't consider it a particularly close friendship.

Les is one of those preachers who you could throw a subject at, and he could preach a sermon about it without preparation. He knew his Bible and knew how to have his audience hang onto every word.

It was a shame that Les would only serve in Bellaire for a short time. He had served me well in terms of a pastoral relationship, someone I could talk to about my time when life had come crashing down on me. He could comfort you with not only words from the Bible but also words from the heart. But his service in Bellaire would come to an abrupt halt when his wife accused him of an incident with his young stepson.

As it appeared his attorney was about to have successfully defended him, he asked for considerably more money, an amount Les could not afford. I took the stand at his trial as a character witness. But a history of some old white-collar crimes crept in. When asked by the prosecutor if I knew anything about this, I truthfully answered in the negative. He had me right where he wanted me and let me know I didn't know the accused as well as I thought I had. I knew the opposing attorney from previous employment, and he showed me respect by putting this as nicely as he could without losing his sting.

I visited Les at the Nelsonville Correction Center during his four years of incarceration. It was a minimum-security facility for males over fifty years of age. One beautiful spring morning I waited in my vehicle in front of the facility. Out came Les and a guard, who walked him to the car to send him on his way. I drove him to Columbus Airport. I don't remember where he was headed but figured this was the end of our friendship. He was a free man now and headed toward "the rest of his life," and I was happy for him.

The one thing I do remember about this time was him telling me he had one other repeat visitor. It was a Catholic priest who was employed at my alma mater, Wheeling Jesuit College. Somehow, they had met professionally and developed a friendship. The priest was a true friend, which he showed by making the two hundred-mile round trip to Nelsonville on several occasions.

It has been my experience that most so-called "friends," in this type of situation, tend to use you and then lose you. A couple months had passed and I wondered what had happened to Les. I knew most of his family had abandoned him because of the charges that had been brought against him. We were in the same boat, both sinking after having had our children turn against us. While the reasons were different, we were each on our own now with little, if any, family support. All I could do was pray Les would find peace. And he did, somewhat, but it was temporary.

About a month went by and no word from Les. Then one evening came a phone call. He had settled in the DC/Virginia area. He sounded good. No matter what happened from here on, he was a free man. He would eventually fall in love with a woman I knew virtually nothing about. I met her when she came with Les for mine and Linda's wedding. They stayed here for a night, and then I never heard of her again. Hopefully, it was a good thing for Les.

A trip to Columbia for a revival, and Les seemed to be all the way back. He was happy now and continuing God's plan for him. He secured employment, but his past kept creeping up on him.

Then came Rosa. They had met in her native Columbia, and eventually she came north, and they were married. Rosa was just what Les needed—someone who didn't question his past. Rosa is now a US citizen. She did things the right way. She is a hard worker, many times working two jobs.

I hadn't met Rosa until a few years ago when they came to visit me while I was a patient at Pittsburgh VA hospital. I was suffering from the complications from the prostatectomy. She was still learning English. But I could understand most of what she said if she spoke slowly.

Then she prayed. I didn't understand anything she said, as she prayed in Spanish. But she poured her heart into the prayer, and I knew God understood every word. When she finished, we all had tears in our eyes as a result of her intensity.

My healing was slow, but I was as convinced as much as Rosa was that God still had a purpose for me. He heard her prayer that autumn afternoon, and he answered it. Slowly but surely, he answered the many prayers from all over the country. More on that later.

A phone call comes every few weeks. Yes, Les has never forgotten my friendship and support through the ensuing years. I say that, not bragging by any means but, rather, repeating his own words every time I talk to him.

So why pick out this particular friend to write about? Simply because, just as Paul Welton did in the beginning, Les has continued Paul's mentoring of one called into the ministry who was starting from scratch. Yes, degrees in psychology and counseling were a good start, but this didn't help me preach the gospel of Jesus Christ.

I felt like placing an ad in the local media titled "Rookie in Need of a Mentor." But in the end, it wasn't needed. The most unlikely one to answer the ad that wasn't even placed was a Catholic priest. Whod'a ever thunk it? Paul got me through the beginning, but his sudden death from a heart attack could have been devastating to my attempt at the ministry.

Then, along came Les! It wasn't that he hadn't been there before, but now I would have to learn from phone calls. I am a hands-on person. You know, those questions they ask at hospitals and doctors' offices? I understand needing to know the answers to those questions in situations such as job interviews. But when I'm lying there only half-conscious, I don't give half a damn about how I best learn things. Nevertheless, I would unceasingly say, "Hands on."

But now the instruction I was receiving wasn't face-to-face as it had been with Paul. With Les, it was over the phone. Like I had with Paul, I was learning what I wanted to learn and not what a different denomination believed in. Teaching a rookie Presbyterian who was eclectic by one who had a strong Baptist background couldn't have been easy. Over the years, I've learned that Les and I are on the same wavelength. And as did Paul, Les respects my beliefs and convictions if we differ a little on a certain subject.

God has a plan. That is the only answer I get when I ask why Les and I met. When he mentions what I have done for him, I always reply by reminding him that he has helped me even more. While I won't be long remembered as a great evangelist or even a little country church preacher once my time has gone by, God has led me to touch at least a few souls. And without someone to guide me through times when I had doubts or was angered by those I serve, that wouldn't have been possible. I recognize who God sent to lend a listening ear and offer advice—advisers who would never tell me, "Do it this way because it works for me."

As I keep mentioning, so many events have crisscrossed in my life that it is impossible to place all events in chronological order. So, bouncing back and forth is a necessity even if it is a little confusing. Therefore, I rearranged chapters here from their original order and placed the following chapter next.

Chapter 19

In this chapter, I've included a sermon I preached in August 2002. The title, "My Brother's Eyes," speaks for itself. The sermon repeats a story I have already told but examines it from a completely different perspective. So, please refrain from skipping over parts of it because you will do yourself an injustice. Scripturally, "My Brother's Eyes" draws from Ecclesiastes 3:1–8 and John 15: 9–17.

If you were attending Pilgrim Baptist Church in my hometown of Bellaire on the morning of this sermon, these were the words you would have seen on the face of the bulletin: "This is a day to celebrate the proof that 'hate' is not a word in God's vocabulary. We are all one with God. His boundaries are without limits. The Bellaire Clergy Association wishes to help break down barriers in religion, race, and whatever else we use to distance ourselves from one another."

Most of the members of the association had no idea what church they were assigned to for this special day until they received their notice in the mail the previous week, basically because most of them couldn't attend the weekly meetings. But immediately after learning of our planned "pulpit swap," I began working on my sermon.

Now, let me assure you that you didn't get the grand prize through a drawing. Nor was it a case of the most experienced pastor getting the assignment, as I had just received my calling in 1998. What Bobby, the pastor of the church of which I was assigned, knew about me was the story of an experience in a far-off land that would eventually shape my life and my destiny. This invitation wasn't as much to preach a sermon as it was to tell a story, the details of which he knew part of, though he'd never heard the entire story.

This was my sermon:

> I grew up on 38th Street here in the small town of Bellaire, Ohio, a predominantly white neighborhood, yet an integrated one, as the Thomas and Carter families were my neighbors. So, I grew up not knowing much about racial strife and issues outside my neighborhood.
>
> I volunteered to join the navy after my junior year at Bellaire High School, and during summer 1965, I left for basic training. I became a hospital corpsman (known as a medic in the army and air force) and eventually ended up serving as a neuropsychiatric technician on the hospital ship USS *Repose*. Though working on the psychiatric ward was my primary assignment, the most memorable experiences I have come from working triage during my "off duty hours."
>
> Early in my tour, I was awakened to racial tensions—not only to their existing back in the States but also to how alive they were in Vietnam. I began to treat soldiers, wounded not by the enemy but, rather, for wounds inflicted on them by our own soldiers.
>
> The bullet and shrapnel wounds from the enemy were accompanied by severe beatings from within our own ranks. On the streets of Da Nang and other major cities, white soldiers were being attacked by black soldiers, and black soldiers were being beaten by white soldiers. And this was topped off by light-skinned and dark-skinned black soldiers fighting each other.
>
> What was this *world* coming to?
>
> What was this *war* coming to?
>
> Then the abuse carried over from the wounded to those treating them in triage or in the emergency

room. For the first time in my life, I began to turn prejudiced. I began to look at the situation from a white person's perspective. I was tired of trying to help mend somebody's wound, only to have them make a racial slur at me. I was forgetting everything my parents had taught me about God being color blind— about God not caring about a person's nationality or political views or the color of his skin. I was forgetting to turn the other cheek.

Yet, deep inside, I knew these were not real soldiers. Although many may have been heroes in the jungle, these men who bore hatred for their fellow countrymen were idiots. Their comrades died in combat, died defending their country and all the people in it—of all nationalities, of all races, and of all political views. They died defending their country, defending me, defending you, defending our children and our future generations.

Before I would get into actual hatred for anyone different than myself, God showed me that every soldier I treated had something in common. The blood they shed was red. As many soldiers as I cared for and as many bodies as I processed, I never once experienced the sight of white blood or black blood ... Methodist blood or Catholic blood.

Yet, there remains a racial prejudice in America today. We need only look at any major city to see a hatred between Americans ... just because people tend to put hyphens between nationalities or color. We are *all* God's people. We must teach our children that we are *all* children of God and that God is color blind and blind to ethnic background and blind to all differences among His creation!

As a combat veteran, I often use a quote from Abraham Lincoln's Gettysburg Address. Please listen to these words from the perspective that, at all my Memorial Day speeches, most of the veterans and their families are Caucasian. I address this point as a challenge to them, calling for us to honor *all* who have given the supreme sacrifice and challenging them to prove to the world that we can love *all* people. In Lincoln's words, "From these honored dead we take increased devotion to that cause for which they gave the last full measure of devotion; that we here highly resolve that these dead shall not have died in vain."

In this matter, I trust that history will never forget that soldiers from every walk of life fought side by side ... and bled side by side.

On December 27, 1967, a young marine was mortally wounded at a battle in Quang Tri province, Republic of South Vietnam. He was immediately given a dose of morphine by a corpsman in the field and then evacuated along with several members of his unit and flown to hospital ship, the USS *Repose*.

From the chopper, he was taken into triage, examined quickly by a doctor, and then the doctor told the assisting corpsmen (including myself) to take him "to the corner," which was the place patients who had no chance to survive were taken to die while the attending corpsmen returned to treat more of the wounded. So, needless to say, many soldiers died a lonely death in that forlorn area of the room. Yes, it was better than dying in the snake-infested jungle or being tortured at the hands of the enemy.

But at this point, a young corpsman who had taken the Navy Corpsman's Oath—to "keep as many men at as many posts for as long as time as possible"— broke that oath and returned to a dying comrade known only to him as "Williams."

As he had started walking away, the corpsman saw his patient lift an index finger as if to motion him to return. When he did come back to his fallen comrade, the young corpsman's life changed forever.

The dying patient was forming his lips, desperately trying to say something with what little strength his body could muster. Within a few seconds, the corpsman realized he was trying to utter the word *prayer.* All the dying soldier wanted in life's closing moment was somebody to pray for him!

It was at this point that an officer came up to the corpsman and gave a direct order to abandon the dead and return to the incoming helicopters. And the young man disobeyed a direct order, leaned over a fallen hero, and prayed. Here were two Americans living and dying on foreign soil, for reasons they might not have agreed with, yet both defending the freedom their fellow Americans enjoyed.

One was a marine; the other, a sailor.

One was Baptist; the other, Presbyterian.

One was a combatant; the other helped save lives.

One was black; the other was white.

One was dying; the other was just beginning to understand life.

The corpsman wouldn't discover the identity of "Williams" for thirty-one years—after dealing with post-traumatic stress and having his world ripped apart by the trauma of reliving the events of all those who were transported to that triage site, whether living, dying, or in unidentifiable parts. But after thirty-one years of research, he would put pieces of the puzzle together and discover that Williams was, in fact, LCPL James E. Williams, Jr., of Oklahoma City, Oklahoma.

While I do not suggest anyone do what I finally decided to do one day, I used self-hypnosis to recall what another marine said to Williams. I knew he called him Williams, but through the hypnosis, I learned he'd said Oklahoma, when he told his dying comrade where he would be going home to.

In summer 1998, this middle-aged Vietnam veteran would travel to Oklahoma to visit the grave of a fallen comrade after a phone call to the sister of the deceased man had convinced him he had finally tracked down the correct Williams. A meeting had been arranged with his sister, but the death of their father was to curtail the meeting until the following year. Locating the cemetery association, I would find the location of Williams's gravesite.

My good friend Father Paul Welton would travel with me. He had a new Toyota, a little cramped for a long trip, but we traveled light. And off we went. We would meet each morning outside our motel rooms. Paul got up early and performed morning Mass, which I discovered was a rule priests must follow daily, no matter where they may be.

We reached the cemetery around noon. It took only a few minutes to find the flat slab of marble announcing that here lay the remains of LCPL James E. Williams, Jr.

The Oklahoma sun shone brightly that particular day. Not a cloud in the sky. The sun's rays shone brightly on the commemorative stone. Not a chirp from a bird. Total silence. I had, indeed, found the grave, and I spent several minutes with head bowed.

I thought several years ago that I had said my last earthly goodbye to my brother. But one more time I would say goodbye. I saluted, and this time knowing I had, indeed, said my final farewell, I turned, with tears in my eyes, and walked away. The next time we are connected will be in a place where war no longer exists. There will be no death no hatred, no fighting, and no tears shed.

Once I'd said goodbye to my brother in arms, Paul and I would drive home by the southern route, as neither of us had been to Texas, Louisiana, Mississippi, Alabama, Florida, or Georgia. We also managed to hit the Carolinas and Tennessee, which Paul had never visited.

The following summer, volunteering to work on building homes for those who had been devastated by the spring tornadoes in Oklahoma (of all places), I returned to Oklahoma to meet Williams's sister and mother and calm their fears after thirty some years. I assured them that their brother and son had not been tortured and that he had not died alone in some forsaken jungle but, rather, in the arms of a brother who he did not know he had until his eyes were ready to close in death.

A disturbing fact that shouldn't have surprised me was the story of a fallen son's possessions being returned by our government. James's bloody uniform and boots were returned to the family just as they were on December 27, 1967. I need say no more except that, each time I thought I couldn't be more appalled by the United States government (specifically the military this time), I was always in for one more surprise.

We were two brothers who were as far apart as two men could possibly be in earthly ways. One of those brothers would return home and then be called into the ministry when he touched the name of "James E. Williams, Jr." on the Vietnam Memorial Wall on Veterans Day 1998.

Sometimes, I wish I could tell this story and pretend I was a hero. But to feel that way would be unfair—because James E. Williams, Jr., was the hero. He was the other brother, and he sacrificed his life for this ungrateful country. The government he fought for comprised a bunch of power-hungry bastards, led by the greatest bastard of all, who sat in a cozy office and lived the life of a king following the assassination of John F. Kennedy. He put foreign interests ahead of the nation's sons, who would sacrifice their lives (in one way or another). I continue to believe that this man had something to do with his predecessor's death on a street in Dallas on November 22, 1962.

The fallen marine is the hero. As John 15:13 tells us, "Greater love has no one than this ... that he lay down this life for another."

He reaffirmed to me that Jesus Christ doesn't care what our differences are in life. We will burn in hell or live in heaven with others of every faith, every background, and every color.

Hours after kneeling at the Wall on November 11, 1998, a sinner was called into the service of Almighty God—through a brother who had died thirty-one years prior.

When this old corpsman looks at the obituary he carries in his wallet at all times, he is reminded of that day many years ago when he embraced a complete stranger and became the last person that young man ever saw. He looked into his brother's eyes and met the eyes of God.

Might I remind you that God is watching you in the last place you expect Him. He will send a guardian angel to you at the time you least expect it, and it just might be the last person you expect it to be.

I would like to end this message by quoting Jesus from the familiar message of "The Sheep and the Goats." This is from Matthew 25:40. "I tell you the truth ... whatever you did for one of the least of my brothers or sisters ... you did for me."

Amen.

Chapter 20

"For I know the plans I have for you", declares the Lord, "plans to prosper you and not harm you, plans to give you hope and a future."

—Jeremiah 29:11

I began writing my memoirs in 2000. At times, I would review them, adding, deleting, and correcting entries. It is now 2020, and I suddenly realize the time is now or never if I am to finish what I started two decades, and what seems like a lifetime, ago. There are many things I didn't think to write as time went by. Looking back, I try to fill in some blanks. "The rest of the story," I guess, more or less, began in 1980 when a devastating but fortunately not deadly flash flood hit parts of Belmont County. As a new hire within the county, I was asked if I would place all other job duties aside, create a damage assessment unit, and supervise the unit. The good news was I would get all the overtime I wanted, plus many hours more than I would have liked. One thing I wasn't able to manage well was some time for rest. But my time aboard the *Repose* had taught me well how to manage what little time I had away from the job. The bad news was that I only ended up with one part-time clerical worker. Fortunately, there were no deaths or serious injuries involved. This would be a precursor to the 1990 flash flood that devastated the county. More on that later

Once I got back on solid ground at the agency, I formed the first welfare fraud unit in the county. It took some time to go from collecting overpayments to begin taking cases to court. Too soon, I would discover the world of politics.

After the initial welfare fraud trial, I was interviewed by a young reporter from the local newspaper. He quoted me in the interview as stating, "The County finally got a trial to court and was successful in its prosecution." He knew full well the word *finally* was referring to the fact the county had hired me to do a job and that I needed some time to set things up in order to file charges, schedule the case, and actually present it in court. But in an attempted power move, he ended up misrepresenting the quote and making it appear that I had blasted the county prosecutor and directing the word *finally* at him.

The following morning when the news made headlines, my boss called me and said not only was the prosecutor upset, the county commissioners were irate. I asked her to get me an appointment with the prosecutor immediately, which she obliged. Within several minutes, I was in his office explaining that everything I told the reporter was meant as a compliment to his office and to him personally. At this point, he told me to go ahead and go back to work; he knew the editor of the newspaper and that they were good friends. He called me back within an hour and notified me that the reporter had been fired immediately, and his statement would be retracted in the next day's edition. It was.

However, one item had not been retracted. On the editorial page, each edition ran something called "Old Man River." It was a sentence commenting on any number of subjects. This time it was political, as usual. I'm paraphrasing as I am not sure of the exact words:

> Kurt Turner,
>   Which office will you be running for in the next election?
>
> Yours truly,
> Old Man River

The only good to come out of all this was that my name was not only well-known in Bellaire but had also become a household name in the county. Those committing welfare fraud in Belmont County now knew the name of their enemy.

Eventually, the newness hit an expiration date, and welfare fraud cases no longer seemed to be a top priority with the prosecutor's office. Maybe it was due to the fact that it wasn't really a challenge. Every case I presented was a "lockdown"—a foolproof case the judge pretty well knew the outcome of before the case was presented. That, in no way, implies the judge had predetermined the outcome. He knew, if I wasn't absolutely sure fraud had been committed, I would take it to small claims division and just go after a lesser amount. There would be adjudication but no threat of incarceration.

The county prosecutor too often had more important things to attend to on trial days. Finally, Judge White asked me if I would want to present the cases myself. I was up to the challenge. I never lost a single case. Most defendants pleaded their guilt before the judge pronounced them guilty. A couple of individuals were sent off packing to prison. But as long as they were willing to make payments as directed, the judge and I both knew keeping them out of prison saved the State of Ohio big bucks.

When it came to the point I wasn't eligible for a raise as investigator, I applied for a supervision position in a new pilot program. At the same time, we were forming the county's first union. I was elected president, and things flowed even better than expected. I took one case to the Ohio State Labor Relations Board. I went up against the agency director and county prosecutor. At one point, the judge asked my boss a question. He replied, "Your Honor, as much as I hate to say it, Kurt can answer your question better than any of us." At that time, I was certain I had won my five-dollar bet with him. Two weeks later he walked into my office, laid a five spot on my desk, and walked out. Case won! Bet won!

Immediately after that, I was made an offer I couldn't refuse and moved up the ladder from union president to administrator and was awarded the position I had applied for. I knew I would have to resign my office with the union, but I was given more responsibility and a significant pay raise.

Eventually, after my third neck surgery, I would end up supervising the fraud unit once again. After my fourth cervical discectomy, I would never return to work. At that point, I had no inkling as to what purpose God had laid before me. So, as a consequence, I fought to remain on the job.

As a result of my physical exam through the Bureau of Workers' Compensation, I was notified that I could not return to gainful employment because of the many surgeries that were due to my two back injuries. Unlike the majority, I would fight to go back to my job, rather than collect disability payments for the rest of my life. I filed for a hearing, which was held at the state office building in Columbus.

I was told to be there for my appeal at 10:00 a.m. Little did I realize, my hearing was set for 1:00 p.m. but my attorney wanted me to sit through a couple of prior hearings so I would be familiar with the hearing process when mine came up.

The two prior hearings were appeals to be granted permanent total disability, unlike mine, which was the exact opposite. I wanted to return to work. They didn't. Though it seemed like a waste of time to me, those two hearings were actually entertaining and ended up well worth the extra time I spent there that morning.

The first hearing was presented by an attorney for a woman who'd filed a back injury claim on her job as a maid at a motel. Her case was doomed by the second question asked by one of the two hearing officers. She spoke very little English, so she was basically asked yes-or-no questions.

"Were you notified that your job was to be terminated soon?"

"Yes."

"Was your last day to be the day after you claim you injured your back?"

"Yes."

Did you immediately seek medical attention?"

"No."

"How many tests did you have done, such as a CT scan or an MRI?"

"None."

Have you been prescribed pain medication for your condition?"

"No."

"You will be notified by mail as to the outcome of this hearing!"

I don't know if she even had the sense to pick up on the judge's demeanor.

Next up was a case attended by the claimant's attorney. The truck driver had lost his employment as the result of a number of maladies, which were filed under a workers' comp claim also seeking permanent total disability. I think the attorney was there only because he was being paid to represent his client, regardless of the outcome.

"Is your client present for this hearing this morning?"

"No, sir."

"Is there a reason for his absence?"

"Yes, sir. He is unable to travel and to sit here because of this back condition."

"When and where did the specific back injury take place?"

"There was no specific time. It is a result of climbing in and out of the cab for many years."

"Do you know what your client's weight was when he began his employment?"

"I have no idea."

"Well, I do. "(He proceeded to quote the weight from his job application. I believe it was under two hundred pounds.)

"Do you know how much he weighs now?"

"No, sir. I don't."

"According to this physical paid for by the State of Ohio concerning this claim, he weighs 305 pounds."

Here, the attorney made a mistake that made me cover up a laugh when he asked, "So, what does that mean?"

"Sir, you know as well as I do that means your client decided to quit this gainful employment, sit around all day and eat, and expect two hearing officers to have a pity party and allow him to live off the taxpayers of the State of Ohio for the rest of his life!" (This may not be an exact quote, but it's very close to it.)

The judge concluded by saying, "You may step down. And you will notify your client that he will receive written notice of our decision within two weeks."

I was not able to hear one of the judge's comments to the attorney as he stepped down and passed in front of the bench. I'm sure I witnessed the attorney crack a slight smile at whatever comment was made. I'm also sure he was expecting it.

So, now it was lunchtime, and everyone took off except for yours truly. I was familiar with Columbus, just familiar enough to know not to go very far and end up being late for my hearing. So, I stayed right there in the hearing room by myself for about forty-five long minutes.

One of the judges came back a little early and sat down beside me. He said, "I have a question for you, Mr. Turner."

Knowing the legal process (what can or cannot be used against you), I asked him if my attorney should be present for my sake. He laughed and assured me my case had already been discussed between the two judges prior to the day's cases and that the result was a foregone conclusion.

He was probably about ten years younger than I was. His question was about my education. He noted that he also had a degree in criminal justice. We discussed the different schools we'd attended. It ended up being a pleasant discussion. Then my attorney walked in and made some comment. I didn't hear what he said, and that may have been intentional on his part. The two looked at each other, turned to look at the confused expression on my face, and then both burst out laughing. Obviously, my conversation with the judge was approved by my attorney as just that, a discussion.

But before my attorney walked in, the judge had already told me that, unless something earth-shattering transpired during the hearing, the state would back the doctor's observation and belief that, because I was constantly in pain, I was now a liability to my employer. The decision was a tough one since I had acquired an education and worked so hard at my two professions. Of course, the outcome also prevented me from returning to my employment at the college.

To this day, I continue to do as much volunteer work as possible and to never give up. I am a firm believer that most people who retire and sit back and become lazy sign their own premature death certificates. I live in constant pain. Most people don't realize that working around the house, mowing grass, and cutting firewood on good days prevents some of the pain I would encounter by sitting back and taking it easy. If I let my spine and muscular system lock up on me due to a lack of exercise, then I am doomed to the walker/wheelchair the doctor at the pain clinic predicted for me at an early age. Had he realized my stamina and willpower, I doubt he would have made the remark.

One thing I need to make clear is that I do not accept pay for the services I perform, work for which most people do accept gratuities if nothing else. I do not cheat the system and don't need to. I enjoy my ministries, or I wouldn't be participating in them. At times when old injuries and surgical intervention pain gets bad enough, I am not obligated to get up in the morning and "go to work." I have been offered jobs to work for pay "under the table" and have refused. I refuse to accept money for funerals. Unless a mortuary is in dire need, I only perform funerals for those I knew well. Even then, I refuse to accept gratuities. I want to remain a productive member of society through my ministries. The sources of my disability payments are well aware of services I perform for the good of the community. And I stand no chance of being discovered participating in any of the illegalities I once made a living catching other people doing.

PART FIVE

Chapter 21

"I can do all this through Him who gives me strength."
—Philippians 4:13

Having been forced into early retirement, I had no thoughts whatsoever of sitting around enjoying the easy life. I was living in a small apartment and felt closed in. But it was something I could afford, and I spent the first winter there with my thermostat set at around fifty. I spent a lot of time squirrel hunting, since all I had to do was walk down over the hill from the apartment. I managed getting local TV channels and then cable from my landlord. Once spring came, I did some fishing in the pond located next to my hunting grounds.

But I needed something to do that had a purpose or substance. Hunting and fishing were fun, but I wanted to give back to society. I had worked all my life, beginning at a mom-and-pop grocery store and delivering newspapers at around age thirteen until I joined the navy at age seventeen. Then was the stint at Arrow Block Plant, where I learned to operate a forklift and end-loader, run the machinery that made the blocks, and do a little bit of mechanical work. Then came the other jobs previously mentioned, including teaching at the local college and working for the Welfare Department. As political correctness came into fashion, the Welfare Department became the

Department of Human Services and, later, the Department of Job and Family Services.

My bachelor's degree came in handy here and then the master's degree for teaching college courses. But in the end, I began to feel they were now useless. I felt like the proverbial octopus with seven tentacles.

In the summer of 1995, I went to the Belmont County Emergency Management Agency, just to drop in and say hi to Dick Quinlin, who was now the coordinator for the county agency. It had slowly advanced from what duties I performed in the 1980 flood. I was responsible for coordinating each entity in the county that dealt with disasters. This was housed in a building my crews helped build when I ran the community work experience program while with the Welfare Department.

After a few visits there, Dick and I became good friends. I began doing paperwork as a volunteer. But before I took a chance in doing something I wasn't supposed to, I contacted workers' comp and the VA. I was told I could volunteer, as long as I didn't do any lifting or anything that might aggravate my back injuries. And of course, I couldn't receive any type of pay. I didn't have a schedule. Therefore, I didn't have a volunteer "job" per se.

Then came the day that would be yet another "life changer." Dick asked me to come into his office. We talked about different things for several minutes. Then he said, "Kurt, you have a master's degree in psychology or counseling, don't you?"

I then became a member of the International Critical Incident Stress Management Foundation.

First, I will regress and tell of the event that precipitated the forming of the CISD (Debriefing), now CISM, as other areas are just as important as the debriefing itself. "Defusings" take place mostly on scene as an event unfolds. One-on-one's are just as they are named, talking to a single person about an event or events.

The event of one evening five years earlier would immediately impact much of Belmont and surrounding counties. Though it would take seven years, that event would be the precursor to the Belmont County CISM team.

Chapter 22

"Listen, I tell you a mystery: we will not all sleep, but we will all be changed—in a flash, in the twinkling of an eye, at the last trumpet."

—*1 Corinthians 15:51–52a*

Please be advised that I am in no way writing about the historical aspect of the flood described in the following event. Books have been published about the flood, along with many magazine and newspaper articles. The following is my personal account and my personal experience. This is about my experience and my perception. Others may not see things as I did. I certainly did not experience the horror of discovering and retrieving mangled bodies as others did. They have had their own stories to tell. Through the years, I have heard many of those accounts as I sat and listened to those very people. They each have their story, their own experience, and their own perception, which may be different than mine. We each had a purpose there.

In almost every college course I taught, whether psychology or social studies, I spent at least one hour on "reality versus perception." No two people experience an event exactly the same. It isn't about who is right and who is wrong. I can assure you, most of those who experienced combat situations perceived events much differently than others. No two of us in that category experience and perceive the event identically. As a prime example, you will discover that my statistic of deaths caused by the flood will differ from a historical viewpoint.

Just to give a short geographical layout of the area, Shadyside, Ohio, lies on the extreme eastern border of the state, along the Ohio River, which separates the state from West Virginia. It is located amid the foothills of the Appalachian Mountains. Therefore, unlike a river flood, the force of water is exceptional compared to the velocity of the flow of a river, while contained in its banks. Those who have never visited exceptionally hilly areas cannot comprehend the difference in the two types of flooding. River floods have been predictable for many years, even in downstream areas, where rainfall has been insignificant. Flash floods are exactly what the name implies. They appear in a flash, "in the twinkling of an eye."

The ground was saturated in June from an exceptionally wet month of May. That evening, rainfall estimated from five and a half inches to nine inches (depending on source) fell over the area between two creeks—Wegee Creek and Pipe Creek.

A wall of water, estimated at six feet, roared down the creeks and then backed up at their respective mouths. Sources agree that about eighty homes were destroyed. Several were swept off their foundations and turned into rubble that, within minutes, would be floating down the river. Another 250 homes were damaged, many severely.

Debris, including major appliances, tires, material from destroyed homes, trees, and cattle were swept into the river, where they piled up at the Ohio River dam at Hannibal, Ohio, approximately thirty miles downstream. Eventually, divers would recover two bodies there before the wickets were lowered and the debris was swept downstream.

Other areas had heavy damage, and I do not minimize damage done in those places. However, they were not a part of my experience, and it is not fair for me to tell about their impact.

Wegee Creek and Pipe Creek were the hardest hit. Wegee eventually flattens out just west of Shadyside. Pipe Creek, originating in the hills to the west, forms very close to the beginning of Wegee. Its mouth, like Wegee, empties into the Ohio River, just south of Shadyside.

Two of the deaths occurred along McMahon Creek, just north of Shadyside. The source is located near the other two. Both victims were young children.

A memorial along Wegee Creek honors those who died as a result of the flash flood of June 14, 1990. The names listed on it are:

Edna Andrecht	Debbie Graham	Dorothy Moore
John Andrecht	Don Grimes	Jim Moore
Scott Balsei	Mary Grimes	Kerri Polivka
Roger Denoon	Danny Humphrey	Rose Ramsay
Mary A. Gatten	David Humphrey	Donald Webb
Stephen Gatten	Sue Humphrey	Tiffany Webb
Timmy Gatten	Jerry Krupa	Jim West
Sophie Glazewski	Patsy Krupa	Naomi West
Bart Graham	Novalee Mellott	

June 14, 1990, was a day that began like any other June 14 in the Upper Ohio Valley—hot, humid, and lots of sunshine. Only God could foresee the devastation that would occur that evening—an evening that would change many lives forever.

I was coaching my daughter Carrie's softball team that evening. We were in St. Clairsville, which is located near the center of Belmont County. The skies began to darken. Hot, muggy days have the habit of precipitating thunderstorms in this area. So, nobody paid much attention to the darkening skies above.

As the fifth inning came to a close and the girls took to the field to begin the sixth, I mentioned to the home plate umpire that the sky had turned an ominous black in almost a circle around us, especially to the south and east. Following a discussion between umpires and coaches, it was decided the best course of action would be to call the game and have everyone head for home.

An hour or so later the torrential downpour began. Looking out of my kitchen window, I could see my slag driveway begin to deteriorate. By morning, it was gone, down to the base of sandstone rock with gullies deep enough the driveway was nearly impassable.

Even at that, I certainly didn't expect the top news story I witnessed the following morning as I turned the TV on. CNN was reporting up to two hundred deaths in the Shadyside area, where two streams emptied into the Ohio River. With that are being only about three miles from my home, I figured there was a massive mistake in reporting. So, I ate breakfast and headed to work, as usual, witnessing no major damage heading northwest.

I would soon discover the news report was blown out of proportion as far as the number of casualties. But the damage and loss of life was still something previously experienced with mine disasters in this area of rural southeastern Ohio.

Arriving at work, I was immediately approached by the agency assistant director. Her words were, "The county commissioners just called and said for you to report to Dick Quinlin immediately. When you get to Shadyside, you will be directed where to go."

I began to think there was some substance to the news reports. But because of the little damage around my home, except driveways and maybe some basement flooding, it still seemed likely there was little chance we'd be dealing with a major disaster.

Turning off the State Route 7 exit at the north end of Shadyside, I encountered an Ohio State Highway patrolman who was blocking traffic, with orders to turn back all unauthorized, unmarked vehicles. Here I sat in my little yellow Chevy Escort with no markings, as the agency did not own any vehicles at the time. Even though I was no longer working investigations, I continued to carry my badge with me. After I'd shown it and a proper county government employee ID card and explained the commissioner's phone call, he let me through and told me where I would find the incident command center.

Amid all the flashing lights and other government vehicles, I found a place to park at what seemed like a mile away. Thankful to find a place to park at all, I followed the crowd to the command center, which was set up in a tent in the grassy area between lanes of the main drag, which had served, recently, as Route 7.

I found one of the commissioners immediately and asked where I could find Dick Quinlin. He said there was a line a mile long waiting to see him. To my surprise, he put an arm around me, led me around the line, and said, "Hey, Dick, Kurt Turner's here."

Dick finished with the person to whom he was currently speaking, turned, and said, "Kurt, I need you to try your best at separating local, state, and federal government entities." Then, his next statement was that he had no idea how I was going to achieve that and keep them off each other's backs.

In that instant, I knew one disaster was about to lead to another. If you don't get it, try telling state offices that county officials are calling the shots, and then tell the feds they are answerable to state and county officials. It was my job to, as politely as possible, explain that and the fact that county officials knew the area; the people; and, most importantly, the local resources that would arrive from all over the eastern half of Ohio, northern West Virginia, and western Pennsylvania.

To my surprise, most of the players were trained at teamwork, willing to shed their hierarchy. Keep in mind, I used the word *most*. I figured I would be out of the agency for a few days, working eight- to ten-hour shifts away from the office. It soon became apparent this wasn't going to be the fact. Bodies were already being discovered. Shelters would need to be set up for various reasons, mostly for feeding survivors and responders.

Immediately, one of the local schools was set up for families of the missing to endure the long wait to see if their loved one(s) were on the list of bodies recovered. I tried to get back there just before the top of the hour every hour and look at the list so I could take each family into a room set aside for this reason and break the news to them, rather than they seeing the name of their loved one appear on an impersonal sheet of paper. But the hours rolled on, and with other responsibilities at hand, local pastors assisted with this task. What a terrific blessing were those pastors and others from the community who assisted in so many ways.

By late afternoon of that first day, the main staging area had been transformed into substations, alleviating unnecessary traffic going into the main area. Fire and EMS (Emergency Medical Services) reported to the fire station. Government officials met at the city building. Others, such as the Red Cross and people helping out with feeding the masses, were located in one of the school gymnasiums.

With all this happening, it just so happened to be the first day of a summer quarter class I was scheduled to teach at what is now Belmont College. There was no way I could be gone that long, so I drove the twenty-five miles to school, introduced myself to the class, went over the syllabus, canceled the class, and returned to Shadyside. I would discuss my decision with my supervisor the following day. The school officials were very supportive and agreed to pay me for my two classes that week and canceled the second class for me. The following two weeks, I would leave Shadyside, head to school, stop by home on the way back for a quick meal, and then return to Shadyside for a few hours, before heading back home for an average of about two hours of sleep.

For two weeks, I would spend only enough time at my office to sign employees' time slips and whatever other forms needed reviewing and signing. Traveling became a hazard. It was becoming more and more difficult to stay awake. On the second Friday of the event, I drove to work and made it to a picnic table outside the back entrance. I don't know how much time passed before I heard a voice telling me it was raining, and I needed to come inside. I did what I needed to do, such as submit my time card and sign the cards of those who I supervised. Then I was back on the road again.

That first day was hectic but extremely well organized. As search crews began returning, it became evident this was not just a little-larger-than-ordinary flash flood. Early on, names began to appear on the list of bodies that had been discovered.

One incident concerning the list turned out on a positive note. A gentleman approached me at the school. I remembered him from my high school graduating class. Larry asked me if I would look for a certain name on the list. I remembered him from school as a tough guy, although not a bully. That day, I witnessed the "other side" of him. He couldn't bear to see his friend's name on the list. I checked for her name. Fortunately, it was not on the list. I checked on the hourly revision. Still not there. Then Larry came up to me with tears in his eyes, gave me a hug, and told me his friend had been found—alive!

Stories such as this weren't plentiful. But this was one of the exceptions. Unfortunately, the longer a name was missing from the list but the person had not been found, the greater the odds the name would eventually be added.

I spent as much time in that small room as possible on June 15. I knew most of the victims' names would appear on the list early that morning and throughout the day. Available ministers and I would perform the unenviable task of notifying friends and families of the deceased as the list grew by the hour.

While local media were very respectful to emergency and political leaders, those from the large cities were sometimes a different story. Two particular incidents come to mind. One of the major television news giants was purchasing written passes from residents that allowed them to get to their homes if the homes still existed and the roads there were traversable. Passes sold for up to $500. While some of the blame is shared by those who sold their passes, it proves the power of the media to bribe those who are the victims of whatever caused the story they seek.

The other issue was much more personal. A mother whose young daughter was missing was brought to one of the Shadyside schools and placed in a room away from others. She was tremendously distraught and became violent. The local emergency squad had offered to transport her to the hospital in nearby Bellaire. But she adamantly refused. I was asked to attempt to console her. That wasn't going to happen. As I attempted to calm her down, she became more agitated.

Fortunately, a local minister appeared. We ended up being forced to hold her down. We took turns, one holding her down on a wrestling mat that had been provided, while the other tried to talk to her. Then we would switch. Neither of us could console her.

Suddenly, I looked up and a reporter from a Cleveland television station was standing at the door filming the event. I happened to be the one who was talking to the woman at the moment. I jumped up and grabbed the camera. This wasn't a direct feedback to Cleveland. It was what I call a "newsreel" camera, meaning there was actually film in the camera. I told the reporter to remove the film.

He disregarded the "request." Now it was an order. "Remove the film, or I'll trash the camera!"

He tested me one last time. I raised the camera above my head, and just before I was ready to smash it onto the floor, he yelled for me to wait. I held the camera while he disengaged the film. Otherwise, I am quite sure he would have taken the camera and ran with the film intact. There is no doubt in my mind that the woman's reaction would have been telecast all over Ohio and probably to the entire nation as well.

I turned to the minister and told him I thought I had figured out why the grieving mother wouldn't allow the squad to transport her to the hospital.

I went out to find the missing/recovered list. Her daughter was still listed as missing. When I told her that her daughter wasn't at the hospital, she finally agreed to be transported. My belief was that she was afraid her daughter's body was at the morgue at City Hospital in Bellaire. She couldn't have handled that situation, being there while her daughter's body was nearby.

Were there victims taken to the morgue? I don't know if the local hospital could handle anything except those who had passed away while in the hospital (which to my knowledge did not happen). It wasn't up to me to release information as to where bodies were taken. I'll just give credit to all the local funeral home directors who handled the situation in an extremely professional manner and served the community in ways most residents are still not cognizant of.

I might be the only one who disagrees with the number officially named as victims of the June 14, 1990 flood. A mother who would cross to the West Virginia side of the river less than a year later and end her own life because she could not deal with the loss of her daughter, to me, was the twenty-seventh victim.

Chapter 23

"There's got to be a morning after
If we can hold on through the night."

—theme from The Poseidon Adventure, *sung by Maureen
McGovern and written by Al Kasha and Joel Hirschhorn*

As we Americans experienced in 2001, "There's got to be a
morning after." That morning after was September 12. For war
veterans, the morning after was the first morning we woke up
in a bed that was somewhere on American soil. It might have been
following a tour in Germany, France, or Africa; in Korea or Vietnam;
in Iraq or Afghanistan; or in any of the other far-off place our heroes
have served. But the "morning after" in Shadyside, Ohio, was June
15, 1990.

If anyone asked me to run through a list of things that transpired
on day two, it would be impossible. I do know it was one of the most
hectic events I ever experienced. On one hand, people performed
admirably. But as time moved on ever so slowly, certain individuals
who represented their agencies began to disrupt the process. I'll say
again that, overall, for an event of this magnitude, the commissioners;
Dick Quinlin; Mark Badia, who served as incident commander for
fire/EMS; Shadyside Fire Department's fire chief; and many others
would make the county proud. Of course, many politicians were
heavily involved. Many times, I bit my tongue when asked about

politicians. But local, state, and even federal officials played an extremely positive role. Quinlin was told by the county commissioners to acquire whatever resources he needed, and the politicians would sort out who was going to foot the bills at a later time.

The county commissioners told Quinlin to do the best he could to not break the county but to call in any and all resources he deemed necessary. Longtime commissioner Mel Sargus handed Dick money and told him to go get a hot lunch at a local restaurant. He declined, saying, "Thank you, Mel, but I would rather eat with the volunteers and other workers." He was referring to those who were being served meals through local churches, restaurants, and other organizations.

While I had no part in logistics and fiscal concerns, I will say that promises were kept. Belmont County did not go broke over decisions that were made and carried out. I will not name the person or the agency she represented, but as things moved on—and I did everything I could to accommodate everyone from every agency—one person took over half of one of the gymnasiums. There was literally tons of clothing being brought in. Granted, many of the people who were displaced were willing to wear almost anything that fit them. However, a lot of clothing, blankets, and other donations basically amounted to trash that couldn't be sold at yard sales. I was able to acquire volunteers to sort through the donations and separate articles that were not worth taking up space. Things were going smooth until this person requested trucks to begin hauling articles to a dump far from the area. The trash was one thing, but the volunteers were doing a great job sorting usable items from that which was utterly useless. Many items were not being sorted, even though there were volunteers waiting for each load to be brought in. Good, wearable items were being sent to the dump because one person demanded that most items be considered as trash.

When I complained about the situation I was told I could not override decisions made by an international organization. I knew Dick Quinlin had much more important things on his mind than a dispute that might seem petty to some. On one hand, this could be considered petty. On the other hand, my job was to overlook all agencies and control usage of space, which was at a premium. We were dealing with an onslaught of people and very little space in such a small town. Eventually, I was able to meet up with Dick, and he assured me I heard right when I was told what I was there for.

I couldn't stop the truck that was already loaded. But now, with so much more space made available with well over half the clothing gone, I ordered the agency to relinquish three-quarters of the space it had taken over. Of course, that didn't sit well, but I immediately moved other agencies into the space provided. This pretty well took care of all the space needed for all agencies not pertaining to first responders.

The worst part of dealing with the particular agency was when I was told we had enough pizza, so I should tell local pizza shops to stop bringing pizza. She said it was "junk food." When you are trying to feed hundreds of people, you don't hear of anyone refusing good hot pizza. It isn't like we were expecting steak dinners or we had a menu to choose from.

Unfortunately, the woman who had originally been assigned to this position and who represented the local chapter of the agency had been doing a sensational job. I have no idea why the agency had chosen to have someone come in and replace her (most likely, internal politics were at play). But it was the beginning of a learning process for me and, hopefully, for others. Keep it local in a disaster! All help is appreciated by those affected. However, local people are even more effective because "they are one of us."

Then came the fiasco with a federal agency that had sent a gentleman from Chicago. We got along well until he decided to take over the space at the city building that I had provided for the Department of Human Services. I had set up a desk with two chairs on one side and five chairs on the other. I needed space for two caseworkers. They would be dealing with several programs for each client. Food stamps was a federal program. Aid for dependent children was a state program. Plus, there was a county program for single persons in need.

That arrangement failed to meet his approval. The five chairs led to a problem. I was told there was only space for two other chairs, and he moved three chairs and extended his "office space" to where the chairs had been.

When he returned from a meeting, the original setup was back in place. Equipment was rearranged, and the other three chairs were brought back, which led to a somewhat heated discussion.

He made the mistake of asking me why I was so adamant about the three chairs. I told him there were chairs for two parents and three children. Also, when a larger family appeared, more chairs would be brought in temporarily and then removed after the interview. I had purposely waited for him to ask the question about the number of chairs. Psychologically, this placed him on the defensive. I had him right where I wanted him! I then asked him where he was from.

"Chicago," he replied.

"Where do you work when you aren't working for FEMA?"

"I work for a major greeting card company. I write the verses for the cards."

My reply, "Then you should understand people's feelings!"

"What's your point?"

Again, I had him right where I wanted him when I said, "You see, when you return home, you're done with this assignment. It's only a faded memory. You worked with a bunch of strangers. You won't remember one name. You will be done here."

Again, "What's your point?"

"You see, these are my people. I've worked with them. I've coached their kids in sports. I coached one of the victims in Pony League baseball. I sat with his family in a little room yesterday while they prayed Scott would be found alive. You don't know how I felt when I walked back in that little room and shed tears with them when their worst fear was confirmed. Who knows? Someday, I might be sitting on the other side of this desk. I would hope whoever was sitting in my position now would provide chairs for my children. Are you willing to tell parents who have just lost everything that you're going to separate them from their children?"

I give him credit for dropping the issue and saying, "I never looked at it that way."

My point was made, and an argument was avoided! He had not, and he could not have looked at it from the personal perspective that anyone in my position had. He did not remove the chairs again. He and I then worked well together from that point on. When his work was done at Shadyside, he got word to me that it was his last day there. I managed to free myself of other duties and went to see him off. I was very satisfied that we shook hands, and his departure came on a friendly basis. I was not there to show authority or to piss people off. I was simply carrying out my assignment. His assignment here was finished successfully with no lingering negative feelings

At that point, I could never have realized that my decision-making and, even more, my follow-up actions, would lead to promotions and to life-changing events later in my careers (both professionally and as a volunteer with emergency management).

Chapter 24

"My God, my God, why hast Thou forsaken me?"

—Matthew 27:46b

And then came an event that made me question my decision-making for years after. It was the day I did what I had sworn in November 1968 I would never do again.

Because of my role over the previous ten days or so, Quinlin requested I be able to do a flyover above the affected area in an Ohio State Patrol helicopter. Of course, political dignitaries and such had first dibs, as if they were in line for a flight over the Grand Canyon.

One early evening, I had just sat down for dinner with my family for the first time in a week and a half when the phone rang. My chance had come as a take-it-or-leave-it opportunity. "We have about a fifteen-minute window of opportunity before a front comes in to get a chopper in the air and back safely."

It was decision time for the old Vietnam vet who had sworn his flying days were over. I had no fear of dying but, rather, of what it would be like on the way down during the crash. But I had ... well, it's difficult to say ... I had a good time flying in choppers in Nam; here there was no danger of being shot down.

"I'll be there in less than fifteen minutes!"

Out the door, into the car, and down old Winding Hill Road, I was onto State Route 7 and into the landing zone at the south end of Shadyside in ten minutes.

The chopper was nothing like what I had experienced before. It was very small with a glass "bubble" that ran from where the top of a windshield would be in a car to under the feet. It didn't seem very sturdy, but if the patrol used these things daily, then the pilots trusted them; and that was good enough for me.

Up we went and headed east. I had never used headphones in a chopper before, and it took a few moments before I was able to get used to speaking with my lips practically touching the mic. I was up front in the only seat other than the pilot, and a gentleman from the Ohio State Emergency Management Agency was in the only seat behind us.

I had never seen the area from above but was very familiar with the roads and outlay of the terrain. As we circled the outer perimeter of the affected area and headed west, things looked bad, but nothing like what was to come.

Although the rain had come down in torrents and soaked the land, the outlying area residents were victims of washed-out driveways, severe basement flooding, and damage that might seem devastating to the property owners. But circling left began the visions that took me back to Nam. Houses were not only moved from foundations but had actually been swept downstream. Parts of mobile homes, cars, appliances, trees, and objects normally considered immovable found their way down the affected streams and many into the river. Even a bathtub had floated into the river containing a young girl who was subsequently rescued. It was a miracle for a family that had little hope of having their little girl's body recovered, let alone seeing her alive again. Others were less fortunate, as several bodies had been swept into the Ohio River, some downstream to the Hannibal Locks and Dam. One farm was left devastated, and even the river was strewn with corpses of cattle and other farm animals.

The fear of flying was long passed by now. Those words of Jesus as He was suffering and dying on the cross rang out to me. I could hear the voices of those crying out just days before, directly below me, uttering those same words, "My God, my God, why hast Thou forsaken me?"

A woman I worked with told the story of her sister and two nephews being washed away in their mobile home. Vickie was in Columbus at a training for the agency's new computer system that week. She was sent a message to return home immediately. I don't know exactly what she was told, but I do know why she was summoned home.

As the water in the creek roared, Vickie's father heard the noise and knew something was amiss. He hurried to his daughter's porch and began pounding on the door. He could see his daughter washing dishes and his two grandsons playing in the adjoining room. None of them heard him, and he just stepped off the porch and scurried toward his own home, which was at a slightly higher elevation. He watched in horror as his daughter and grandsons were swept to their death, perishing before his very eyes. He had barely escaped death, as he stepped off the porch just in time to avoid the rampant waters.

At the funeral home, I signed the visitor log but chose not to go in the room to view the bodies. I had a lot of work to do yet and felt it would be better if I wasn't picturing the lifeless bodies of a nine- and eleven-year-old.

By this time, response mode had ended, and recovery (the last phase in disaster protocol) had begun. It was time for cleanup. In such a massive recovery project, there were headaches upon headaches. Townships were overruled by county policy. County was overruled by state. And of course, all were subject to the Federal Emergency Management Agency's (FEMA) regulations. Fortunately, I had very little involvement in this phase, but I was constantly aware of the turmoil.

This isn't to say anyone was wrong, as everyone did their best to remove all obstacles. This included thousands of tons of woody debris (from trees, homes, sheds, and so on); metal; and flammable liquids, such as gasoline or motor oil; and even ammunition. Many people in this area were hunters and practiced firing weapons so they legally had ammo in their homes. Spoiled food became a hazard. The list goes on.

The recovery period lasted for months. By the time the leaves began their yearly descent to their final destination, some sense of normalcy prevailed. Of course, this doesn't minimize the psychological aspect of dealing with the loss of loved ones. And the many had been forced to move in with relatives or seek public housing until other arrangements could be made to restore or rebuild homes.

Many occupants did not have flood insurance, and their losses were totally non-reimbursable. However, though I was very sympathetic with the plight of those misplaced, my involvement had ended, and I was back to investigating welfare fraud and teaching in the evenings.

Chapter 25

"Now this is not the end. It is not even the beginning but it is perhaps, the end of the beginning."

—Sir Winston Churchill

Life is a story of twists and turns. One day, some of us awaken to find the result of all those twists and turns. For some, it is regrettable. Some wake up one morning and decide they cannot deal with what those twists and turns have dealt them. Others go on reliving what they have been dealt, living in constant misery.

Having dealt with the nightmares from post-traumatic stress, the loss of two terrific jobs, a divorce (which included the loss of my two children), my mother's death and then my sister's subsequent death, and the loneliness of living in an apartment with the thermostat set just high enough to keep pipes from freezing, three events would end the old and present me with a new beginning.

Although I had known Linda from my employment, we began a new chapter in our lives. After Mom died, I needed someone to cut grass at her home until I sold it. I offered Linda's son Jason the job, and Linda brought him down once a week. As we talked during those times, we got to know each other better, and an even closer friendship developed.

Soon after that came the second event, which was the call to ministry. This gave me goals to work on and kept me busy. But I thought it was only one ministry to which I would be called. An end to my "old life" had developed into a new beginning. I still lived a life of emotional and physical pain due to the PTSD and back problems. Neuropathy and restless leg syndrome were getting close to unbearable. Keeping barbiturates (prescription) to a bare minimum, I dealt with the pain day and night with medications other than "painkillers" (such as Tylenol). I vowed to keep active and just bear the pain.

Then came the offer to set up and supervise the Belmont County Critical Incident Stress Debriefing team, which I mentioned previously. Affirming that one of my bachelor's degrees was in psych and one of my master's degrees was in counseling, Dick Quinlin asked me if I had ever heard of CISD, or critical incident stress debriefing. I wouldn't need the degree to attend classes and to assist with debriefings, but a master's degree was necessary to become a team coordinator.

I confirmed that I'd never heard of the program. He had been introduced to the program at an EMA directors' yearly convention. Dick explained a little about it and asked if I would be interested in attending classes and possibly forming a team. I decided to take a shot at it. The two main courses were scheduled soon in Pittsburgh. Each was an eight-hour class. The problem was that I didn't have the money to pay for the classes and lodging. I could have driven home and back after the initial class. But the classes were on a weekday, and it was in an area of very congested traffic. I know those of you familiar with Pittsburgh are saying, "There isn't an area of Pittsburgh that isn't bogged down daily with traffic." But this area had a lot of construction, and I wasn't familiar with that part of the city.

Belmont County agreed to reimburse me for mileage, but that didn't amount to much in this case. I contacted the Upper Ohio Valley Presbytery of which I am a member. The presbytery agreed to pay a third of my expenses if Key Bethel Church's session would agree to cover another third and with the stipulation that I would pay the other third. At that time, there was money available for continued education allowance through the presbytery, as the economy was still stable. So, off to Pittsburgh I went, and my CISD career began its infancy stage.

As a side note, at this time, the program was known as CISD (debriefing) rather than CISM (management). At a later course I took in South Carolina, I addressed Jeffrey Mitchell, founder of the organization, telling him I used "management" rather than "debriefing," as we used more than one application. He later changed the name to "management," as many more team leaders had approached him on this issue. (I don't have the ego to believe I singularly convinced him to make the change.) In his infinite wisdom, he, as founder of the organization, was aware of the advancement of the program—the extent of which he had probably never imagined.

Dr. Jeffrey Mitchell saw the need for the program he'd created as a fireman in Baltimore. His story is very interesting and inspiring. I won't delve into his history, as I am not attempting to tell his story. It can be found through many resources by googling his name or "critical incident stress management" or visiting the International Critical Incident Stress Foundation (ICISF) website. My endeavors within the program are what I have done as an individual and not necessarily within ICISF guidelines. An example is, when I train first responders in managing stress, I am not instructing under ICISF. I am not a certified trainer under the organization. Nor do I profess to be. Under my own education and experiences, I can acquire CEUs for my students, and I make sure I legally separate my ICISF credentials from my individual presentations. Having said that, I credit ICISF with many of the skills I have learned. I am simply stating that I do not want to legally complicate issues, as I am working under separate issues. I use the Mitchell method and represent ICISF when I, or my team, debrief first responders after stressful events.

Back to Pittsburgh. I attended the classes and by obtaining the credentials needed, became Belmont County critical incident stress management coordinator. I also became a member of the Belmont County chaplain team and eventually became coordinator of that team also. The two teams worked hand in hand. But again, for program purposes, we did not introduce religion into debriefings.

"Now this is not the end. It is not even the beginning of the end but it is, perhaps, the end of the beginning." I could find no more appropriate words to fit my situation than these from Sir Winston Churchill. What had seemed like the end of everything for me wasn't the end after all.

As "the end of the old beginning", the new beginning would happen and could not have happened for me if my life experiences (good and bad) had not occurred. The old and the new had intertwined. The old painfully integrated into the new.

There is a time we must accept the fact that things will never go back to what once was. An apparent end transforms into a new beginning. Did it make a brand-new me? Impossible. But as old issues were beginning to somewhat resolve themselves, a new version of the old began to transpire. My ministries opened up a new purpose for me. The cocoon hadn't produced a butterfly, but it had begun a new chapter with a new purpose.

Chapter 26

"There are different kinds of gifts. But they are all given to believers by the same Spirit. There are different ways to serve. But they all come from the same Lord. There are different ways the Spirit works. But the same God is working in all these ways and in all people."

—1 Corinthians 12:4–6

To believe I could preach without the Holy Spirit from the pulpit—or console an individual over a personal loss or direct events related to first responders without that guidance—would be an act of heresy. It is the same Spirit that gives us the gifts God decides are appropriate for each of us as individuals. Often, as in my case, these may not be the ones we would have requested or even hoped for. To pray for a gift from the Spirit is fruitless. He, and only He, decides which gift or gifts we will receive. A common fallacy among Christians is that, "I have never received one of those gifts." If you believe, then God will lead you to do His will in at least one venue. Sometimes, it is difficult for a Christian to recognize one of these gifts. We think it is either something we have trained hard for and accomplished on our own or something that just happened, and we don't recognize the source. At some point, we need to put on the brakes of life's speeding locomotive and look at why we made the decisions we did and who got us through the preparations to receive the gift.

Another fallacy is to believe we can pick and choose the gifts we deem most suitable for ourselves. If I was obnoxious enough to ask God for a gift, it would be the gift of music. I tried to learn music at an early age. I tried several musical instruments and, even up to a couple years ago, tried to get the hang of playing a guitar. My problem—Mr. T just can't get the hang of reading music.

I could pray for that as a gift, but I know better. That isn't what God chose for me. I am thankful he chose to present me with more than one gift as it is. Who am I that I should defy scripture and ask for more?

Satan has tempted me several times to ask for the gift of being able to play music, not to mention read it. The only tunes I can decipher are those I am familiar with because I've heard them over and over. I couldn't possibly, by any stretch of the imagination, pick up a hymnal and begin singing. Just to make sure the devil doesn't get through to me, I wasn't given a voice for singing anyway. To make things worse, my four neck surgeries necessitated the surgeons to go through my throat, and after one verse of "Anchors Aweigh" my voice is shot.

So, I know to accept the gifts with which the Spirit has presented me, and I am totally satisfied (not that I would complain if music was added).

When I speak of the gifts I've been blessed with, I am in no way bragging or taking any credit of my own. I believe that, if you brag about something you do well, then you mistakenly credit yourself and discredit and disrespect the Holy Spirit. Then it is Satan who takes credit for the gift. And he is very willing and able to do just this. Yes, I am pleased with my accomplishments and some of my actions, but it would be blasphemy if I took the credit or if I pounded my chest and bragged that I was responsible for my accomplishments. Even in many of my failures and my darkest moments, I have learned valuable lessons I had no way of teaching myself. Look at your bad days and learn a lesson God is providing you. I only have to go back to the deaths of my mother and sister to realize God gave both of them a blessing, and He gave me a valuable lesson. Neither of them died in a nursing home, and I was there with them in their homes when the angel of mercy arrived, all because I had lost my employment due to the two spinal injuries I sustained.

The first gift I was aware of came early in life. I had no idea why I wanted to join the navy so badly and become a corpsman. But as it ended up, I couldn't have accomplished more if I had been a Navy SEAL. The Holy Spirit, unbeknownst to me, had presented me with one of the greatest gifts a young sailor could receive. Again, no credit toward myself. The gift of "healing" was slowly being introduced to me. It wasn't complete yet. It was a long, drawn-out process of learning medical, lifesaving, and comforting skills I would end up practicing the remainder of my life.

One might argue that *healing* is not specifically listed in any translation of the Bible (at least not in any I am aware of). However, in my humble opinion, not being a theologian, I believe healing is a conglomeration of several gifts. Those include the recognition of the power of prayer, knowing what to pray for, and knowing how to pray in a particular situation, all of which are topped off through faith. Combined, these present as the gift of being in a state of grace. Jesus referred to this when he stated in Acts 1:8, "But you will receive power when the Holy Spirit comes upon you."

I furthered my skills through neuropsychiatric school. And my advanced education enabled me to not only comfort soldiers in time of deep distress but also, at times, talk individuals out of attempting suicide and possibly harming others.

Serving on a psychiatric unit aboard a Navy hospital ship sounded like a fairly easy assignment under combat pay. Some of it was very easy, while combat stress sent more marines than usual to the unit when action in the field intensified. During those times, which was more often than not, incoming casualties also rose to extreme levels.

With the constant sounding of, "Flight quarters," which meant unloading casualties, living, and KIA those (killed in action), stress levels became highly significant. Corpsmen were working regular shifts of their specialty and getting very little rest due to incoming casualties. It would have been great to have men assigned to that specific duty. Yet, each one of us was dedicated to saving as many lives as possible. These men wore a different uniform than we did, yet we were brothers fighting for the same cause. Note that I still have no idea what that cause was!

Many times, the moment of healing was within moments of the soldier arriving in triage. Life-and-death decisions were made more times there than doctors face in a normal hospital setting. Sometimes they hit as often as incoming rounds. You never knew how many were coming in or where they were coming from. To this day, I wonder how many of the medical staff who were Christians realize the gift they were given. It is sad to hear someone tell how they saved a life and gave no credit to anyone but themselves. I have "assisted" in saving lives countless times throughout my time as a navy corpsman and at least three times afterward as a civilian. In each situation, I could only perform under the guidance of the Spirit because, "Apart from me ye can do nothing" (John 15:5). As a counselor, the Spirit has led me down many paths with a suicidal first responder or any individual contemplating ending their life because the stressors of life have become overburdening.

Speaking of gifts, in researching various scriptures, I ran across a Catholic website that claims the Roman Catholic Church does not list healing as one of the gifts of the Spirit. (This is only a notation here and not in any way a disagreement with any religious beliefs.) The resources I visited use scripture from Isaiah, Romans, Corinthians, and Ephesians to come up with a list of these gifts. Different translations can complicate things when studying the Bible. I will not attempt here to go into what those far above me in theology may attempt to decipher. Whether you want to call this counsel, understanding, or wisdom, it doesn't matter to me. I call it a combination of whatever the Spirit presents at that particular time. I will let God define whatever it is to be called because this mere mortal has nothing to do with it except following what is laid out by a far superior being. God uses us for the good of others in a way where He is supreme commander, and we only choose whether or not to let him overcome an earthly moment to participate in the glory in which He heals someone.

When the Elders of the church practice "laying of hands," I lead in the prayer for healing. But my last commentary in the prayer is that God provides healing in the way He sees fit, which isn't always exactly what we intend to pray for. Many times, that prayer is answered by the person dying very soon. In that case, God answers in His way of relieving pain and suffering because He knows how miserable the person and the person's family would continue to be. So, death can be a relief, rather than a curse. Too often, I have submitted to a dying loved one or parishioner's request to ask God to take him or her into His eternal hands and relieve them from their physical suffering. But still, I utter those words, "If it be Your will."

To this day, I believe my gift of healing was embedded in my experience of James Williams. Much of my life is predicated in those few moments aboard a ship, half a world away from home. God led me to understand what a dying young marine was trying to communicate to me. With only one guess remaining before this voice was forever silenced, God led me to understand that one word—*prayer.*

Most Americans are familiar with FDR's speech drawing us into WWII, "a date that will live in infamy." That date, of course, was December 7, 1941. Just twenty-six years and twenty days later, I was to have the Holy Spirit interpret a single word that, to me, will be locked into my memory.

My perspective of 'healing' is quite different than that of so-called "faith healers." I am not arguing against them in any way. Most of them say they are healing through the Spirit, and I certainly give them credit for that. But, first of all, who is to say it is my wish and my prayer that will be answered in the way I want? I cannot argue a person's fate when God is in control. Therefore, in praying for healing, I am making no attempt to change God's will for a person or situation. However, I certainly believe in the power of prayer. I have felt the presence of the prayers of others while near death in a hospital bed. If those prayers weren't pleasing to God, I would not have felt their presence.

Which prayers does God choose to answer? And which does he hear but reject? I guess those with the gift of "piety" might come closest to answering the question. The word *piety* is defined in my thesaurus as "the quality of being religious or reverent."

While I certainly consider myself "religious," I do not consider myself as having the gift of "reverence." That sounds confusing, but I submit that that gift belongs to those who are much more knowledgeable of the scriptures than myself. I only took one class on religion in my eighteen years of formal education. That was because, in order to graduate from a Catholic college, I had to take at least one course based on the Catholic religion. It ended up being more of a history class, which made it much easier for me to get an A. I jokingly submit that, if it would have been a class on Catholic doctrine, I would probably have failed the course.

So, back to the definition of piety. I believe every Christian (as opposed to so-called Christians) has the gift of piety, just by virtue of having been baptized into the death of Jesus Christ and having accepted him as Lord and Savior. (What type of baptism is accepted by God is a matter of each individual's own belief). One last thing I would offer is that saying you're religious and God's acceptance of your religion may be two different aspects of acceptance. Fortunately, I can leave it at that because I am not the one to judge whether or not you are actually religious. Neither am I to judge the eternal acceptance of religions other than my own. My hope for each person is that you will be led by the Spirit to believe and do what God leads you to do, and you will be judged on that premise. I also believe that goes for me too. I will not be judged compared to your beliefs and actions, so please do not judge me according to yours.

Chapter 27

"Assisting those who experience normal reactions to abnormal events."

—goal of the Belmont County Critical Incident Stress Management Team, taken from ICISF

I mentioned critical incident stress management in chapters 18 and 23. International Critical Incident Stress Foundation (ICISF) is an international agency of which the Belmont County, Ohio, team is affiliated. Any remarks stated within this book are those practiced by our local team (Belmont County) and neither reflect in any way nor are meant to coincide with rules, regulations, or practices of any group or individuals, whether related to ICISF or any other organization.

I previously mentioned my classes are not labeled or intended to be a part of ICISF. We do adhere to ICISF guidelines and attempt to honor all regulations and practices under its guidelines. However, if any practice not in complete adherence to those regulations is mentioned, it is not meant to reflect on ICISF but, instead, solely on Belmont County CISM. In other words, any team in almost any situation has to make the best decision in critical circumstances and do the best it can. While all my ICISF training has been extremely comprehensive, there is always an event that has some component that has not been explicitly addressed. In those situations, the leader takes responsibility for making the most adequate decision according to his or her training and experiences. And it is, therefore, possible that the decision would not be the one ICISF would have made. We do our best according to ICISF and other trainings we have attended, to accommodate each first responder to the best of our ability in each incident.

I previously described the inception of the Belmont County CISM team. After several classes in several eastern states, I decided it was time to roll out the proverbial carpet and get the team rolling.

We already had a chaplain team in place, so Denny was already onboard. As a fireman who was familiar with Jeffrey Mitchell from the Baltimore, Maryland, Fire Department, he was the only one in the county who was familiar with CISM. He headed up the chaplain team until I took over those reins a year or two later. He remained a member of the CISM team, but health issues kept him from being active.

After training Brad Johnston, who had joined the call to ministry at about the same time I did, I was able to get some help with calls. Technically, Brad was a member of the peer support part of the team because he had no formal ICISF training at that time.

Next came Tony Johnson, who was employed at the local state rehabilitation center (prison) or BECI (Belmont Correctional Institution). I had met Tony when the facility opened, and I toured the prison with Dick Quinlin and a few EMA staff members. Dick and I were invited by the warden for a few training sessions and were on scene for an actual incident, at which time we were placed in the incident command center.

In conversation with the warden, I learned the prison had its own version of a critical response team for staff, used during and after incidents such as riots. It was then that the warden summoned Tony and introduced us. I immediately accepted my new friend as a partner of our team. Tony, who is a hostage negotiator, has an electrifying personality. He has become a true friend and a valuable team member.

During a severe flooding incident in 1998 in the small town of

Barton, Ohio, Brad and Tony both proved early on that they had my back when things went downhill. In the late evening of the first day of the flood, we were told the governor of Ohio was flying in to visit the scene. I expected a Blackhawk helicopter, as that was the usual mode of transportation for government officials. Lo and behold, here came the *chop-chop*, *swish*, *swish* of a Huey helicopter. The scene and the incident immediately took me away from my task at hand. Back came USS *Repose* and the choppers landing on the flight deck, all over again. I didn't do anything irrational, but Brad immediately saw the "thousand-yard stare" I emitted. Though Brad was second in command (CISM), he immediately gave me a gentle about-face shove and told me to go home for a few hours.

Fortunately, he was quite aware of my history and was doing me a huge favor. I went home, changed into my swim trunks, and headed to the hot tub in pouring down rain. After forty-five minutes or so, I got out, showered, and watched a few innings of a Cleveland Indians baseball game on TV for another hour. By then I had recovered and left to return to Barton, which was only about twenty minutes from home.

I realize this sounds strange to most people who haven't dealt with PTSD. Those who have experienced it or are familiar with those suffering from it understand it only takes one stressor during a certain event to take the one who suffers from it back to its point of origin. Had I known a Huey was to arrive that evening, I would have prepared for it by going to the fire station until it landed. It was the unexpected that triggered the alarm. Most will not understand that it is the sound and not the sight of the Huey that affects me. I would like to explain that to you, but I can't and won't even attempt an explanation.

Learning to cope with PTSD and overcoming it are two completely different animals. Coping is minimizing the affects, knowing when to back off for a while and clear your mind. Thank God, I am able to do that, but it doesn't make it any easier when the moment strikes.

After returning to the scene, I stayed all evening into the next morning, with a gentleman whose wife had been swept away in the flash flood. A counselor from another county agency, and I took turns sitting with him. Word finally came that she had been swept about seven miles downstream into the Ohio River. Her body had been discovered by a search and rescue crew assigned to the river. The woman I was working with told the man about his wife. It was heartbreaking, but at least he had affirmation of what he knew the result would be. One consoling detail was that her clothing was mostly intact and that her body, amazingly, had not been dismembered or damaged significantly.

I spent the rest of that morning at the family residence notifying other family members and friends.

This was where Tony Johnson was initiated with the team. Tony was the only member who was not at the scene all night. The fire chief requested a debriefing during the second evening of the event. Brad and I had been too involved in the event to be a part of a debriefing, let alone act as leader.

I knew the fire chief well. "Mick" and I were friends and had known each other as first responders for several years. I explained who I had in mind to lead the debriefing. There was only one potential problem that presented itself with the situation.

Barton is a small town hidden in the hills of the Ohio side of the Appalachian Mountains. It is what we call a motorcycle town or "redneck" zone.

I asked Mick, the Barton fire chief, to let Tony come down to lead a debriefing as Brad and I were too involved at the scene. A quick call to the warden, and Tony was available to leave for part of his afternoon shift for as long as we needed him. I had no fear whatsoever that things would not work out, since nobody knew Tony. I introduced Tony, and the rest was history.

The emotions of the first responders were calm, and the debriefing was a total success. The Lord had a vision that something good would come out of this disaster. Sometimes, we don't accept a person or group because we have never been introduced to them. The Lord had led me to use my experiences in Southeast Asia to teach people that because others look "different" from us doesn't mean we are right, and they are wrong. Hopefully, all of us learned a valuable lesson, one way or the other as we experienced the hand of the Lord in action that night.

John Looney, whom I previously mentioned as my VA counselor, serves as the team's clinical director. Our friendship goes back about twenty-five years. He is a valuable member of the team, although job duties limit his ability to respond except in critical instances.

Each team must have a director with a master's degree in counseling or psychology and a clinical director currently employed in that field with the same credentials. John fills that requirement. He has called me several times to assist him with debriefings on the West Virginia side of the river. One was requested by a SWAT (special weapons and tactics) team, after a person well known to them had literally blown his head off while standing directly in front of several members of the team.

When we had a horrendous (oil) well field death in Belmont County, I had been called to the scene, where I talked to all the workers who were present at the scene of the accident. Later that day, I received a call from the oil company and was asked to hold a debriefing the following morning. I called John and told him there would be between sixty and eighty workers there, and I needed help badly.

There existed extenuating circumstances, as company owners were flying in from states such as Texas, Louisiana, Arkansas, and Oklahoma. Typically, they would not be allowed to attend a debriefing, as they hadn't been on the scene during the event. Because they had dealt directly with the family of the deceased, I made an exception and allowed them to be included in the debriefing.

I prayed we could deal with the massive number of workers/owners. This was a first for me. I had dealt with a lot of issues concerning debriefings, but this massive number was an extraordinary challenge. We couldn't break it down into groups, as time was an issue, with the multiple companies involved. With a lot of prayer and experience behind us, we pulled it off. Afterward, everyone was very appreciative and seemed to be dealing much better with the tragedy than when they had first entered the building.

One thing that impressed me was the concern for the family of the deceased, some six hundred miles away. The assurance by the company owners that the family was being taken care of in very capable hands quelled the workers' fears. I wonder if those fears were based partly on a question that would easily come to mind at a time like that. What if that victim was me? How would my family be taken care of? That was a question we couldn't have answered ourselves. Trying to do so would have only garnered us lost respect, as we'd have been trying to tell them something we had no proof of and, obviously, would have been making an assumption.

The next member of the team to come along, lo and behold, was the one who'd gotten me into this in the first place. Dick Quinlin had helped me out in debriefings as a peer member who had experience in just about any first responder duty one could think of. Dick had made sure the rest of us went through the entire 700-level class of the incident command structure. Now, we were working together as not only first response but also as follow-up to events.

Darby Copeland became the newest member of the team. He had volunteered with the team for several years. This interest was piqued through the several relevant positions he'd held, including EMT, flight nurse, law enforcement, and membership on different boards concerning first response. He received a doctorate in education and is now the superintendent of a technical school near Pittsburgh.

Despite his employment and first response activities, I could always count on Darby as a peer leader. Known by just about everybody in Belmont and surrounding counties, Darby was the one to receive many CISM calls, rather than EMA or myself. Whenever I didn't understand fully what someone was talking about, I would glance over to Darby, who was much more knowledgeable than any typical first responder.

So, here I was. I had Brad, Tony, Dick, and Darby, each of whom I trusted to be placed in charge of any situation that could possibly arise, day or night. But they were not certified in critical incident stress management. One day, an email from ICISF popped up on my computer screen—ICISF classes were being offered in Pittsburgh. It was like a message from heaven. However, and a huge however, there were two obstacles:

1. The availability of all four of the men for a weekend in February 2019
2. Funding for the classes

Fortunately, the Belmont County Emergency Management Agency had received a grant from one of the gas and oil companies operating in Belmont County. It was not specifically earmarked for anything related to CISM. Through the cooperation of EMA Director Dave Ivan and the company involved, money was set aside for CISM, and all four men were able to clear their schedules for the two days.

I began to wonder if my group of kids were going to graduate from the two classes. Every half hour, my text alert sounded, and I was getting messages that the boys were throwing jelly beans at each other. And I won't repeat some of the ornery messages. At least they were having fun and getting through the classes. They were so experienced in CISM that the necessary classes for certification were a mere formality.

By late afternoon that Sunday, I had four experienced ICISF members who were now legitimate leaders and were allowed (they were all certainly already capable) to conduct debriefings on their own. This was a blessing for me, as I was now relieved that requests for debriefings would no longer necessarily have to be scheduled around my availability, due to both mine and Linda's health. At times, this had been an issue due to my medical conditions and, most recently, Linda's cancer issues.

Lately, we have added Donna Gacek as a peer member and, hopefully, soon as a team leader. Recently, Kellie Bonham completed the ICISF courses and is now a team leader.

One true supporter I would like to mention is the current (as of this writing) Belmont County 9-1-1 director, Bryan Minder. He lists the CISM team in each quarterly newsletter and makes our availability known in as many ways as possible. Past 9-1-1 directors have worked with us but none has been as proactive as Bryan. Having departments aware of our program is the tip of the proverbial iceberg. If nobody knows we are available, we are not going to receive calls. The entire 9-1-1 staff has done a great job in getting the word about our existence out to neighboring counties.

Also, Becky Horne, executive administrative assistant for the Belmont County EMA, has provided help with any and all clerical issues above and beyond those of her job description. Dave Ivan and Glenn Trudo, EMA director and deputy director respectively, have provided invaluable assistance on Belmont County Emergency Management Agency's end.

PART SIX

Chapter 28

"Whether therefore ye eat, or drink, or what so ever ye do,
do all to the glory of God. Give none offence, neither to the
Jews, nor to the Gentiles, nor to the Church of God."

—*1 Corinthians 10:31–32*

As with the previous chapters, the events of this book are not exactly in chronological order. Too many events in my life have overlapped, bisected, and intersected each other, to the point it is impossible to list all events in sequence. So, I decided to select this section to tell some of what I have learned in life. My beliefs may be much different than yours, which is OK. Each of us has experienced different lives. We may have different skin color, opposite political stances, dissimilar economic issues, distinct religious practices, and a thousand other differences I could list. Please respect my differences as I respect yours. If we were all alike, we would be clones. There would be no reason to sit down together to "shoot the shit" (back to military times).

Even identical twins do not have the same life experiences. Therefore, at some point, they see certain things much differently. What a boring life it would be if we all saw everything through the same eyes!

You may believe in the same God I believe in yet still interpret the Bible much differently than I do. You may believe in an entirely different God, as do those in Asia who surrounded me for a year of my life. They were not my enemies because of their religious beliefs. Many who read this may not believe in any God. I do not challenge you on those premises.

This book is my story. As they say, "It is what it is." I couldn't change it any more than you could change your past.

Many Vietnam veterans—no, I should say all of us—have different stories to tell. Some brag about their time spent there. Others refuse to talk about their experiences at all. They will take their story to the grave. I honor those who, like myself, chose after many years to relate to others what the politicians put us through, only to have our troops eventually turn tail and run like hell out of the jungles to the awaiting planes. Many of us who served during that war suffered physically and mentally for the rest of our lives—for nothing but the ego of many politicians, including, in my belief, one Lyndon Baines Johnson. The picture that constantly comes to mind is the sailors on the helicopter carriers pushing the aircraft overboard in order to make room for the South Vietnamese attempting to escape the wrath of the North Vietnamese during the days known as "the fall of Saigon."

I grew up in the Methodist church, and for reasons previously mentioned, I ended up in the Presbyterian Church, USA. The reasons were not at all over philosophical differences, but simply as a matter of convenience. I had no idea, nor did I care what the difference was between the two, or between any other Protestant Churches as far as that was concerned. I had accepted Jesus Christ as my Lord and Savior and am no more concerned than He is with what church an individual chooses to attend. I will qualify that statement by adding that those churches that do not follow scripture and are self-serving are not included in my acceptance of "churches." I will not give an example of those I do not associate with. It is up to God to decide what is acceptable to Him. In the present state of affairs, we are all entitled to our own opinions. I will leave it at that.

As a Christian, I was ridiculed often because I wasn't among the "in crowd," especially once I reached high school age. I didn't smoke or drink and never once touched weed or any illicit drug. I took one drag on a cigarette one night when a bunch of us were camping out below the cemetery. One of the older boys lit it and handed it to me, and I took a drag. It did absolutely nothing for me, and I thought of all my mother had sacrificed for me and my sister. I handed it back and was ridiculed the rest of the night. But I never looked back. I was so proud of myself that I had the nerve the following day to admit to Mom what I had done. To my surprise, she hugged me and told me how proud she was of me. I had just passed one of the early tests of growth and maturity at the age of eleven. Those of you who are smokers, don't take offense here. You have every right to smoke all you desire. Remember, this is my story; it's not about what I think others should or should not do.

No, I'm not trying to convince you that I was or am now an angel. I'm the one who put sand in the constable's gas tank after he harassed us kids night after night for sitting on the sidewalk, which my mother owned. It was evening and not late at night. We weren't loud, and none of the neighbors had ever complained about our presence. One night, Mr. Constable walked up to the corner and began harassing us. Mom came out on the porch, blew up, and really let him have it in front of all of us boys. She told him to get off her property and stay off. He stormed away and went home, which was two houses away, the house he had purchased from Mom after Dad's death. Fortunately, he didn't get a chance to mention to Mom that his cruiser's fuel system was clogged. Years later, when I confessed my deed to Mom, she had a good laugh. So, my angel wings were gone (probably long before that). But I was never in trouble with the law growing up or as an adult.

I attended church regularly until an event that occured aboard ship. My friends Stan and Ray decided to go to Christmas Eve service. Stan being Jewish and Ray Catholic and myself as a Protestant all walked in the chapel together. We got there early and took seats in the second row from the front. Much to our chagrin, when the officers started to arrive we were told we would have to sit in the back. We got up and walked out because we were under the impression that, in church services, rank doesn't matter. My anger wasn't with God. It was with the chaplain who arranged the seating placing rank above all else. I don't remember attending services again aboard ship, yet it was a spiritual encounter aboard the USS *Repose* that would largely define my life and, eventually, my purpose in life—or, I should say, God's purpose for my life. The event I'm referring to is the incident with James E. Williams, Jr.

But the Christian life is about forgiveness. Yes, many memories still haunt me. But none go unforgiven. Yes, LBJ, even you!

Chapter 29

"We command you, brothers and sisters, to keep away from every believer who is idle. We worked night and day, laboring and toiling so that we would not be a burden to any of you. We did this, not because we do not have the right to such help, but in order to offer ourselves as a model for you to imitate. For even when we were with you, we gave you this rule, the one who is unwilling to work shall not eat."

—*2 Thessalonians 3:6–10*

Few people can understand post-traumatic stress disorder. Many create their own diagnosis in an attempt to cover up their misdoings. Just because someone has suffered a traumatic event does not automatically qualify them for such a diagnosis. Yes, they might have nightmares at times, and certain events may trigger fierce memories. It isn't something that presents immediately. Usually, the vivid memories pass in time and dwindle to, more or less, bad memories, relived only at times when extreme stressors appear. Such stressors may trigger memories of past events for a short time and then disappear completely. Unfortunately, this is not always the case.

I am a firm believer that a diagnosis given by a professional such as a psychologist or psychiatrist is not necessarily valid. Many times,

PTSD is a label (rather than a true diagnosis) given to someone who presents as a victim, as it is easily faked without testing. It is easily given as a diagnosis as if the provider is saying, "I don't know what the hell is wrong with you, so I will blame it on past experiences you claim traumatize you."

Everyone, by the time they reach a certain age, has been presented with traumatic experiences. But everyone doesn't necessarily become obsessed with the issue many years down the road. While another traumatic event may trigger a psychological reaction, the memory soon fades away, once again.

I also believe the condition of "bipolar" has become a "catchall" label when a professional is unable to come up with a diagnosis. This certainly does not mean I don't believe the condition exists, but a bipolar diagnosis is a replacement for what we knew as manic-depressive back in the day. Heaven forbid in our society that we use the term "manic" applied to a person's condition. As a neuropsychiatric technician, in my military experience, our psychiatrists would use the term to mean a person had severe mood swings. I saw instances where a patient moved suddenly from a severely depressed mood to uncontrollable laughter, or vice versa. These weren't happy-go-lucky people who were jovial until their supply of weed, heroin, or whatever ran out, suddenly becoming depressed because they didn't know from where their next fix was coming.

As with PTSD, I do not claim the condition does not exist or that there are few people actually suffering from the malady. I just cannot accept the fact that lazy people who have no desire to be productive in society should be diagnosed as bipolar, solely as an excuse to claim disability and sit around the rest of their life causing their own ups and downs and attempting to control them by legal or illicit drugs. I know several people with this diagnosis who I have no doubt have been correctly diagnosed, yet they continue to be successful, productive citizens.

I guess what I am trying to say is that we have become a society that accepts any excuse to sit back and enjoy taxpayer contributions. Yet, many of our troops and first responders go without the protective gear they need and deserve because too much money is earmarked for taking care of those who have no desire to serve their country or help the economy by being productive. We support entirely too many people who are fourth- or fifth-generation welfare clients, whose learned-behavior begets yet another generation of slackers. Now, post-COVID-19, so many people are getting "free money," courtesy of our government, that businesses are closing due to the lack of people willing to work for a living.

Having worked as a welfare fraud investigative chief, I know what I have experienced in human behavior. But I do desire to stress that I do not believe the welfare system should cease to exist. There are certainly many who deserve to be taken care of by the system. Those include the unfortunate, rather than the lazy—the injured and disabled, the unemployed, and I am sure there are other categories, but you get the point.

One belief held by many is that those who comprise certain socioeconomic groups are lazy, bound and determined to live a life of receiving welfare checks and whatever other freebies they can obtain from the government. Speaking from hands-on experience, I can say there are many families who live off welfare programs from generation to generation. Hopefully, at some point, a member of the family will break the generational curse and step up to the plate and accept a real job.

I certainly would be untruthful if I denied this existed when I was a welfare fraud investigative chief or that it continues to exist all over the nation today. However, and a very strong however, I can verify in my experience that I could not generalize any group, defined by categories like race, religion, or creed, who were particularly guilty of fitting into this category. It was more of a family thing or even a family tradition than any other factor.

I'll give two cases in point. I grew up with a friend who was Jewish. Bob came from a family where the mother was what we now call a "stay-at-home mom." This was typical of the few Jewish families with whom I was familiar. It was also typical across most categories of families at that time. As long as the husband had a decent job, he was the wage earner, and the wife took care of the kids, cooked, did laundry, and so on. If you aren't an old geezer like me, then trust me, that's the way it was no matter your ethnicity. I don't know a lot about the Jewish religion today as compared to my studies of the Old Testament times. But Jewish families take care of their own. Brothers or brothers-in-law would step in following a family disaster, such as death of the wage earner; catastrophes, such as floods; and other tragic situations. I did not know of a single Jewish family who applied for assistance the entire time I worked in the welfare system.

The second case is the so-called African American family or individual. First, let me state that I don't consider anyone as an African American because their ancestors came from Africa. Before you are tempted to call me a racist, just hold on a second and hear me out. I am a descendant of English, Irish, and German ancestors. I am not an English Irish German American. I do not call myself that or wish to be called that. Yes, I am proud of my ancestry as you should be also of yours. But my point is, I am an American. I was born in the United States of America, despite where my grandparents were born. I am a citizen of the United States of America. I am a veteran of the United States Armed Forces. I am an American, period!

I despise hate groups. Look at where Hitler's hatred of Jews and poor German and Polish families got his country before, during, and after World War II. There is no place for white supremacy groups, any more than there is room for the gangs whose goal it is to rid their neighborhood of people of a certain religion or ethnicity.

Back to my second point. How many times when I was investigating an individual for welfare fraud did I hear, "Why don't you pick on so-and-so and check out the Lincoln he drives?" Sorry, but I usually knew the guy in question and that he was black. The truth was that, although he drove a Lincoln, it was twenty years old, and he had to put a great deal of money into keeping it running, so he could drive to work. He was putting more money into the vehicle than its listed book value.

So yes, I did get racial remarks. But they were the exception.

Misery loves company, and I had little respect for someone who transfers blame onto someone else, especially when that person is a law-abiding citizen who happens to be different than you.

I had no idea what segregation was when I was growing up. As I mentioned in chapter 19, there was a black family who lived above us (above as in on a hillside) and another family who lived next door. Had I lived down South, I may have, indeed, understood racial inequality and injustice. But in my little eastern Ohio town, we played together and fought each other as young boys everywhere did, frequently. The only time I ever heard the N-word was when the Thomas kids fought among themselves. Yes, as a white kid, I thought that was funny. But it didn't translate into us calling them that or other racial slurs. To their credit, I never heard them using racial slurs against us white kids. I am not saying that never happened in Bellaire or other towns in the area. I didn't run around with kids far from my block, so residents in other sections may have experienced life completely different than I did. But that's something I learned in the service, as early as boot camp. There was a lot of hatred between almost all ethnic groups. While in Vietnam, I even witnessed beating some of the lighter-skinned black marines took from darker-skinned men of their same race.

Speaking of naive, the flames of racial distress were all around. But I was raised in an exceptional area that had failed (fortunately) to follow what seemed to be the norm. I thank God for that, because some of the people in my life became good friends who I did not look at as "black" any more than they looked at me as "white." One of my best friends, Tony Johnson, who I mentioned earlier as a member of my CISM team, has been very instrumental in teaching me about diversity. No, I'm not talking about what you may consider as diversity. The word *diversity* doesn't mean black versus white or Protestant versus Catholic. It is much more complicated, yet much simpler than that. It simply means casting aside what the other person looks like or how and who they worship. Look beyond the surface and into the soul. Then if you don't like the person, you simply keep your distance.

An elderly woman asked me one morning after church service what she should do about a certain situation. "I go to the mall every Thursday with Sally" (name changed), she told me. "I used to enjoy the trip. But lately she has become overbearing, and I don't want to be around her any more. As a Christian, am I wrong in feeling that way?"

My answer was that God loves all of us. He expects us to love each other, no matter what principles come between us. But I believe the Bible teaches us to distance ourselves from someone before hatred sets in. Who says God would choose our side in a situation like this? Maybe the other person feels the same way about us. Let God do the judging. And don't tempt Him to make a major issue of the situation. Keep your distance. But pray for the other person. Just don't make the mistake of telling God to make the other person just like you, as did the Pharisee in Luke 18:10!

Why do we need foreigners to fill jobs while unemployment figures continue to expand? I am not speaking of those who are here legally, but those who are here illegally and supported by the rich in exchange for cheap labor. There is a problem here that needs to be remedied. As I stated previously, our elected officials need to stop the rhetoric and start fixing things that are broken (especially our southern border). If one party comes up with a good idea, the other automatically rejects it. If the other party had come up with the same exact idea, it still would be rejected. We the people have become pawns to those we elect, who become rich because of self-interest. Yet, for some reason, we tend to keep those very people in office.

I refuse to talk politics. But in my opinion, there needs to be an agreement within our political system as to who should have first crack at jobs within our borders. If a citizen is willing to perform a certain job, I don't believe in bringing another person across the border illegally to do the work. However, I do understand that many Americans are not willing to do certain jobs, such a manually gathering crops. It is an issue that needs to be resolved, rather than just allowing anyone to cross the border. I am not decrying immigration. But we need direction as to who crosses the border and what they will do when they get here. Until politicians can sit down and agree on some principles, we are being overrun by illegal aliens, many of whom are criminals who other governments want to get rid of. The amount of illicit drugs crossing our southern border is completely out of control and is killing hundreds of our citizens daily. I do realize those taking the drugs are just as much at fault for ingesting them.

Disagree with me if you wish. I respect your stance on issues. I don't ask that you agree with me, only that you also respect my right to opinions.

I was taught from a young age that hard work is not a curse but, rather, a strength. I became indoctrinated into doing small chores as a young child, taking on increasingly more difficult tasks after my father's death. Then came the work on my grandparents' farm, which for a preteen, seemed like a forced labor camp. But I will never regret all the work I have done in my life. I do not even regret my time at Arrow Block, working outside in both summer heat and subzero temperatures. It was a valuable experience and the hardest I ever worked in my life. It was a miserable time but also a time of great experience.

I regret the two spinal injuries, which will persist the rest of my life. But I learned valuable lessons from that also. I learned to deal with pain without becoming addicted to painkillers, as several of my friends experienced in their inability to deal with a life sentence of pain and discomfort.

I never had a single thought about not returning to work after my first back injury, even though my doctors advised me to remain on disability and complete my bachelor's degree. Then, after my fourth lumbar disk surgery and a decision by workers' compensation to not allow me to return to work, I had already earned a master's degree and wasn't about to let it go to waste. I'd worked too hard for that degree to sit back and take it easy for the rest of my life—a life I figured would only exist a few more years because of the premature death of my father due to heart disease. Yet, after open heart surgery and three cardiac ablations, I continue to live in the humble satisfaction that Paul spoke of in 2 Thessalonians.

Chapter 30

A Time for Everything
"There is a time for everything,
and a season for every activity under the heavens,
a time to be born and a time to die,
a time to plant and a time to uproot,
time to kill and a time to heal,
a time to tear down and a time to build,
a time to weep and a time to laugh,
a time to mourn and a time to dance,
a time to scatter stones and a time to gather them,
a time to embrace and a time to refrain from embracing,
a time to search and a time to give up,
a time to keep and a time to throw away,
a time to tear and a time to mend,
a time to be silent and a time to speak,
a time to love and a time to hate,
a time for war and a time for peace.

—*Ecclesiastes 3:1–8*

For a long time, this scripture has been familiar to me. However, it meant little to me until sometime after my return to the World. One day, the words struck me like a bolt of lightning. I wish I could remember what that day was. I am quite sure it was a patriotic holiday of some sort. I can tell you that, on my first trip to the presidential laying of the wreath on Veterans Day sometime in the late '90s, a military chaplain read this scripture prior to President Clinton's speech. Later that afternoon at the Vietnam Veterans Memorial, not one but two other speakers read the same passage.

This had become one of my two favorite passages sometime before that, but the fact that it was read, not just mentioned, three times during those two services amplified the meaning of the words that became dear to me forever.

The other passage is Matthew 28:16–20, known as the Great Commission. I read this passage in closing the sunrise service each Easter morning. It, too, has a meaning deeply imbedded in my soul. It is a challenge not only to the eleven disciples but also to all of us, as disciples of Jesus Christ. As you read it, if you are not familiar with the words, read it in silence and determine if Christ is speaking to you through these words:

The Great Commission

Then the eleven disciples went to Galilee to the mountain where Jesus had told them to go. When they saw Him, they worshiped Him; but some doubted. Then Jesus came to them and said, "All authority in heaven and on earth has been given to me. Therefore, go and make disciples of all nations, baptizing them in the name of the Father and of the Son and of the Holy Spirit, and teaching them to obey everything I have commanded you. And surely, I am with you always, even to the end of the age."

Back to the Ecclesiastes passage. Solomon, in all his wisdom, put life's entities in such eloquent perspective. There is not only a time for everything and a season (of our life) for everything but also an antithesis. To me, He simplified a statement that could have read, "If there is light, there must be darkness. If there is day, there must be night. If there is good, there must be evil". If you believe in God, you must also acknowledge that Satan also exists. I could go on forever, but I think you get my drift.

I do not think two people could sit down, discuss, and agree on exactly what each of Solomon's statements mean. It is a matter of perspective. We each see things differently, at least to some extent, according to our life experiences. I realize I made this same statement two chapters previously. But I am looking at it now as an old Vietnam veteran who had different experiences and events than other Vietnam vets. I am not implying my experiences were worse than others, or at least as bad as many others. The magnitude of specific events isn't the issue.

Pick any two people in the world. One might be from the Arctic Circle, and the other, from a luxurious island in the middle of the Pacific Ocean. Or take two people of very similar backgrounds. They will probably agree on colors if you show them a paint chart (unless they are color-blind like I am, with some shades of coloring). But ask them which color they like best. They might like the same color of carpet or paint for a certain room. But they will certainly not agree on color preference for everything. Even our own preferences for things change over time. There is a time for everything under heaven. But things change.

Time is not constant. Consider the fact that the last breath you took before reading this sentence is gone. It has been exhaled, and a new breath has reached your lungs. With this new breath, you might experience a new aroma. You may enjoy it. Someone else in the room may be offended by it. (No, I wasn't thinking of that type of odor.) Linda and I both had a general dislike for roses. Why? Because it takes us individually to losing a parent at an early age. At that time, there were very few flowers at a funeral home except for roses. Although the dislike hasn't entirely dissipated, the negative emotional reaction isn't as strong as it once was. Things change. Time progresses. Old hurts are alleviated over time. On the other hand, old friendships may have turned into new enemies. Someone once said something to the effect of, "There is a good chance your worst enemy was once your best friend." There is a season for every activity under heaven. Life changes sometimes as seasons change.

One message I interpret from Solomon is that nothing remains constant. So, you say, "I love my spouse the same as on my wedding day". I doubt that is an accurate statement. If you don't love him or her less, then the love has probably grown even stronger over time. For everything there is a season, and seasons change. Hopefully, as we grow older, our wisdom increases. We learn just about everything by experience.

Now that I have rambled, hopefully enough to get your attention, I will express how I reflect on Ecclesiastes 3:1–8 in relation to my own life experiences. Hopefully, this will lead you to sit back and do the same. While you read this, you will reflect on your own life experiences. If not, then at least maybe you will see fit to do it at a later time. How many times did a parent punish you for the same offense before the proverbial light bulb in your head lit up and you finally got the point?

Sometimes, we learn from our life experiences, and sometimes we fail. The path we take guides our future. We can blame others for failures all we want. But if we fail to learn from our mistakes or bad decisions, we are doomed to failure. Solomon's message is that certain paths will lead us to a life of emptiness.

Solomon's statement is that we have the ability to discover our true purpose in life. How do we find our true meaning in life? Some believe in karma. Some believe in existentialism. Others believe in predestination, to the extent that whatever happens, happens.

Solomon teaches us the true purpose in life is wisdom. This book is an essay about life's true meaning. Its negativity grinds us down to the grave when we try to find our true meaning through knowledge, pleasure, and other earthly matters. We can gain the wisdom of the top educators throughout history. But all knowledge results in emptiness without the satisfaction of knowing that what we are doing is whatever God's purpose is for us in life.

As we read throughout the Bible, our way and God's way are likely to take two different paths. It is easy to seek pleasure and live a life of self-satisfaction. That seems to be the norm throughout history and especially present times, where we are a generation that claims, "It's all about me." Sometimes, the more we search, the more we realize that wisdom eludes us. Solomon reminds us that, at our moment of death, we have nothing to take to the grave.

Throughout the first two chapters of Ecclesiastes, each subtitle concludes with the word *meaningless*. The very first is, "Everything is meaningless." That is followed by wisdom, pleasures, and folly and, finally, toil. All is meaningless if we are not subservient. No matter how hard we work, without God there is no lasting reward for our work.

While reading most of the book of Ecclesiastes, it is likely that one will interpret nothing but one of the most consistent messages of "meaningless." However, thank God, when we put everything together we realize that, with faith in and obedience to God, everything becomes the opposite—*meaningful*.

My following interpretation of scripture is my own and meant to represent no viewpoint of any specific religion, including my following of Presbyterian beliefs. I do not see exactly eye to eye with those beliefs in all circumstances. Having grown up with a Methodist background, I still adhere to some beliefs that differ slightly from the Presbyterian Church. I respect everyone's right to believe how they see fit, as long as those are true beliefs and not shortcuts to cover up one's actions and falsely interpret scripture to cover someone's actions by false pretense.

I'll cover one more point here. My priest friend, Father Paul Welton, who I spoke of earlier in this book, was the best teacher I could have been provided with at the onset of my ministry. Paul and I agreed to disagree on certain points, but there was never a question of our respect for each other's beliefs.

I don't think my personal beliefs should challenge those of any Christian's religious beliefs. Please remember, I am not a theologian and do not make any claim as such. I am taking these few verses that are extremely significant to me (as an individual) and merely placing them into an interpretation that fits or coincides with my own personal experiences.

You, the reader, have every right to express your own feelings according to your own life experiences. What a blessing it would be to me to discover that you are inspired to author a book, telling your story and interpreting the same biblical passage in your own terms.

Chapter 31

"A time to be born and a time to die."

—Ecclesiastes 3:2a

God has a plan for each person he has ever or will ever create. However, to be a successful Christian, it is imperative that we accept this plan, rather than set sail on our own ship. For each individual, where does it all begin? At birth, of course. So, that is where Solomon begins. "A time to be born."

Who are our parents? What are their traits, beliefs, strong points, weaknesses, professions, and residency? What is their hierarchy in the community? I couldn't begin to finish this list. There are as many implications as there are variables.

God brings us into this world with an individual plan, having known us before we were born. He is already prepared to deal with our weaknesses and lack of resources for accomplishing our goals in life. Our life cycle begins with birth. Our ensuing experiences come at different times.

There is a very important theme here. Notice that the verses are not deemed to be sequential. There is, of course, one major exception. It doesn't take a genius to realize that verse two is the exception. Obviously, a time to be born precludes any other event in anyone's life. When Solomon wrote the book toward the latter days of his life, we must realize this blessing of great wisdom he had did not come from books but, rather, from experience and from listening to and obeying God.

Verses 2b through 8 are experienced at different intervals for each individual. You would be hard-pressed to meet someone who can run down these seasons of life in the order Solomon listed them. Likewise, the chances of someone who experiences them in the same order or the same fashion as you is impossible.

The author of Ecclesiastes could have gone to great lengths to explain this. But in his great wisdom, Solomon included the seasons of life as inclusive, rather than sequential.

Timing is important in almost every aspect of life. It is as different for each of us as our fingerprints. We have all heard the phrase "timing is everything." It relates to what time period we were born, where we were born, and many of those things I spoke of previously in this chapter. We have no control over when God chose to place us on this planet, which He created billions of years ago. If you study creation, just take "billions" with a grain of salt. I will not challenge your estimate of how long ago God created this earth or even how many years have faded into eternity since he created humankind. That is far beyond my expertise, and in simple words, I could not care less.

"A time to be born" begins Solomon's observations, in which he so eloquently describes his lessons related to the seasons of life.

Just as a note, let me assure you I did not fail to consider the second part of verse 2a at this time. With all respect to Solomon, I will change the sequence slightly only for the purpose of this book by using that section of the verse to end my summary of these first seven verses of Ecclesiastes 3:1–8.

Chapter 32

"A time to plant and a time to uproot."

—Ecclesiastes 3:2b

Unlike the first verse, we have some control over the remaining verses. A time to be born is totally out of our control. That was taken care of by our parents nine months prior. Now, as we begin to mature, we begin to show some accountability for our actions.

As I mentioned previously, the verses are not meant to be sequential. Many will overlap. Sometimes, a mixture can provide anxiety or even fear. But God has a plan for each of us, and each experience is appropriate for a certain time. Yes, at times we question why God appears to contradict himself. But we must have faith in His timing in all seasons of our life. And we must have faith that He will not lead us down a road and abandon us. He will tie all things together and give us peace through His perfect timing.

Again, it is important to remember God loves each of us, even when we are burdened by lack of faith, doubt, fear, and resentment that others seem to be far better off than ourselves. These can lead us to turn from God and lead us down a road of despair and barriers to His plan for us.

Do you think Billy Graham grew up on a straight and narrow path along which God timed his seasons in a way that he never questioned his purpose? If you happen to think the Reverend Graham had it easy all the way through life and God provided the seasons exactly the way he would have liked, read his story and you will realize that the main difference between the reverend and others who face difficult trials in life is that he had a stronger faith than most of us. Despite setbacks and though that faith may have waivered at times, as with all Christians, that very faith allowed God to control his seasons of life, instead of him trying to tell God what his needs were. I can only wish I could have as much faith as the one I consider the greatest spiritual leader of our times.

Let's get to our current verse. What does "a time to plant" mean? Are we planting flowers today? How about soy beans, wheat, corn, or maybe sunflowers? Whatever your geographical location is, the choice is yours. Maybe you have a greenhouse and raise tomatoes from seeds to sell in the spring.

Spring is a favorite season for many of us. It is an exciting season. The temperature is warming up. New growth is appearing as buds on flowers and trees after a long, dormant winter.

Then there is summer. It's not necessarily as great a season for people like me who suffer from psoriasis and skin cancer caused by Agent Orange. But at least I don't look out my office window as I am doing right now and look at twenty-two inches of snow and ice that has accumulated over the past two weeks. That is good news for those who enjoy winter activities, such as building snow people and snowmobile activities.

Continuing with summer, it's a season for cutting grass, chopping firewood, and other outside activities that continue from spring. When I was younger, I believed my skin was indestructible. What young boy is going to be the sissy of the group and pour on suntan lotion like the girls do? Certainly none in the group I grew up with! Now, my skin is ravaged with age spots, which are unattractive, although that part doesn't bother me. I'm not out looking to impress others with my skin tone (let alone my looks).

Then comes my favorite season—fall, or if you prefer, autumn. Yes, the garden is done producing and the flowers wither and die, but now comes the season of beautifully colored leaves, announcing that nature is taking a rest for a few months before new life begins to spring up all over again.

My point here is that weather and seasons are cyclic and predictable. But even then, sometimes we have an earlier than usual winter or maybe a summer in which temperatures remain warmer than normal for an extra couple of weeks. Nature will give a little, but the seasons will come and go as always, and each season will follow the predictable path. And guess what? We have faith in God taking care of this, and we know we cannot control the weather seasons.

Back to planting. We know what to plant in different seasons. There are a few crops that aren't planted until fall. We don't control that. We go along with that fact, and if we wish for these crops to grow and flourish, we plant them accordingly. So it is with the seasons of life. Some things are predictable, but God's appointed season for each individual is mostly unpredictable. The question here is, When is it the time to plant, in terms of our Christianity, rather than green thumbs?

God will provide us with the "seeds" to plant as Christians. He will provide the season in which to plant them. But the seasons differ with each individual. The seeds of our faith may have been planted earlier in life, and we may have missed out on God's message that He has a plan for us. Sometimes, those seeds need a little more watering and tender loving care. I certainly do not, in any way, compare myself to Billy Graham. If I did, I would lose the contest before it began. But using him as an example, the Reverend Graham understood his calling during his early teens. He answered that call to understand the seasons of life and followed God's call into ministry almost immediately. For myself, the seasons were there, but I failed to recognize them.

My main concern during my teenage years was to graduate from high school and head off to complete my military obligation. I had no idea how that would work out. Maybe I would be a laborer for the rest of my life, which was apparently my path until certain seasons appeared, and I began to go with the flow. God had a plan for me, and so did Satan. Satan's plan was much easier to follow. Blame my war experiences for any excuse I needed to make, rather than face responsibilities. Blame my injuries on bad luck, rather than turning them into something positive. Feel sorry for myself and blame God for the wrong steps I took in life and try to get others to feel sorry for me. I could go on forever, but hopefully you get the point.

I am humbled that I can share with you the message that God waters and cares for us, just as He does the plants and trees of the fields. The difference between being humble and being proud is that, for a long time, I was letting Satan score too many points. God didn't plant those seeds in a silver platter. He made me search for the meaning of each seed. If I was proud, I would tell you I overcame all of Satan's curveballs because I had the Wisdom of Solomon, and Jesus Christ saved me because he feels I am someone special. But the humility in my life comes from the fact that I am a sinner, not a saint. Jesus did not save me because I am Kurt Turner. He saved me because He humbled me into accepting what I am, not who I am. At some point, we must recognize the seasons God provides for us. As we go through those seasons, we will see that it isn't a scripture of positives. It isn't a scripture of having done everything right, so we don't have anything to correct in our lives. But I will cover those verses in time.

It doesn't take Einstein to figure out what the term *uproot* represents here. Using my own example, my humility isn't based on my having been able to uproot many of the misgivings I've had during my life. Rather, it's the fact that I've had to uproot circumstances to accomplish things, due to having let Satan control some of the seasons, thereby allowing bad seeds to be planted in the first place. In some instances, I refer to God having planted our seeds. In others, such as here, I refer to bad seeds that were planted by either Satan or myself. Please do not mistake the word *planted* as necessarily meaning planted by God. Wouldn't it be terrific if we could blame God for all the seeds we have planted, both good and evil?

Sometimes, we have to uproot deeds we have done. Sometimes, we have to uproot lies or falsehoods we have believed and fallen for. It could be what we have come to recognize as "fake news." Uprooting of prejudices of one type or another and letting go of stigmas isn't easy. Satan isn't about to let these things go easily. That is what faith is all about—faith that God will help us and faith in ourselves that we are able to let go of things we once had a firm grasp on.

There is a time for each of us to accept God's timing and let go of the past and uproot our old selves. God will give all of us a chance to atone for our sins and our doubts. We must accept His perfect timing by being humbled into giving up the past. Some of us will accept that season. Others will reject it. Some are given a second chance, but that isn't something to rely on. This is where pride sets in, and we believe we can tempt God to let us go on living until a ripe old age, when we no longer deal with our ego and can humble ourselves at the end of our life. I am not saying God will refuse to forgive you at the last second. I am merely warning that our last second might come long before that ripe old age when we are ready to sail into the sunset.

Chapter 33

"A time to kill and a time to heal."

—*Ecclesiastes 3:3a*

I will not even attempt to guess how many times, as a counselor or as a pastor (or when combining the two roles), I heard a combat veteran or law enforcement officer express the guilt they carry for the (to them, unforgivable) sin of killing one or more enemies in combat.

I refuse to let someone off the hook by translating a word or sentence from the Bible in order for them to feel that God accepts what they did because Pastor Kurt figured a way for them to skirt around the issue. This is my interpretation of the biblical answer to this dilemma. I only speak of this issue through my own belief. Theologians might debate the answer as to whether or not the soldier has broken the sixth commandment, "Thou shall not kill" (murder). I take the stance on the issue of my own accord, based on my personal beliefs.

Do I believe murder has been committed during wartime actions? Absolutely! I have personally spoken with veterans and heard stories ranging from marines sweeping through a village to helicopter gunners proudly talking about gunning down mama-san and papa-san while they were planting or harvesting rice in the fields of Vietnam. Similar stories exist from probably every war ever fought, whether by American GIs or allies or enemies.

Do I believe this is a sin committed in the true interpretation of the sixth commandment? Absolutely! Killing for fun fits the definition of murder. Returning fire, whether as a military personnel or as a law enforcement agent, does not constitute murder. Yes, you may have killed a human being, but my honest feeling is that the word *kill* was probably misconstrued somewhere in Greek, Hebrew, or whatever language your choice of Bible translation originated from. Again, believe whatever you want to believe. I believe there is a significant difference between murdering someone and taking a life when using self-defense as a means of self-preservation.

I am not going to preach a sermon on repentance here. This isn't a lesson in forgiveness for our sins. I am only dealing with the issue of differentiating between killing and murder as an act of war.

If I wasn't trying to keep the focus of this book on my military and personal life experiences, I would address the issue of abortion at this point. The only part I will address is whether or not killing an unborn child is self-defense, aka the difference between to kill and to murder. I obviously have a stance on abortion. But if I had the answer to that question in every instance, I would be as wise as Solomon himself.

I cannot imagine a physician of any sort not following "a time for healing," rather than "a time to kill." Yet, as I think of it, I am reminded of several instances where a doctor or nurse has intentionally killed patients for one reason or another. The latest, which is close to me, is the Clarksburg, West Virginia Veterans Hospital, where a nurse murdered several of our heroes. Maybe some were deathly ill, but a hospital is a place to heal, rather than a facility to send people to die, especially when death is not imminent. Even when it is imminent, a hospital is a place to comfort the person until natural death presides.

Having stated the exception, I'll add that the remainder of us would love to have the gift of healing. Too many times, we fail to credit those who bring healing by surmising one has to be a certified health or skilled psychological professional in order to facilitate healing of a stricken individual. As "healing" is specified as one of the gifts of the Spirit, it is something we should not pray for. The Holy Spirit provides gifts to individuals as it sees fit. Spiritual gifts are not selective, except by the Holy Spirit. We should each accept the gift(s) we are assigned and use them to our utmost ability. Others will take care of the rest.

I could write an entire book on the subject of what circumstances entail the gift of healing. However, again, I am not delving into theology and will attempt to stick to personal experiences, as not to offend those who would argue over circumstances where they think they have received this gift.

My desire to become a Navy hospital corpsman had nothing to do with hoping to receive a gift handed to me by the Holy Spirit. Had I wished for it, I have no doubt I would have been rejected. Did I earn it by graduating from hospital corps school? Absolutely not! How about when I graduated from neuropsychiatric school? Again, the answer is no. How about college degrees in psychology and counseling? One more time, the answer is a resounding *no*!

Now for the $64,000 question (that will test your age). Do I believe I have been provided this gift solely through the desire of the Holy Spirit? The answer is yes, I do. It has come to me not by way of degrees, not by the fact that I am a minister, and not by anything whatsoever that I have done to deserve it or anything else provided by my own accomplishments. It is through the act of the Holy Spirit and the grace of God. In no other way have I received this gift. It is nothing to brag about, for it does not come from within. I believe that, if I was to brag about any gift I have received from the Holy Spirit, I would be condemning my own soul. So, I do as Paul tells us and brag on the Spirit that it uses a sinner like me in its plans of goodness provided to others.

It was a dreary day in late March on the shores of Lake Erie that I was presented with my diploma as a navy corpsman—something I had dreamed about and pursued since my early high school years. Though I was careless with my studies in high school, having taken college prep courses such as biology and chemistry made corps school a little easier. For the first time since fifth grade (when my father died) I had an ambition and a goal in life. I went straight into NP (neuropsychiatric) school, which was more of a time of learning than helping patients work through their healing process.

While I didn't see it then, I was preparing to assist in healing young marines (some navy personnel) in a different way than I had imagined when I decided the navy was my first goal in life. Once I was handed my certificate as an official NP tech, I would begin helping to heal others in a way that had previously been foreign to me.

I want to stress here that I never healed anyone. And no matter what role I may play in any incident in the future, I will never heal anyone. My two navy schools prepared me to accept a role in healing. But clearly, I would never be the primary source of healing. The Holy Spirit would be the primary source of healing, and I would only achieve what the Spirit would lead me to do as its earthly assistant. Even at that, most of the time I would be under the guidance not only of the Spirit but also of doctors, nurses, and other corpsmen.

I could make a lengthy story on how many people I was called to assist in healing by the Spirit, but it would tend to lean toward bragging. Let it suffice to say I felt the presence of the Spirit many times while a healing process was in effect. Many times, I would not realize at the time where the Spirit was leading me. Although, I am sure that happened many times, I don't even care that I realized it; it is not and was not about me. It was about the person who received the healing touch. And while I might have assisted in the delivery of that touch, I was far from the true provider.

Long before my training in the ministry, I realized all healing isn't physical or psychological. The other type is spiritual. The prime example in my life is the experience with James E. Williams, Jr. I won't rehash the story I already told. What I will do is tell you that God used me on that dark, rainy night by leading me to assist in fulfilling a young dying marine's final wish. It wasn't a wish for fame and glory as a fallen comrade and true American hero, who lay dying in the arms of a complete stranger. As I looked into this fallen marine's eyes, as I mentioned previously, I looked beyond those glossed-over eyes, which were victimized by pain and morphine. The

Spirit guided me to look into his soul and understand his final wish in life—a wish for prayer. That prayer became the last words he heard on this side of his final resting place, a peaceful cemetery outside Oklahoma City, about twelve thousand miles away.

You can call it anything you want. We each have a right to our own opinion, even if it by far surpasses the belief of another. To me, it was the sincerest sense of healing the Spirit ever involved me in—an event that would eventually carve out my future in many significant ways. I can say that it was the event that defined me as a man of God. Unfortunately, there were many bumps and roadblocks I have no desire to remember that delayed my realization of the shining moment that would, in the future, guide and inspire me to becoming the person I am now and not the person I had been in the past.

I helped in lifesaving events during my tour of duty on the USS *Repose*. And I have been able to provide lifesaving techniques as a civilian, by being in the right place at the right time (or, actually, by being where the Spirit led me to be at the time it chose). For all of it, I give thanks to God that I could be there. At no time will I take credit for being there of my own accord. God led me there and provided lifesaving assistance for those persons through my earthly help. But in all cases, God is the great healer. It is not me. Nor is it the best brain surgeon on earth.

My assistance in counseling sessions and in my ministry are led by the Spirit. When I am called to a debriefing or to the scene of a tragic incident, as soon as I get into the car, my first order of business isn't to prepare what I am going to say to first responders or to a family. Rather, it is to pray that the Spirit will guide me and members of the team as to what to say and when to say it and what not to say.

To me, that is a gift of healing. It is nothing to brag about and nothing to pound our chest over. It is a gift that, although we may not proclaim it aloud, each of us has received from the Holy Spirit.

There are countless instances where "a time to heal" comes from God without any earthly assistance whatsoever. I won't get into this because I am dealing with life experiences and not theological principles.

Chapter 34

"A time to tear down and a time to build."

—Ecclesiastes 3:3b

Seasons come, and seasons go. For every season there is a purpose. A purpose set by God. The reason for many seasons, we fail to understand. Many we cannot comprehend or accept because His ways are greater than ours—His, a mind we cannot fathom.

So, what season is there that we need to tear down something? Shouldn't Solomon have turned that verse around and started with "a time to build" first? Then he could have moved to tearing down what we have constructed in an earthly way, rather than in a heavenly approved manner?

I am guilty before God. I would be condemned to an eternity in hell if it wasn't for God's grace. If I lived under "the law," rather than grace, and accepted Jesus Christ as my Lord and Savior, my past life would certainly lead to condemnation. No, I wasn't a serial killer or rapist or anything like that. But my existence left much to be desired. I am tempted to go on, saying we all are sinners, and I am one of the fortunate ones to have accepted Christ. But that would be bragging. No, I am excited to know that many have done the same. The truth is that Christ has accepted us. He accepted us before we were born. The question is, have we accepted Him?

When we meet the definition of all those big words in the New

Testament, we are free from the mistakes we have made previously. We're free to "tear down" barriers of a past life and begin to "build" or reconstruct our lives. We can tear down existing walls of prejudices. We can build new relationships and build walls to block old prejudices.

While Solomon is certainly not speaking of a construction company involved in tearing down and reconstructing physical buildings, he is offering an allegory relating to the spiritual, as opposed to the physical. We should recognize the need to step back, reconcile ourselves, tear down old barriers, and build new alliances.

I'll end this section with the Parable of the Seed. In order for a new plant to grow, the old must die for a seed to be reborn. And so, a new season's preparation has begun. The leaves or blossoms wither in the fall and become dormant in the winter. But in the spring, the seed is raised to new life by its Creator and blossoms throughout the summer. Then the cycle resumes over and over.

Our seasons as humans aren't cyclic like those of plants, whose seasons come and go and are repeated annually. We experience different types of seasons. Some contain times of spiritual growth and some contain failures. Our pattern is up and down, instead of cyclic. If we are successful in our spiritual life. we will recognize the season for destroying old barriers and the season for reconstruction—"a time to build."

This reminds me of listening to Bette Midler singing "The Rose":

Just remember, in the winter,
Deep beneath the bitter snow,
Lies the seed, that with the sun's light,
In the spring, becomes the Rose.

Chapter 35

"A time to weep and a time to laugh,
A time to mourn and a time to dance."

—Ecclesiastes 3:4

Many excerpts from the Bible piece this verse together, bringing it into existence. As a whole, I believe it suffices to say that we, as humans with imperfect minds, fail to look at these emotions through the eyes of God.

How many times do we weep when we should laugh? Sometimes, we realize we should be laughing at ourselves. How many times have you wept over a situation that was embarrassing at the time but, later, looked at it as humorous? At that point, we see the situation through the eyes of others.

In the sadness of the moment, we weep as we mourn over the loss of a loved one. God understands our emotions. For heaven's sake, He created them. His own Son looked over the city of Jerusalem and the shortest verse of the Bible tells us, "Jesus wept." This tells me that God does not say we should not weep or mourn. He did the same when he discovered His friend Lazarus had died. Sorrow over life's events is a natural emotion. Look at yourself as a child. Do you think God was upset when we cried because our parents wouldn't give into our demands?

Truly, there is a season for weeping and for mourning, but

eventually it often ends up in a season of laughing and dancing. The mother of a bride bawls her eyes out at her daughter's wedding. But within a few hours, she joins the bridal dance amid the sounds of laughter cascading down the halls of the building.

My personal take on this verse is that I have lost all the members of my immediate family. My father died a very sudden death at a very young age. My mother died slowly of cancer. Then my sister also died of breast cancer at a fairly early age. Each passing was followed by a season of weeping and mourning. But in each case, I was able to begin a new and much more pleasant season by laughing about pleasant memories involving each family member. As a Christian and knowing all of my family members were also Christians, I could place things in perspective and laugh along with those old memories, knowing that, at their deaths, each of them gave the angels in heaven cause to rejoice and to dance as a soul had arrived at its heavenly abode. A new season began for them and for me.

Chapter 36

"A time to throw stones and a time to gather them, A time to embrace and a time to refrain from embracing."

—Ecclesiastes 3:5

I have been bouncing back between the New Revised Version and Life Application Bibles in choosing which translation better fits what I want to say. Just as a note to the reader, I have referred to one or the other and have not made up my own version in any situation.

This verse may well have come from someone familiar with vineyards. As often as the writers of the Bible mention wine, we can assume that some writings are based on things that might go right over our heads, unless you live in wine country. Am I sure that is what Solomon is referring to? No, but in my research, I have discovered that is what seems to be a widely held opinion. I certainly did not come up with that on my own. I seldom drink a glass of wine, let alone know about throwing stones dug up from preparing to plant vineyards.

So, wiser people than myself conclude that, after the stones are thrown or scattered, they may be used to build walls or small buildings. Who knows? They might be used to build a shed where grapes are stored or crushed to be made into wine.

So, how do we translate this into our own daily living? I can remember more than once getting into trouble with my friends when we got caught throwing stones at things we shouldn't have. This certainly wasn't a constructive type of throwing as it was meant to be in this setting.

When I look at this verse and attempt to decipher the true meaning, I can only reminisce about throwing the proverbial stones in my life that held me back from following the right path. Sometimes, we stumble over stones (issues) we don't see. Do we cast them aside or do we go on with whatever stumbling block they provide? I have certainly had enough of those stones pop up in my life. Military life provides an individual with many more choices in life than most of us seventeen- or eighteen-year-olds had ever faced in our previous civilian lives.

Reveille at the ungodly hour of 0500. Really? All we were going to do is march our butts off after breakfast. Then came all the exercising. My muscles didn't get this sore working on my grandparents' farm. And even then, I didn't get up before sunrise. Then there was the putting up with all the bullshit dished out by the company commander. We were too tired for all this nonsense! How about a democracy here and we cast aside some of the stones you toss in our path and make a few rules ourselves? Of course, that is not, nor will it ever be, an acceptable way to raise an army (although things have changed a lot since the 1960s in regard to punishment and harassment). Back then, we were mentally and physically abused. And if you tried going to someone higher in command, the punishment became much more severe.

So, what could we do? We learned to "take it like a man" and cast aside those stones, or stumbling blocks, not realizing we were gathering in those same stones and building soldiers out of them. I went from 117 pounds out of high school to 145 pounds out of boot camp. And I guarantee none of the twenty-eight pounds contained an ounce of fat. I grew not only in physical stature but also in maturity. I learned to say, "Yes, sir," instead of, "No, I don't think so!" Old stones had been cast aside and new ones gathered in to construct a young mature sailor, ready to be introduced into a world far more difficult than the place he had grown up in. Others may have come from areas where they were already tough or they wouldn't have survived. But the gang member mentality was replaced with building blocks from those stones of hatred and bitterness that were refurbished and gathered in.

We were transformed, from a time of embracing our old values to a time when we would refrain from old habits and become military individuals who would set new values, new goals, and new standards.

Chapter 37

"A time to search and a time to give up as lost,
A time to keep and a time to throw away."

—*Ecclesiastes 3:6*

"If my people, who are called by my name, will humble
themselves and pray and seek my face and turn from
their wicked ways, then I will hear from heaven, and
I will forgive their sin and will heal their land.'

—*2 Chronicles 7:14*

As a first responder, I have participated in many search parties. Some end happily, but most have ended tragically. My first thought is, *has the person or persons who are missing been saved?* It isn't up to me to judge anyone, so I only wonder about that individual's soul. No matter how much I pray for them at that point, it is fruitless.

As responders, we are searching for a body, whether living or deceased. As a chaplain, I am usually with family members while the search continues. I have sat with families for a few hours and, sometimes, for several days. As a search drags out, family members tend to talk about the missing person's standing with God.

The verse from 2 Chronicles comes to mind during this time of waiting—waiting in fear as to the outcome. The longer the wait, the smaller the chance of survival. The family usually has an opinion as to whether the missing person has searched for a meaning in life. Have they taken an existential viewpoint as to their existence, a viewpoint as a person who just takes life for granted with no concern regarding life after death? Has theirs been a lifetime of belief that the universe "revolves around me"?

I can tell you from experience that it is much easier on me when I am told that the person in question has humbled him or herself and sought God's face, asking forgiveness for his or her sins, knowing they will be forgiven. It is much easier to talk to the family and to comfort them when the positive season of the person's life has been defined.

My main concern during such a search isn't so much for the physical body as for the spiritual body. Families, at some point, begin to turn from the doubt of recovering a living body to that of the spiritual soul and spiritual hope.

In some tragic events, a body is never found. In some cases, there lingers the question of whether the soul was found. Only God can answer that question, and the surviving family must wait a literal eternity until they get their answer.

As with other verses, I am writing as a veteran and a first responder and not as a theologian. But much of my life is directed by these few verses. I can relate what they mean to me as a byproduct of my life experiences. If you want a theological interpretation, I would advise you to do a google search on the true biblical interpretation. But in most cases, I believe you will look into these verses through a mirror and see your reflection in at least one verse, if not several or all of them.

At the end of a search (notice I used *end*, rather than *conclusion*) where a body isn't discovered under an avalanche, in a body of water, or in a mine deep beneath the surface of the earth, for example, there is a time to give up the search. Unfortunately, some searches end without recovery. The physical body is given up for lost.

All that remains is whether the person's soul has been given up for lost or whether God has heard from heaven (the person has accepted Christ). It is God's decision as to whether there is a time "to keep" or "to throw away" into eternal darkness that determines the destiny of an individual's soul.

"For everything there is a season." Our eternity depends on how we live out the seasons of our lives.

Chapter 38

"A time to tear apart and a time to sew together,
A time to be silent and a time to speak."

—Ecclesiastes 3:7

ll of us were torn apart, whether we wanted to admit it or not. Most of us failed to realize the implications. But one by one, we would find ourselves hit, sooner or later, by the fact that we had seen and done things we were not prepared to see or do as teenagers. Some wanted to go to war to be embedded in battle and to come home and claim the status of hero by virtue of how many enemy lives they disposed of.

I go back to the words of the old instructor from boot camp. "War is hell, and this is war." War tears young men apart (again ladies, except for nurses and I'm sure a few others, I'm speaking of Vietnam, not Afghanistan / Iraq).

For some, the "fun" of battle doesn't subside with age. But I believe that, in all honesty, even those who claim they live with the past with no emotional scars are torn apart. I believe they're either in denial or just trying to make the rest of us believe they were not impacted by killing and being sought after by the enemy to be killed. They don't want to admit they're being torn apart by nightmares and daydreams. Aspects of human behavior cannot be assumed regardless of what some research might proclaim (my opinion). There are exceptions to every rule, especially those pertaining to behavioral implications. So, I am not going to argue with a veteran who sits back and laughs about watching his buddies being blown away by a Claymore mine while riding in a Humvee. But I don't agree with him that he is facing reality.

And yes, I have experienced that in speaking with combat veterans. This was an actual experience. At a dinner table, I witnessed an Iraqi war veteran speaking about the deaths of his friends in this way. When I mentioned he should think about going to the VA for help, he laughed at my suggestion and did his best to convince everyone there how tough he was. I lost all respect for him. Yes, I felt sorry for him to an extent; he definitely wasn't processing terrible experiences and coping with them as a "normal" human being would. But the arrogance of laughing about his so-called friends and the scene he claimed was embedded in his mind was bullshit, stacked high and deep.

I would later explain to his family that I believed he was lying about the event and desperately attempting to have people believe what he claimed to have experienced as a combat soldier, when in actuality, he had no real combat stories to tell. I believe he was crying out for help but was afraid the truth would come out. His life of drug abuse and challenges with maintaining employment may well have been remedied by the VA. Plus, if he was telling the truth, he would have been eligible for VA compensation the rest of this life—with which he could have purchased more coke to snort.

If you visit a VA hospital, you will see many whose lives have been torn apart. You don't need to go into the psychiatric unit to recognize many of them. But the difference between them and the veteran I am speaking of is that they are ready to face their demons. They are attempting to have their lives "sewn back together."

Many of us realize being sewn together after having been torn apart is a long journey—a journey filled with the pain of remembrance. Our demons don't go down quickly or easily. It takes time to tear them apart as they once did to us. Assistance is there if you're willing to accept it. As I constantly remind my students, the first step in counseling is the desire to seek help, coupled with the willingness to accept it. You can feed the PTSD demons through self- pity, denial, drugs, or any other means you choose. Or you can seek help and sew yourself together to become the person you desire to be. Many of my best friends have been torn apart by their profession (not necessarily military) and have picked up the pieces of their lives and sewn them together. Now, they are terrific at helping others who would have continued to struggle with being torn apart.

For everything there is a season. For every darkness there is light. This, like the other verses gives us a choice in life. We can overcome our demons, whether caused during war or anything else. We each have our own battlefields of life, including drugs, gambling, or pornography; you name it. Each of us struggles with our own experiences at one time or another. Believe me, I am living proof that some of us struggle with our past—a past we are incapable of escaping without first admitting we have issues. Then we begin to accept the fact that seeking help does not represent weakness. Then, finally, we accept that help from someone trained in sewing us back together.

I truly believe the worst struggles in my life wouldn't have resulted in what I and others experienced if only I had sought counseling earlier. I don't care as much about myself as I do about the other lives that were affected so drastically. There is light at the end of that tunnel of darkness. The time to keep silent is now, replaced by a time to speak!

Chapter 39

"A time to love and a time to hate,
A time for war and a time for peace."

—Ecclesiastes 3:8

If someone were to ask, "When is it a time to love?" the answer would be easy. In God's eyes, it is always a time to love. So, why would Solomon list "a time to hate" in scripture? I cannot answer for him, but he must have had some particular incidents in mind. So, again I will look at this from a Vietnam veteran's experience. As always, I do not pretend to represent all veterans or even all veterans of a particular war. Rather, I share only from my own perspective.

The historic hippie movement was born in the early 1960s. I see no reason here to delve into the history of the movement, other than to say it was an appeal for love rather than hate. It was the "make love, not war" era of American history. Therefore, protests of the war in Southeast Asia took over what may have been the real essence of the movement. Before long, protests over the war spread worldwide. The ancient peace symbol was prominent everywhere. "Make love, not war," was chanted anywhere the press covered the peaceful (mostly) protests.

To each his own, as far as opinion is concerned. Once more, I am expressing my own opinions, which obviously are agreed with only by those who express the same feelings. I do not condemn supporters of the movement, as they had the right to express their own opinions, whatever they may be.

From the perspective of my own feelings and those of most of my comrades, the hatred of our government was anti-American. We felt the protests were against us. Being spit on when returning to the airport in Seattle confirmed the hatred. We had watched films of the protests, which condemned the dead upon arrival to their native, beloved country. As recently as the conflict in Afghanistan, protestors lined the streets in protest as the remains of our fallen heroes were transported to their final resting place. That is pure hatred. That man or woman died for you and me. I understand the disagreement with our nation's involvement in the wars in Korea, Vietnam, Iraq, and Afghanistan, along with other smaller conflicts in foreign lands. I learned to hate my (collectively, not individuals) government, too, as stated previously. But showing dishonor to those who died for you is as pathetic as it gets. I will argue that with you face-to-face.

As long as protests are carried out peacefully, our constitution guarantees that right. It also protects those who disrespect and dishonor the fallen soldier. I do not want an amendment for every issue the masses disagree with. However, there is a time to hate and a time to love. I hate the path our government has proceeded on in so many directions over the last several administrations. However, I am not willing to be cast into hell by hating the individuals who collectively form that government under each president.

Should we be fighting for people's freedom in far-off foreign lands? I won't even begin that discussion. Should we love those people? Should we hate those we are fighting against? Philosophically, those are open-ended questions we could debate until the proverbial cows come home. But biblically, we are forbidden from hating individuals. God did not say you must love everyone except this or that individual.

Telling people they cannot hate an individual is one of the toughest challenges for a pastor or counselor. Most of us want to make an exception to God's commandment, and I am no exception. I hate the violent acts perpetrated against me. But going to hell for failing to forgive the person is a different story. Did I hate the person during the act? Absolutely! I am a Christian, but I'm no way near sainthood. Let me just proclaim, I am human. In each case, it took time to ask God to forgive my offender, and I trust He understood that just because of the fact I am human, and I have human emotions.

So, that time to hate was replaced by a time for forgiveness, and a burden was lifted from my soul. Those individuals have been forgiven on my part. Whether they have been forgiven by God, by way of asking forgiveness for their offense, is in their hands. How God deals with them is His decision.

Can I say that I actually love those individuals? That's a very difficult process. But suffice it to say, I believe Solomon, in all his wisdom, would claim that asking God's forgiveness for another's actions is an act of love. I cannot speak for God, so I will leave it at that.

Once more, I do not question Solomon's reasoning. I can only say that, if I had Solomon's wisdom, I would personally have reversed verse 8a—"a time to hate and a time to love." But I am not that wise or intelligent, so I will not protest his reasoning. So, although this order messes up my rationale, I honor his order of things—a time to love and a time to hate.

Is there ever a legitimate time for war? That is a matter of perspective. Considering wars such as World War I and World War II, there was no real choice in whether or not to defend our own country. Defending our own nation and allies is one thing, but having thousands of our young military heroes spill their lifeblood on foreign soil over politics is another. I promised not to get political, so I will leave it at that.

One thing we can be assured of is Jesus's warning from the Mount of Olives (as recorded by Matthew in chapter 24):

> You will hear of wars and rumors of wars, but see to it that you are not alarmed. Such things must happen, but the end is still to come. Nation will rise against nation, and kingdom against kingdom. There will be famines and earthquakes in various places. All

these are the beginning of birth pains. Then you will be handed over to be persecuted and put to death, and you will be hated by all nations because of me. At that time many will turn away from the faith and will betray and hate each other, and many false prophets will appear and deceive many people. Because of the increase of wickedness, the love of most will grow cold, but the one who stands firm to the end will be saved. And this gospel of the kingdom will be preached in the whole world as a testimony to all nations, and then the end will come.

The beginning of the first war in history was probably a battle of two cavemen going at it with clubs or maybe even rocks. It was probably as senseless as all the wars that have ensued throughout history. Worldwide peace has been more intermittent than war. I cannot remember a time since I have been old enough to read or watch the news on TV, that the entire civilized world was at peace.

But when Jesus's promise in the gospel of Matthew finally comes to fruition, there will be a thousand years of peace. Then will come the tribulation and great tribulation, which will be the time that Satan is loosed, and all Christians will be the victims of the Antichrist.

I didn't write this book from the perspective of a minister and believer of Jesus Christ, although I state my beliefs and religious viewpoints at times. Although I am tempted to steer into that course, I will stick to the perspective of a Vietnam veteran, by making a single statement to embellish the final word of verse 8—*peace.*

Once all wars have been fought, Satan and all his weapons and followers will have been destroyed. We have one glorious statement that all Christians have to look forward to. This promise comes from John's vision during his time on the island of Patmos, where he wrote the book of Revelation. The words of the Holy Spirit that were given to him are what the culmination of all the sufferings of a devoted Christian come to. This promise comes from Revelation 21:4. "He will wipe every tear from their eyes. There will be no more death or mourning or crying or pain, for the old order of things has passed away."

You cannot spell the word *p-e-a-c-e* any better than that. There is no greater promise than knowing we will never again be reminded of any of our battles. The pain of the Vietnam War won't even be a minor blur in our vision. We will be incapable of remembering anything bad that ever crossed our paths. No physical pain will ever again exist. Nor will mental anguish. Nor will hatred. Every—not most or almost ever—but every single tear will be wiped away. A time for hate will never again exist. God's love will prevail for a time that has no conclusion.

So, that, my friend, is a time for peace.

Chapter 40

"A time to die."

—Ecclesiastes 3:1b

As noted earlier, I will now digress to the second part of the first verse of Ecclesiastes 3. I felt it appropriate not to change Solomon's chronological order for the purposes of this book. Therefore, I am not changing anything except for the current purpose of placing "a time to die" at the end of my personal experience of the passage, not at the end of the scripture itself. I want to make sure the reader understands this purpose because Revelation 22:19 warns about taking away from the words of the book of this prophecy. I am, in no way, changing scripture. I'm only using verses as a background for my life experiences. Think of it this way—when a minister, priest, or other member of the clergy preaches a sermon, he or she does not necessarily follow scripture sequentially.

Western civilization tends to look at death somewhat differently than most people of Eastern culture. I will not get into philosophical differences here, only to say that we tend to fear death more than others. I am not speaking of religious beliefs or fear of the afterlife but, rather, of the process of death. We seem to have more of the fear of the physical act of dying. Linda asked me once if I was afraid of anything, as I'd gotten through some tough times without the fear of dying, which was beginning to seem imminent. I told her my only fears were cancer and large dogs. It was meant as a joke, yet I was referring to the fact that I had been attacked by a couple of German shepherds. Also, I had witnessed the horrible deaths of those succumbing to cancer and a time that I felt I was being left at death's doorstep as a result of my own bout with the dreaded disease.

My point here was to deny the fear of death itself, fearing only the method of my demise. Knowing the next life will be so glorious, I have no fear of what will happen after I die. Death is only a stage of life. Death is the last stage of this life, which transcends into the next and final stage of existence.

In Solomon's eight verses, he expresses seasons of our lives. No two people experience the seasons in identical order. I don't believe he meant them to be sequential, or he would not have placed "a time to die" in the first verse. Only the beginning of life in verse one exemplifies a common first season for all creatures.

Looking at "a time to die" from a personal perspective is probably a little different for each of us, other than it is the last season of earthly life, regardless of religious or other beliefs.

I have a jacket I purchased at a small hooch in Vietnam. You may have seen one worn by a Vietnam veteran or a picture of one on Pickers. On the back is an outline of a map of Vietnam with the words, "When I Die I'll Go to Heaven, Because, I've Already Been to Hell." I couldn't find one in my size, but I bought one anyway because I thought it was so philosophically unique.

As cool as I thought the jacket was, it was early in my tour, and I had not yet learned how true those words would be after a couple of near-death experiences.

Many people are victims of the false belief that we Vietnam veterans believe we are in some way better or more important than veterans of previous or ensuing wars. Oh, I forgot, it wasn't a war, just a "conflict" that claimed the lives of over 52,800 American soldiers.

I doubt there is actually a single one of us who feels we hold any superiority over anyone who fought in a different war. Upon return to the world, we scraped ourselves out of the bottom of the pit we were dragged into. And we vowed we would rise from the ashes as leaders, rather than hang our heads as those who were scorned. All we have ever tried to express is that we believed we were fighting for a cause that was just. History may prove that our war was not justified, but we fought and bled for what we believed in at the time. We were the first returning warriors to be spat on and degraded for wearing the uniforms of the military of the United States of America. We hold no claim as to superiority. Our mantra has become a statement that none who follows will be treated as we were. Our hope is in the future. That hope is that as a time to die draws nigh for those of us who remain, we will be remembered not as heroes or saviors but, rather, as a generation of soldiers who passed the torch, not the bitterness of an ungrateful nation.

So, it is true that each of us has either met or soon will meet our time to die. For our fallen comrades, seasons have come and gone. Many died during battle or from wounds that eventually took their toll. Those who suffer from PTSD but received no physical scars suffer from seasons of agony, ranging from guilt complexes (why did he die instead of me?) to gruesome sights and sounds that invade the psyche in dreams and vivid memories of what seems like a former life.

Every time I see a flag-draped casket, I wonder what the seasons of life held for that fallen hero. I silently honor the fallen for their service, whether they witnessed combat directly or not. Many survivors will carry on their experiences, while others met their final season while refusing to open up about their time for war.

I hope those who experienced the events nightmares are made of will open up before their story is forever sealed by time and never delivered to others. If we fail to tell our story before our demise, it cannot ever be told. Many of us have experienced at least a partial healing by eventually opening up to the events of our story.

I can speak for myself. I might have saved a marriage and a relationship with my children had I openly faced my demons earlier than I did. Not revealing my season, which lasted only a year, destroyed much of the most important seasons of my life. Nobody knew the stories of rape, covering up a live grenade, experiencing the feeling of placing my hand deep into a fallen marine's torso while probing for his dog tag, or praying for a dying soldier who experienced life's final season while I held him in my arms.

The main purpose of my endeavors in critical incident stress management is telling first responders about the importance of opening up, pleading with them to talk about the event in question. You can somewhat disperse the effects of PTSD simply by talking. I am not embarrassed to tell my story of talking to my cat when I had no others I was willing to open up to.

You might just be shocked to realize what your story provides for others. They may discover the power of what you have to say. So many times, I have heard someone say that what they just heard made them realize they aren't the only one who experienced an event very similar to theirs. The old saying that misery loves company comes from a wise person, whose mental health was obviously emboldened by knowing their misfortune wasn't unique. Somewhere along the line, you will find that someone else has had an experience very similar to yours, and you will realize your reaction was normal as a result of such an abnormal event.

A time to die ends Solomon's list of general observations. This first verse represents the heading under which all the other seasons prevail. Seasons come, and seasons go. As we near the final season of life, will we revisit our past and hope God is satisfied by our works? Or will we hang our head and think, *I could have done better*? (I am not speaking of works versus grace.)

We don't have the power to rewrite our seasons unless we atone for our errors before life's season runs out on us. When we take a written exam, we can go back and change our answer. But once we hand that sheet of paper over (I know, now it's online), it is too late to change the answers. The time to correct seasons is now. Now is the future. I know that. I locked in too many seasons too early. But the good news is that, unlike that written exam, we can look back at our mistakes and correct them. Maybe not with certain people, but with God, we can dispose of those negative seasons such as "a time to love" or "a time to hate"—dispelling them into the distant past so we may be accountable no more.

God doesn't lock us into our past. Jesus took care of that at Calvary.

PART SEVEN

Chapter 41

As I sit here in January 2023, having lost Linda to cancer in August 2021, I have pondered over the past year and a half where to go with my story. I planned to add a conclusion wrapping these memoirs up with a perspective on how my past led me to what was then my future

But first, a glance at the past six months, which has been filled with atrial fibrillation and having my heart shocked back into rhythm three times. I told my electro-cardio physiologist there would not be a repeat of that unless it is a dire emergency. In January, I had my third cardiac ablation. My previous two procedures lasted about six years each. I was told I would have the "cryo" method (instead of heat) and an additional extension of the procedure, which would involve dealing with both the upper (as before) and lower part of the heart. Instead, heat was used once again, and another wire was attached to my pacemaker to regulate my cardio rhythm. However, three weeks later, I was so off-balance and light-headed, I ended up in the emergency room. For the second time (once prior to the procedure), I was told I needed to be admitted to the cardiac unit but, because of the number of COVID-19 patients, there was no room for me. I am currently in A-Fib again and am waiting to see a cardiac specialist.

I paused my writing again, as Linda's chemotherapy took several turns—all for the worse. When the second oral chemotherapy failed, we knew it was only a matter of time before the inevitable. She was having her abdominal cavity drained of fluid twice a week. She didn't suffer as badly at the end as I expected, but her life was miserable. Having gone through the last days of my mother's and sister's lives gave me an idea of when to involve hospice. Though a nurse came earlier and spoke to us, we didn't call until the early morning hours of August 9.

Because of COVID-19, the funeral homes were all backed up, so it took a week before we could hold Linda's funeral. I had the honor of officiating her funeral and the privilege of being able to say my last good-bye from the pulpit. I teared up at the beginning of the service, but then the Holy Spirit offered me the peace I had prayed for.

I have kept busy, as my stepdaughter, Chrissy, has spent many hours deciphering what I needed to keep and what to send to Goodwill. Plus, we had a garage sale, and I was able to clear out a lot of things that were no longer useful to me.

I have spent one day a week volunteering at the Belmont County Health Department's COVID-19 clinic, along with my other ministries, including pastoring at Key Bethel Church.

Many of you know the loneliness involved when a spouse has departed, so I am not going to explain how I feel. We always believed I would be the first to go because of my health problems. I keep reliving Linda's words from about a year ago. "Which ever of us goes first, we won't have to wait long to be together again." I thank my Lord and Savior, Jesus Christ that we will be together again. Although the Bible tells us there will be no marriage in heaven, I am OK with whatever God has planned. I also cherish the point Jesus made that there will be no more suffering or pain—no more physical pain, no more tears, and no more emotional anguish. Amen to that!

But for now, life goes on, with only Garfield here to keep me company. No one else is here to greet me at the door when I come home. Now I know why God led us to decide on adopting another cat many years after losing the others and many years into declaring we would never adopt another pet. What a true blessing God provided me with in that little feline monster!

The past six months have provided a time for reflection. I could sit here and feel sorry for myself until God calls me home, but every one of my friends and family could have told you that wasn't going to happen.

Had my intent been to write a detailed story of my life, there would have been many more chapters included. To tell what I believe I can express in a much shorter version. It all began with the plight of the Vietnam War veterans. It was a time when we were finally beginning to get some positive recognition. But we were still the bastards of society. Only the Iraq and Afghanistan wars resulted in a switch to honoring our troops, no matter what war we served in. If that sounds like a backhanded remark toward our brothers and sisters, it certainly is not. It is a thank you to them. It was only due to their recognition by a nation that the nation decided it was time to honor all who survived a conflict or war, whatever society deemed was the correct label. That which our government refused to do, the people did. Was the Vietnam experience a war or a conflict?

Statistics show that twenty-two veterans take their lives daily. If we could pinpoint one reason that number is so high, we could undoubtedly reduce the number significantly. Is society to blame? Is the Veterans Administration to blame? Or is the individual to blame? It's probably a combination of the three. I won't even attempt to place a percentage of blame on those three factors. In fact, there are certainly many other mitigating factors to consider along with these.

I cannot and will not try to speak for anyone except my own generation. Even each Vietnam veteran has his or her own perspective when it comes to the personal impact of the war.

I have always been very explicit that I was not a grunt. I didn't watch as my compatriots were riddled with AK-47 fire or were decimated by enemy grenades and booby traps. If you want to read stories about that portion of the war, there are many other books that have been written that would better meet your expectations than mine.

I have had many marines tell me that my part of the war was psychologically more intense than theirs. I disagree with them. My life was on the line only a few times, including my days of working in maximum security mental wards, both stateside and during the war. I cannot imagine the constant stress and fear combat veterans endured for thirteen months 24-7.

It only took a relatively few occurrences to explain those events that surround my own case of PTSD. Although I faced the stress of being on duty one way or the other 24-7, I applaud those whose lives were on the line constantly.

Chapter 42

As I stated early on, I matured early in life because of the death of my father when I was nine years old. But as in everything else, maturity is a relative term. I grew up facing the responsibilities most boys my age didn't experience. What I missed out on, though, was being brought up by a loving, caring father. I didn't get to learn his trade as a carpenter or to work on vehicles. I didn't even master the task of changing oil in the family car. Everything I learned was through the proverbial "school of hard knocks." As I look back over six decades, I see a young fatherless boy who never learned to defend himself physically. In most aspects, I was far beyond the maturity of my friends because they were not faced with the responsibilities of housework (shared with my sister) and other stuff that came with the situation. I learned to put off going to the baseball or football fields or basketball court until chores were finished.

Physically, I was the runt of the neighborhood and, for that, was bullied—until the day I was determined to stand up for myself. From then on, the bullying was over. The tough guys didn't want to face the chance that a puny little guy like me might just beat the shit out of them. Once word got around that I had stood up to the neighborhood bully, the teasing ceased. I wasn't, all of a sudden, the tough guy I wanted to be. But the other guys perceived me as the guy it would be embarrassing to have stand his ground against them.

So, another step toward maturity was chalked up. But then came basic training. I will not repeat stories I delved into earlier, but I had to start all over, as I was again the runt of the company—that was until I began to add muscle, while others were concentrating on losing fat. My accomplishments in the gym and pool were beginning to be noticed. However, I felt I was beginning to mature socially, as I did what I was supposed to do and didn't want to provoke the tough guys, which would only have gotten me into trouble. Basic training behind me and twenty-eight pounds of muscle later, I no longer worried about how to work my way out of being bullied.

The next step toward maturity was my accomplishment of completing hospital corps school. That may have been no big deal for most. Thousands of other young sailors graduated with a knowledge of first aid; drawing blood; and body parts, their functions, and how to repair them. For me, it was a big deal, as it was the first time I exerted myself when it came to studying and learning. This was a first since the death of my father ten years prior. It was now February 1966.

Neuropsychiatric technician school gave me even more confidence in my maturity. Sixteen weeks of classes, hands-on experience in neurology and psychiatry, and placing second in my class gave me more confidence in myself than I had ever dreamed of. I became a certified neuropsychiatric technician in September 1966.

I finally realized another goal, which was to participate and even excel in sports. Maturity was late in arriving, but I had set my mind on becoming one of the best in every aspect of life. I look back now and can only wonder how far I would have gone if I had made the military a career. The reality is I may well have been buried in a military uniform. So, I don't kick myself too hard when I look back at what could have been.

Basic training, hospital corps school, and neuropsychiatric technician school brought me from a small-town kid who lacked confidence in himself to a young man ready to take on the big wide world. War was something I had not witnessed before. I was totally unprepared for the psychological aspect it would present. I thought I was ready for whatever the United States of America military would throw at me.

Well … almost anything!

And now, I would move from Vietnam to Tokyo to Seattle to Pittsburgh and back to good, ol' Bellaire, Ohio, all within two weeks.

Chapter 43

The coldest winter of my life had been spent on the shores of Lake Michigan (1965–66). The Indochinese Peninsula at 16 degrees longitude and 109 degrees latitude has an average yearly temperature of eighty degrees. When I returned home in November, it was somewhere between the two extremes. But it seemed as bitter cold emotionally as the frigid temperatures I'd endured on the shores of Lake Michigan two years prior.

To top it off, I arrived home just before the Ohio winter began, right where I'd left off one year before. But I was home!

I previously shared memories of my life post-Vietnam. What I wish to do now is convey how living in hell for a year has helped me put my life into perspective through my religion (specifying only Christian as opposed to denomination). I don't think my beliefs would have changed any regardless of minor differences of worship and trivial aspects of how we worship God. Let my statement stand. A Christian is one who accepts and worships Jesus Christ as his or her Lord and Savior and does his or her best to follow scripture as closely as possible. This is my personal working definition, so any theologist out there need not correct me.

Having previously laid out those memoirs, I would like to delve into identifying my own means of exploring the effects of post-traumatic stress disorder according to my own experience and not attempting to be all-inclusive as to the effects of traumatic experiences of others. There is no book that outlines the stages of PTSD or the steps that mark the progression of this disorder. Those books have been written but only speak to the "average" case of PTSD.

While I taught about PTSD in college, I was always very explicit when it came to ensuring students understood it is not similar to heart disease or cancer. It doesn't destroy body parts or cells. PTSD isn't something that can be located in the brain and repaired or removed by surgical means. While its function involves the brain, it is an unseen phenomenon, undetected by a microscope, MRI, or other means used in the detection and progression of physical maladies.

Again, I am speaking from my own knowledge and experiences and not making any claims about or disclaiming any results of studies and research. Having known and counseled numerous veterans afflicted with PTSD, I can be certain that the disorder does not follow a predictable path that can be used to treat each victim. Of course, as in any physical or mental disease, there are similarities that occur in each victim. But while counseling courses and treatments have been designed to be inclusive, variations are necessary to treat each individual. Each individual presents with his or her own specific traumatic experience.

Treatments may vary according to what caused the traumatic experience. Victims of house fires or forest fires differ dramatically, though the origin of the disaster may be somewhat common. Entrapment in a dark cave cannot be compared to being attacked by a grizzly bear or a great white shark. Nor can the treatment be identical.

The first step (again, speaking as an individual combat veteran, not as a researcher, psychologist, or psychiatrist) should be to pinpoint the origin of the trauma. Again, consider a medical comparison. When we treated a leg injury, we first identified the specific type of injury. Did the projectile damage flesh or bone or both? Did it sever an artery or was there venous bleeding? Was the projectile still embedded or did it pass through the leg? Was there debris in the wound? Had infection set in? How long ago did the injury occur? I could go on forever. The point I'm attempting to make to the reader is that post-traumatic stress has just as many questions to be answered as a physical wound.

When I speak about my own PTSD, I am not attempting to

speak about that of my brothers and sisters who were traumatized by some aspect of war. No two people experience identical situations. Even if the event is shared by two or more individuals, there is one fact that I always point out. No two people experience the event alike. It is very important to realize we deal with our experiences from our own perspectives. No two people, not even identical twins, share how they experience an event. The same event will affect each individual in different ways even though the event is what it is. Our life experiences dictate much of how our brain thinks; therefore, the interpretation of and reaction to events are unique to each individual.

The first time I recall realizing I was dealing with PTSD was when Chris mentioned I was spending hours staring out the window, totally unresponsive to what was going on around me. This was very significant, as it was extremely rare for me not to be actively involved with the kids. If not, I was cutting grass, shoveling snow, or doing remodeling work around the house.

Leaving Da Nang and spending almost two weeks in Spokane, where it was much cooler and then arriving home in November in Ohio provided a little bit of a transition from the heat of Southeast Asia. But the weather in southeastern Ohio could have been below zero, and I would have welcomed it.

After finally being home once my military endeavors had concluded, I don't remember Thanksgiving Day or Christmas that year. I really don't remember much of anything until I sought employment and the aforementioned fiasco at the employment office. I quickly awakened to the craziness of the finance business in my quick stint with Midland Finance. Then came the harsh reality of the labor force and life in the labor union.

At first, I had little time to pay much attention to my surroundings outside family and work. But soon, I began to realize the bitterness of the war in the periphery. There was little in the way of negativity in a blue-collar area that didn't particularly embrace our overseas involvement; nor did people here complain much about it either. However, the newscasts of the large cities crept over those of us who had served our country honorably. To us, our cause was just, but an ungrateful nation looked down on us as if we'd created the war so we could return as heroes. The hell of war placed us on a slippery slide. We wanted to come back and slip unnoticed into the society we had suddenly slid away from. But society viewed us as assholes who had gone where we shouldn't have agreed to go.

Most of us let the country's mood and anger fuel our own anger against society. Others joined the protest movement. While those who returned with animosity against the government had even more right than others to protest, they were doing to those currently deployed what others had previously done to them.

What a screwed-up mess! We were victims of a generation who sat in the proverbial bleachers as the game went on and cheered less and less for the members of their own team.

So much for the past. I will attempt to make some sense of how all these events and emotions brought me to where I am today.

Now, I will go beyond the war, beyond my education, and beyond all the things that were poured into a mixing bowl and stirred into my current ministries.

Chapter 44

The beloved cartoon character Popeye was famous for saying, "I am what I am, and that's all that I am." So it is with me. I can look back and see individual events that led me where I ended up in life. Some good, some not so good. There are things I should have done differently, things I shouldn't have done at all, and things I should have done but failed to accomplish. But on the bright side, there are the times I made the right decisions. I am not going to discuss which is which. I did what I did and became what and who I am. When I look back at my life, I do as everyone else does. I wonder, What if?

What if I'd decided not to enlist in the navy?

What if I'd gone through my enlistment without orders to Vietnam?

What if I'd failed to go beyond what I was committed to do in life and left out the things I did more or less voluntarily?

What if I'd reenlisted? (This is the one question that has run through my mind over the years more than all the rest put together.)

What if I'd looked back at my lack of achievements in high school and decided to pass on college?

What if I hadn't met Linda?

I'll quit at this point except for two more events—(1) God leading me into my ministry of critical incident stress management and (2) His calling me into the ministry in His church.

Each of us can "what if" ourselves until we are blue in the face.

At this point, I wish to discard all the what-ifs I passed on, for whatever reasons. Some were decisions I alone made, and some were based on actions or requests of others. We all live with decisions we made not to do things and wonder later, what would have been? We can dwell on those decision points and lost possibilities and sometimes agonize over them until they become a neurosis. This can be healthy to a point. But I would eventually accept that which was and not that which could have been. Myself, I try to put them behind me because I can't go back and change them now. I look at each decision as an opportunity to be what I became, not what would have or could have been.

I am what I am, basically for two reasons—the things I chose to do or chose not to do and the things God chose for me, many of which I rebelled against at the time. Take, for instance, my early call into ministry and my ministry at Key Bethel Church, which I wanted no part of beyond Christmas season 1999. This is no statement about the wonderful friends I have served over the years. It only has to do with the way the presbytery handled the situation. That soon became a blessing to befriend everyone who walked through the doors of the church. I couldn't ask for a greater congregation.

When I look back over the past fifty-seven years of my life, most of my endeavors (except for my upbringing) seem to culminate from my experiences from October 31, 1967, to October 31, 1968—a year of hell. Yet, it was also a year of experiences that can never be replaced or forfeited. It was what it was and cannot be erased. As I said previously, it is the single year that had the greatest impact on my life. It represents the good, the bad, and the ugly.

The greatest single impact on my life was my experience with James E. Williams, Jr., on December 27, 1967. This day will live on in my memory forever. It was a day I did not speak about for about thirty years. Then it became the focal point of my life. Opening up, I realized it was this memory—my experience with a man who was so different from me in so many ways (and, eventually, a brother in Christ I knew only for a few brief moments)—that would guide my life. Much of the man I am today is the result of those few moments that seemed at once to pass in a heartbeat and to last for hours. Those few passing moments of sadness and of pride (in Christ's presence, not myself) were followed by years of wondering. Were the last words he heard the appropriate words for a dying United States Marine who had given his life for all of us? Had he actually heard those words? Had he been able to comprehend their meaning? "A time for every season" was wrapped into a single life-altering event.

I've never been to heaven, so, I cannot explain, let alone understand what God's purpose was and is for me. But through trials and tribulations too numerous to begin to share, for mistakes and sins too numerous to explain, I yield to Jesus's prayer, which He gave us. "For Thine is the kingdom, the power and the glory forever." In that, I have accepted the role He gave to a sinner and that, through the blood of Jesus Christ, who I have accepted as my Lord and Savior, He has forgiven my iniquities, has forgiven those who have trespassed against me, and has led this sinner to the place where I left off with the time I spent with Williams. Some will disagree with my belief that I have been given the gift of healing, since I don't have an MD to go along with the other initials after my signature. Call it what you may, as I really don't care what others believe.

If you have never been to a debriefing, a defusing session, or a one-on-one session as a first responder, maybe you should talk to someone who has been there. While every session may not be individually successful, it is very rare that some sort of healing does not occur. Therefore, I am convinced that every member of my team, regardless of his or her particular faith, has been given the gift of healing by accepting a role in stress management for first responders and others assisting in or following a horrendous event.

I am not a fan of so-called faith healers. But I do believe in spiritual healing. My aforementioned mentor Les and I have held many discussions on this topic. We agree that praying over someone or praying with them can lead to spiritual and bodily healing. But it doesn't occur during many of the televised events, where a show is put on for what amounts to a paycheck for both the false prophet and the one who walked into the building, was presented with a walker, fell over backward, and then had the false prophet toss it aside and proclaim a star for his crown.

As a young navy hospital corpsman, I learned healing methods and was there for those in distress, using skills I had learned. I helped save lives during seizures, injuries, and other emergent situations as a member of civilian life. (Regarding all of those situations, I'll add an "asterisk." God saves lives, while those in the medical field and clergy only assist.)

The other life-shattering event I mentioned—the incident with the live grenade—haunts me and will haunt me to the grave. (There were many others, but they did not play as big a role in my life as these two). Those moments with the grenade constituted a major event in my life and forever will as long as I live. The nightmare is about what could have and would have happened, except by the grace of God.

The nightmares will never end. Neither will the bitterness over a psychiatrist who practically called me a liar until he gave me the Mississippi test and then admitted he finally believed me. I am not a hypocrite who says to forgive others and then fails to do so myself. The doctor gave in once I passed the test and was the key factor in my receiving a 100 percent disability rating. The VA obviously believed him, but that has not led to receiving a medal.

Why didn't I bring this event to the forefront earlier? My mind repressed it all those years until I began to focus on my life aboard the USS *Repose* and other places in the Far East. I undoubtedly also suppressed it, as I intentionally refused to tell anyone, even my family, what changed me from that tour of duty. It cost me a Navy Cross medal, as I established the reality of the event through a VA psychiatrist fifty-four years later. But the fact that I had no witnesses to confirm the event after all that time was the reason no medal was forthcoming. The event was proven to have happened, but so many years later, no witnesses were still around. The doors of my mind had slammed shut. They remained closed for too many years to backtrack the images into acceptance of recollection as to what really happened half a world away.

The nightmares were there, but their meaning was hidden in the repression/suppression factor. When my psyche was ready to deal with all this, the memories returned. And I had to begin dealing with remembrance all over again.

Why is there no record of these events in my VA medical file? Everything else is there. The overwhelming factor is that the results of the Mississippi PTSD scale was given to me only after I related the incident to a psychiatrist whose notes seemed to have disappeared from my medical records. However, the test results were transcribed, along with the statement that scores were consistent with severe PTSD. Those are part of my record, which I obtained before they conveniently disappear.

When I was recently given the name of the psychiatrist who gave me the test, the search for anything contained in my file stated or signed by "J. F." came up as "not found." My mind will not be at rest until this issue is resolved or until I die. It looks like the latter will be the first to occur. But I still haven't given up hope and will persist in my quest. Why was I provided the name of a psychiatrist who treated me but whose name vanished from my files?

As for James E. Williams, Jr., I still have nightmares about my time with him. However, the fact that the Veterans Administration has accepted my story gives me some peace of mind. My visit to his family and his gravesite in Oklahoma calmed my soul to a great extent.

I look forward to my trip to heaven to meet Jesus in person and to be reunited with my family. It won't be very long until that happens. I do not fear death. To me, it is a stage of life—the final stage on this earth. Death is only a transition from this imperfect body and mind to perfection within a spiritual body.

I look forward to meeting Michael Burns, who included my story in *A Battalion of Angels*.

Most of all, I look forward to being reunited with Linda, whose battle with cancer claimed her earthly life on August 9, 2021.

I sit here at the conclusion of my book listening to the song Linda chose for her funeral, "I Can Only Imagine." There are always a few words that one remembers from a song you are not very familiar with. The words to that song that are engraved in my memory are,

"Will I dance with you, Jesus?" My belief is that yes, my love, you will. And, so will I. But I probably won't be singing "Bridge over Troubled Water" this time, as I did while dancing with you and Justin at Spencer's wedding!

As for the immediate present, I look forward to my future, which is guaranteed by the Blood of the Risen Christ.

As of yet, ***I'VE NEVER BEEN TO HEAVEN, BUT I'VE BEEN TO OKLAHOMA!***

AUTHOR'S BIO

Kurt Turner was born in 1947 and raised in a small town alongside the Ohio River. After high school graduation, he fulfilled his dream of becoming a navy hospital corpsman. Knowing this would lead to his orders to Vietnam, he accepted whatever fate lay ahead. He arrived in Da Nang on Halloween 1967, leaving the USS *Repose* on Halloween 1968 with a psyche full of the things PTSD is made. Many horrific events were repressed (some suppressed), revealing themselves only in future years.

When a string of negative events uncovered memories of the past, a husband and father became lost in a downward spiral, dealing with divorce, the loss of his mother, and the loss of two professional jobs due to earlier back injuries. His battle to keep both jobs was ultimately lost.

Eventually called into the ministry, he turned his negativity into several ministries. However, an incident in which he covered up a grenade with his body while running through triage and tossing it into the South China Sea as it exploded, saving the lives of staff and patients in triage, resurfaced. This incident came to life, released in full force, once it came time to no longer repress thoughts and memories of the distant past.

His story became a dichotomy between religion and the horrors of war, as seen through Ecclesiastes 3:1–8.

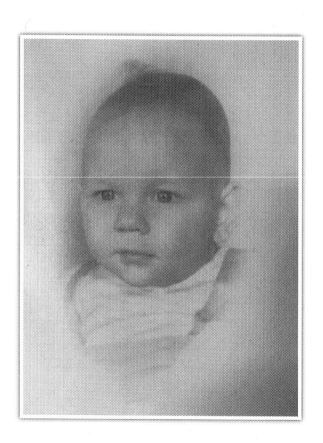

Author at eight months

Basic Training

Author aboard the USS Repose, Tet Offensive, Feb. 1968

Wounded Marines Arriving at USS Repose, Jan. 1968

Chu Lai, May, 1968

Author at Work in the Psychiatric Ward C-2

South China Sea, April, 1968

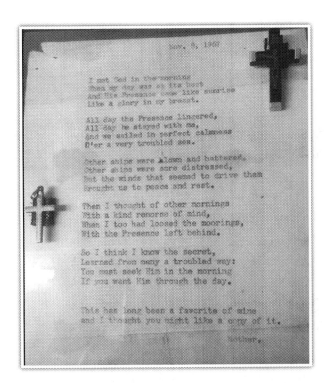

"I Met God in the Morning", Ralph Spaulding Cushman
Mom sent me this poem with her cross which I kept with me.

Geneva Conventions ID card

Saying Good-Bye to the USS Repose (AH-16), Oct. 30, 1968

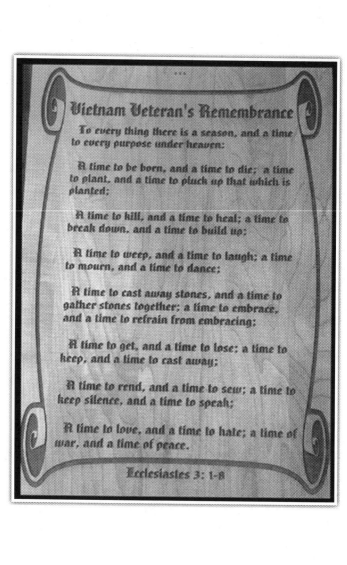

Vietnam Veteran's Remembrance

To every thing there is a season, and a time to every purpose under heaven:

A time to be born, and a time to die; a time to plant, and a time to pluck up that which is planted;

A time to kill, and a time to heal; a time to break down, and a time to build up;

A time to weep, and a time to laugh; a time to mourn, and a time to dance;

A time to cast away stones, and a time to gather stones together; a time to embrace, and a time to refrain from embracing;

A time to get, and a time to lose; a time to keep, and a time to cast away;

A time to rend, and a time to sew; a time to keep silence, and a time to speak;

A time to love, and a time to hate; a time of war, and a time of peace.

Ecclesiastes 3: 1-8